D0915931

Creativity, Innovation, and Quality

Also available from ASQ Quality Press

Mapping Work Processes
Dianne Galloway

The Reward and Recognition Process in Total Quality Management
Stephen B. Knouse

Quality Quotes
Hélio Gomes

Show Me: The Complete Guide to Storyboarding and Problem Solving
Harry I. Forsha

Show Me: Storyboard Workbook and Template
Harry I. Forsha

The Change Agents' Handbook: A Survival Guide for Quality Improvement Champions
David W. Hutton

Team Fitness: A How-To Manual for Building a Winning Work Team
Meg Hartzler and Jane E. Henry, Ph.D.

Integrating Reengineering with Total Quality
Joseph N. Kelada

Avoiding the Pitfalls of Total Quality
Charles C. Poirier and Steven J. Tokarz

LearnerFirst™ Process Management software
with Tennessee Associates International

To request a complimentary catalog of publications, call 800-248-1946.

Creativity, Innovation, and Quality

Paul E. Plsek

ASQ Quality Press
Milwaukee, Wisconsin

Creativity, Innovation, and Quality
Paul E. Plsek

Library of Congress Cataloging-in-Publication Data
Plsek, Paul E.
  Creativity, innovation, and quality / Paul E. Plsek
    p. cm.
  Includes bibliographical references and index.
  ISBN 0-87389-404-9 (alk. paper)
    1. Creative ability in business.   2. Technological innovations.
  3. Total quality management.   I. Title.
  HD53.P58   1997
  658.5'62—dc21   96-40946
                                                      CIP

Trademark Acknowledgments
"Directed Creativity," "Creative thinking for serious people," and "If you can think, you can think creatively" are trademarks of Paul E. Plsek & Associates, Inc.
Many of the designations used by manufacturers and sellers to distinguish their products are claimed as trademarks. Where these designations appear in this book and ASQ Quality Press was aware of a trademark claim, the designations have been printed in initial caps.

10 9 8 7 6 5 4 3 2

ISBN 0-87389-404-9

Acquisitions Editor: Roger Holloway
Project Editor: Jeanne W. Bohn

ASQ Mission: To facilitate continuous improvement and increase customer satisfaction by identifying, communicating, and promoting the use of quality principles, concepts, and technologies; and thereby be recognized throughout the world as the leading authority on, and champion for, quality.

Attention: Schools and Corporations
ASQ Quality Press books, audiotapes, videotapes, and software are available at quantity discounts with bulk purchases for business, educational, or instructional use. For information, please contact ASQ Quality Press at 800-248-1946, or write to ASQ Quality Press, P.O. Box 3005, Milwaukee, WI 53201-3005.

For a free copy of the ASQ Quality Press Publications Catalog, including ASQ membership information, call 800-248-1946.

Printed in the United States of America

∞ Printed on acid-free paper

American Society for Quality

Quality Press
611 East Wisconsin Avenue
Milwaukee, Wisconsin 53201-3005
800-248-1946
Web site http://www.asq.org

Contents

🔣 ☺ ⸮ ✗

Preface

Creativity and innovation are essential to business success as we prepare to enter the new century, yet the quality management literature is virtually silent on these topics. The purpose of this book is to give quality management practitioners current knowledge on the topics of creativity and innovation, and to show how creative thinking can be used to advance the practice of quality management in organizations today. The overall objectives of the book are to enable the reader to

- Understand recent advances from the field of cognitive science and describe how these advances unlock the creative potential in everyone.
- Recognize the underlying theory behind various tools of creative thinking.
- Develop his or her own techniques for generating creative ideas on demand.
- Use creative-thinking techniques to stimulate innovation in the context of the challenges commonly encountered in the practice of quality management.

Overview of the Book

The book is organized in four parts, with a prologue and appendix. The prologue sets the stage for the rest of the book by presenting a concrete example of what I call directed creativity. *Directed creativity,* as I define it here, is the deliberate mental action needed to produce novel ideas in targeted areas. I purposefully chose to start the book with a concrete example of creative thinking applied to a quality management issue to make a point: *This is a creativity book for results-oriented, action-bent people who need to get something done.* I hope that you will appreciate this application and action bias throughout the book.

Part I presents the case for bringing the tools of creative thinking and innovation into the quality management literature. Chapter 1 describes five generic factors driving the need for innovation in organizations today, two key challenges, and five reasons why practitioners of quality management should be interested in innovation. We will see that the goals of innovation and quality management are congruous.

Having made the case for innovation, part II takes a step back to present some essential theory of creativity. C. I. Lewis (1929) and W. Edwards Deming (1993) have taught us that learning cannot take place without theory. We cannot hope to learn how to direct ourselves to be more creative without some understanding of the theory of creativity and the workings of the mind.

I believe that this section on theory sets this book apart from most of the popular literature on creative thinking. Most books on creativity present tools and methods only. These authors seem to assume that the reader will accept the methods and apply them on the basis of faith alone. This never worked for me, and I do not think that it will work for the largely analytical thinkers who are typically involved in quality management. This book stands apart from the crowd by presenting creativity for serious, analytically minded individuals.

Part II on essential theory comprises two chapters. Chapter 2 begins by presenting the insights that we can gain from the definitions of creativity and innovation, and then goes on to describe the processes of creative thinking and the mechanics of mind. Practitioners of quality management know that the quality of the output (in this case, creative ideas) depends on our continual improvement of the underlying processes (the mechanics of mind). In chapter 2, I will distill more than 50 years of research from the fields of the cognitive sciences down to a set of core concepts that support directed creativity.

Chapter 3 concludes the theory by describing heuristics and models for directed creativity. A *heuristic* is a rule of thumb that guides thinking and leads to expertise in an area. For example, the Pareto principle—search for the vital few—is a heuristic in quality management. There is no guarantee that we will find the vital few, but it is generally useful to think in this direction. Similarly, we will examine eight heuristics that summarize the accumulated experience and research from the field of creative thinking. Models are a step beyond heuristics. As practitioners of quality management know, models indicate flow and sequence. They guide thinking over time. I will review various models from the creativity literature and present a synthesis model that we will use to guide our thinking in this book.

With a good grounding in theory, we are ready to move on to the tools and methods of directed creativity—the subjects of part III. Chapter 4 opens this section by describing the three central principles that underlie all the tools of creativity. While other books on creativity hint at these principles, I believe that this book is the first to articulate them clearly. The key point here is that once we know the principles behind the tools, we can generate our own methods for creative thinking that are uniquely suited for our specific needs. I will show you how.

Chapters 5 through 7 describe the variety of tools that support the four phases of the directed-creativity cycle. Chapter 5 focuses on the tools that help prepare the mind for creative ideas. Chapter 6 describes the methods and attitudes that enhance imagination and the generation of new ideas. Chapter 7 covers the practical development of creative ideas and outlines the challenges of putting them into action. Throughout these chapters, I will stress the dual themes of inventing one's own methods and understanding how these apply to the issues we face in the pursuit of quality in our organizations.

Part IV is the culmination of the book. While the entire book is about applying directed creativity in quality management, part IV really drives home the applications. In chapter 8, I will describe how we can help our organizations be more creative in process design and reengineering efforts. Many practitioners of quality management find themselves leading or facilitating such efforts, and many are frustrated by final designs that are not much different from the current processes they were supposed to replace. Fortunately, there are specific tools that we can apply in such efforts to increase the probability of generating truly innovative designs.

Chapter 9 continues the applications focus by examining specific creative-thinking techniques to enhance customer needs analysis. Chapter 10 presents methods that will help quality managers contribute creatively to new product and service design efforts. Chapter 11 describes creative problem solving. The purpose of these applications chapters is to enable readers to see that creative thinking is a widely useful and easily accessible skill. It is my firm hope that the methods of directed creativity will become part of the generally accepted techniques of quality management.

Chapter 12 concludes the book with my thoughts on the future of these methods in the pursuit of quality. Finally, the appendix contains several resources and bibliographies to aid your continued practice and learning.

Some Personal Notes

I hope that you enjoy reading the book as much as I have enjoyed preparing it. It is a major milestone for me in a journey that I began several years ago and that I believe will continue for some time.

Like many quality practitioners, I have a strong background in the largely analytical methods of quality management. After receiving electrical engineering degrees from Texas A&M University and Brooklyn Polytechnic in the late 1970s, I took a job in the Quality Assurance Center of the AT&T Bell Laboratories—the organization where quality pioneers like Walter Shewhart, Harold Dodge, and others practiced. I progressed through various engineering and management positions in Bell Laboratories and was the founding manager of the AT&T Corporate Quality Planning Office during the 1984 breakup of the Bell system. In 1985, I went out on my own as a consultant. In 1987, I coauthored the Juran Institute's *Quality Improvement Tools* training series. I have since taught quality management and statistical methods to literally thousands of managers in several industries.

The more I practiced quality management, the more I noticed the occasional failure of analysis. Slowly, I began to understand Deming's (1993) teaching that "the most important numbers are unknown and unknowable."

Around 1991 I began my serious study of innovation and creativity. As you can see from the bibliography, I am not kidding when I say serious study. I read everything I could get my hands on. This book summarizes what I have learned so far. I am sure that I have much more to learn, but I am firmly convinced that *creative thinking is something that analytical people can and must master.* Our organizations need innovation in order to thrive into the next century. We can help, but we must learn first.

I want to thank my family—my wife, Belinda, and sons Jonathan and Ryan—who have put up with my travels over the years and with the time I spent writing this book. Drs. Glenn Laffel and Donald Berwick have encouraged me greatly. Dean Lea has been a good friend who always wants to know more about what I have been doing and who continually stimulates my creativity. The staff of ASQ Quality Press and the various manuscript reviewers have also contributed greatly to this work.

There are the many organizations and colleagues who have given me experimental grounds and teaching platforms for my work on creativity. Special thanks to Penny Carver and the Institute for Healthcare Improvement; Barbara Kavalew-Spreadbury at the SSM Health Care System; Cynthia Majewski at the Ontario (Canada) CQI Network; Elizabeth Lowe, Nigel Sewell, and Peter Wilcock with the Quality Forum in London (England); and all my many friends at the Fletcher-Allen Healthcare System; HealthPartners; Cedars-Sinai Medical Center; the University of Michigan Medical Center; the Baptist Health Network; St. John's Medical Center; the Henry Ford Health System; the Mayo Clinic; Carroll County General Hospital; Newton Memorial Hospital; Gillette Children's Hospital; the Maryland Hospital Association; VHA, Inc.; Kaiser-Permanente; Hanneman University; Green Mountain Power; and ASQ.

I hope you enjoy the book. I also hope that you will share your successes and failures with me in the same spirit that I am sharing my learnings with you. Please write, visit my Internet web page, or e-mail me at the addresses below.

Paul E. Plsek
1005 Allenbrook Lane
Roswell, GA 30075
paulplsek@aol.com
www.DirectedCreativity.com

Prologue: An Illustration of Directed Creativity

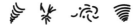

When you come to a fork in the road, take it.

Yogi Berra

An organization that runs like clockwork is great—if your goal is to run around in the same circle forever.

Anonymous

If you normally skip over book chapters entitled "Prologue," I urge you not to do so now. The topic of creativity and innovation is so shrouded in myth and so misunderstood by most people, that I believe it is imperative to begin with a concrete example of what we mean by *creativity*.

In this book, we will confront directly the myth-and-magic view of creativity. Creative thinking is not a zap from out of the blue. It is not magic. It is not silliness. Innovation is not something that only other people can do. It is not necessarily large-scale change. It does not require advanced degrees or secret laboratories. In contrast, we will see that we *can* purposefully practice creativity in our organizations. We can be innovative whenever we choose to be. These are the key messages of this book. The following example will start us on a path of concreteness as we explore the usually ethereal subject of creative thinking.

Creativity Versus Stuck Thinking:
The Story of the Medication Errors

"Do you ever reach the point where there is just nothing else you can do . . . where you just have to accept some level of error in a process?" The head nurse asking the question was the leader of a team in a hospital that had been working on reducing errors in delivering medications. Her frustration is a common one—I call it stuck thinking.

The medication error team was a model of the scientific approach to quality improvement. They had gathered data on the problem, used the Pareto principle to identify the vital few types of medication errors, constructed cause-effect diagrams and flowcharts, collected more data, identified root causes, implemented remedial process changes, and measured improvement. They were successful with every error type they focused on except one: medications not administered on time.

"What we found," the team leader told me, "was that most of these timing errors occur simply because the nurses get busy and forget to give the medication at the prescribed time. If it is more than 30 minutes late, we call it a medication error."

Based on this observation, the team had developed a log sheet with all of the patients' medication times written in chronological order. This was clearly posted at the nurses' station. As it turned out, however, the nurses were too busy to look at it! The team found itself back where it had started.

"We talked about it at our last meeting," the team leader continued, "and concluded that we cannot afford to hire more nurses to relieve the workload pressure. We will continue to emphasize the need to check the medication log frequently, but I think we are at the limits of the improvements we can make on this type of error. The nurses work hard; I see no reason to demoralize them with even more pressure."

Here was a quality team that clearly was stuck and at the limits of its analytical thinking. As I listened to the team leader's review of the analysis a simple idea occurred to me. "Have you ever seen the little digital clocks that your can stick to your refrigerator or dashboard? Most have an alarm feature, and you could buy 15 to 20 of them for less than $100. Instead of compiling a medication time log, why not set the alarms for the medication times and stick them to the patients' charts? When an alarm goes off, someone will hear it, even if she or he is busy, and be reminded that it is time to administer a medication."

The team leader stared back at me intently with a surprised smile on her face. "That's a creative idea," she said. "It might even work." It did.

An Introduction to Directed Creativity

Of course, the idea of using little alarm clocks to remind nurses when to administer medications is not astounding. I am not suggesting that I am a brilliant creative thinker for having come up with it. I tell the story because it is typical of getting stuck and getting unstuck in thinking. It is a concrete illustration of the paradoxical conflict between analytical thinking and creative thinking in the pursuit of quality.

Reflecting on this and other situations like it, we can clearly see that there are limits to traditional analytical thinking when it comes to solving nagging problems or generating breakthrough ideas. What we need, it seems, is the ability to be analytical when the situation calls for it and creative when the situation calls for that. Both skills are critical for success.

Personally, this simple realization of the need to be able to use both analytical and creative thinking as the situation demands was a major revelation for me. I am an engineer and have worked in the field of quality management since 1977. I love analysis. I believe in the power of analytical methods. Unfortunately, I had also always believed that only certain people were creative, and that creative thoughts came from out of the blue. Further, many of the techniques recommended for stimulating creativity seemed silly to me—not the type of thing that a serious, scientific, analytical person like myself (and others engaged in quality management efforts) would want to take part in. So, while I could see the need for it, the notion of creative thinking on demand seemed an impossibility. The more I reflected on it, the more I realized how little I knew.

While I do not know what thinking process I used to come up with the alarm clock idea, I now know that the team could have gotten unstuck on its own through the use of directed-creative thinking. A directed-creativity process for the medication error situation might have proceeded in the following manner.

- Realize that analytical thinking has reached a stuck point.

- Clarify the focus or concept that requires new thinking. (In this case: I need a way to remind busy people when a certain time has come.)

- Review the current facts. (We have tried to remind them with a time log, but that failed.)

- Look carefully at the current situation to identify elements that could be modified to yield a new approach. (We have tried reminding them visually. Sight is only one of our senses; hearing, touching, tasting, smelling are others. We have used a paper time log; a large white board or a computer screen is another option.)

- Restate the focus by modifying an element and looking for an association. (How could I remind a busy person about time through hearing rather than sight? The mental association of the concepts of reminding, time, and hearing leads us to identify an alarm clock as a mechanism. We could go on to think of other ways to utilize other senses or modify other elements of the situation.)

- Develop the idea further to meet practical constraints. (For example, it must not cost too much; it must be flexible, portable, and easy to associate with individual patients. A stick-on alarm clock is one way.)

- Express it, develop it, try it out, and see what happens.

These processes of directed creativity are based on modern theories of how the mind works. Furthermore, they utilize ordinary thought processes like noticing, associating, remembering, and selecting. No special genius is required. Finally, while the end product of the thinking is creative—a new idea—the thought processes have a logic that makes them appealing to serious, scientific people.

While the thinking process just outlined is not a universal sequence that can be applied to all situations, it does illustrate five mental actions that are common to many successful creative thinking endeavors (see box). First, it is often necessary to stop and clarify the focus that requires creative thinking. By stating the focus broadly—"I need a way to remind busy people when a certain time has come"—we give our minds both a fixed point from which to direct our thinking and a wide space in which to come up with alternatives.

Five Mental Actions in Directed Creativity

1. Clarify the focus with a broad problem statement.

2. Recognize the concepts in the current situation.

3. List alternatives.

4. Make mental associations.

5. Develop ideas into practical realities.

Being clear about the current reality and looking carefully to notice the underlying concepts behind the common things around us is a second critical element in directed-creativity thinking. Often, we fail to pause and consider how or why something works or fails. The medication time log was a good idea, but it failed. If we stop and think about why it failed, we might realize that an underlying assumption was that the nurses would find time to look at it. We found that they were too busy, which, of course, brings us back to the original problem. The key insight here is to notice that the failed solution relied on the sense of sight to do the reminding.

Listing alternatives is a third key element in the creative process in this situation. Recognizing that reliance on the sense of sight had failed, we can list our other senses and consider them as alternative ways of reminding. Careful reflection on this list of senses would lead us to notice that while it is difficult to look at something when you are busy, it is easy to hear something even when you are otherwise occupied. This is not an earth-shaking insight. So why didn't the team members think of it? I believe it is because our minds tend to race quickly past it on the way to the only approach we can think of; for example, the way we remind people about things in a hospital is by writing them down on a log sheet. So, paradoxically, stuck thinking does not necessarily mean that thinking has stopped. A better metaphor is to say that our thoughts are racing toward a repeated collision with the same brick wall! Listing alternatives helps us slow down our thinking, look around, and find an alternative side street to turn down before we hit that same brick wall again.

This example also illustrates the fundamental thinking process of association. When we associate the concepts of reminding, time, and hearing, we come up with the idea of using an alarm clock. Association lies at the core of all creative thought.

Finally, this example illustrates the importance of further refining our ideas in order to make them truly useful. Many good ideas are never implemented because our first impressions of them make them seem unappealing. Since, by definition, a creative idea is a new idea, we cannot be sure what mental model people will conjure up when we first express it. For example, imagine a row of bedside alarm clocks with big brass bells on top going off at various times. This mental picture would certainly lead to immediate rejection of the alarm clock idea as too goofy. Rather than prematurely rejecting the idea, however, we should consider the alarm clock suggestion merely a seed of an idea that must be further refined. In the development process, we can address practical issues such as cost, fit with the environment, need for flexibility, and so on.

Creative thinking is needed in the pursuit of quality for the simple reason that sometimes it is useful. When we are stuck in our thinking—whether trying to solve a problem, redesign a process, develop a new product or service, or delight a customer—it may not do any good to simply think harder. If our analytical thinking has locked us in to a particular approach that is unfruitful, thinking harder is analogous to driving faster into the same brick wall in hopes that we will break through it. While there may be a slight chance of success with this brute force approach, wouldn't it be easier to drive around the wall or construct a ramp over it? Driving around or over the walls in our thinking is the creative approach. Learning how to do that is the purpose of this book.

PART I

Why Bother Learning About Directed Creativity?

CHAPTER 1

The Need for Creative Thinking in the Pursuit of Quality

It is necessary to innovate.

W. Edwards Deming

Maybe the Hubble telescope wasn't broken . . . maybe the universe really is blurry.

Jay Leno

It might seem that creative thinking and quality management will not mix well. After all, quality management is based on science, the application of statistics, and the use of analytical methods, while creativity is about wild ideas that come from out of the blue—isn't it? Surely, quality management and creative thinking have little in common—right?

Wrong. As we will see, the two disciplines have plenty in common. Quality management is fundamentally related to the success of an enterprise—and so is innovation and creative thinking. It is becoming increasingly clear in our fast-paced business world that creative thinking and the production of new, innovative products and services are essential for future success. While the advocates of quality management and the advocates of creative thinking might sometimes seem to be at opposite poles, their objectives are the same.

Five Factors Driving the Need for Creativity and Innovation in Organizations Today

Why should organizations today be concerned with fostering creativity and innovation? At one level, the answer seems obvious. Surely, few would be against creativity and innovation.

When we examine organizations closely, however, we must conclude that the need for creativity is not so universally supported as it would seem it should be. For example, in their book *Driving Fear Out of the Workplace,* Ryan and Oestreich (1991) describe the many ways that modern organizations and management structures stifle new ideas.*

Based on interviews with 260 people at 22 organizations, these authors note that fear freezes many people in their thinking, that many organizations foster a play-it-safe culture, and that most organizations have better rewards for firefighting and reacting than they do for innovative ideas.

True innovation requires an uncommon willingness to stick one's neck out. That will take some effort. If we want innovation in our organizations, then we must be able to articulate forcefully the answer to the question: why put forth a special effort to be creative? The example in the prologue gives us one answer: because it is sometimes useful to be creative. We can say more than that (see box).

Superior long-term financial performance is associated with innovation. The largest, most successful companies in the world today recognize that innovation, change, and new ideas are essential ingredients in the recipe for success. Consider, for example, these quotes from the CEOs of the top three corporations in the world on *Fortune* magazine's 1995 ranking of firms based on the amount of wealth they have created for stockholders (Fisher 1995).

> *If you think you are going to be successful running your business in the next ten years the way you did in the last ten*

---

*I use the author-date citation method throughout this book. A date following an author's name indicates that the reader can consult a reference cited in the bibliography for more information on the topic under discussion. Repeated mention of the author's name in subsequent sentences is a continued citation of the same reference.

Why Should Organizations Be Concerned with Creativity and Innovation?

- Superior long-term financial performance is associated with innovation.

- Customers are increasingly demanding innovation.

- Competitors are getting increasingly better at copying past innovations.

- New technologies enable innovation.

- What used to work, doesn't anymore.

---

years, you're out of your mind. To succeed, you have to disturb the present.

—Roberto Goizueta, Coca-Cola

I'm convinced that if the rate of change inside the institution is less than the rate of change outside, the end is in sight. The only question is the timing of the end.

—Jack Welch, General Electric

Swim upstream. Go the other way. Ignore the conventional wisdom. If everyone else is doing it one way, there's a good chance you can find your niche by going in exactly the opposite direction.

—Sam Walton, Wal-Mart Stores

These leaders clearly value new ideas. They would attribute at least some of their organization's long-term financial success to its capacity to innovate. These organizations, and other companies on *Fortune's* list, illustrate Peter Drucker's (1995, 60) point that "innovation [is a] . . . core competence . . . that every organization needs."

Customers are increasingly demanding innovation. Past innovation drives the need for future innovation through the marketplace mechanism of customers. Today's customers are experiencing innovations all around them and have, therefore, come to expect further innovation. For example, the customer who routinely uses her bank's ATM system for complex financial transactions cannot help but be frustrated by the arcane systems she experiences when interacting with her utility company or an educational institution. Similarly, anyone who purchases one of today's technologically sophisticated television sets is driven to expect useful technological upgrades in other products. As the expression goes, "If they can put a person on the moon, why can't they . . ." (fill in the blank with a complaint about some product or service).

Customers' needs and expectations become increasingly sophisticated as they experience new ideas in the world around them every day. While they may not understand the difficulties inherent in adapting these new ideas to other products and services, trying to explain this to them is not likely to be a useful strategy. Customers today know from experience that someone will come along someday with just the new concept they are looking for. When that happens, they have no strong need to be loyal to their old producer. If you can't innovate and someone else can, why should the customers stay with you? W. Edwards Deming (1993, 8, 10) summarized it this way.

> *It will not suffice to have customers that are merely satisfied.*
> *A satisfied customer may switch. Why not? He might come*
> *out better for the switch. . . . The moral is that it is necessary*
> *to innovate, to predict needs of the customer, give him more.*
> *He that innovates and is lucky will take the market.*

Competitors are getting increasingly better at copying innovations. It is important to note that the fact that customers are demanding innovation does not necessarily mean that your organization has to be the one to bring it about. The follower strategy is appealing—let someone else be the innovator, but then quickly replicate what they have done. Today, many organizations have become quite adept at this follower strategy. The presence of these effective innovation copiers in the marketplace further drives the need for innovation. Because the copycats are so good, we can no longer simply sit back and expect to reap a long-term stream of profits from new products and services. Therefore, to paraphrase Joseph Juran's (1964) famous statement about the need for continuous quality improvement, it is the *rate* of innovation that is decisive. The organization that thinks it only needs to hit it big with one major innovation is deluding itself. Effective competitors, coupled with demanding customers, drive the need for continuous innovation. Continuous innovation, like continuous quality improvement, will not happen without focus, leadership, and structure within an organization.

New technologies enable innovation. A fourth answer to the question "Why should organizations be concerned with creativity?" is similar to Sir Edmund Hillary's response to the question, "Why did you climb Mount Everest?" "Because," Hillary replied, "it is there." Organizations should purposefully innovate simply because they can. If they don't, someone else will.

There is a rich history documenting radical business innovations driven simply by the availability of new technologies. For example, it is not clear that customers were demanding a better system of lighting when Thomas Edison developed the light bulb and the electric power distribution system that makes it practical. The natural progress of the advancement of science made electric lighting possible and, in some ways, made the invention of the light bulb inevitable. As a result of this new technology, the thriving gaslight industry of the nineteenth century became irrelevant. In *Mastering the Dynamics of Innovation,* James Utterbeck (1994, xxiv) chronicles the history of technology-driven innovation in this industry, and a variety of others, and concludes that "failure to innovate is a prime source of business failure."

Henry Petroski (1985) recounts a similar but more modern tale involving the Keuffel & Esser Company (K&E). K&E, you may recall, was the world's leader in the slide rule industry. Petroski (1985, 191) notes that, "As late as 1967, K&E commissioned a study of the future that resulted in predictions of domed cities and three-dimensional television in the year 2067, but that failed to predict the demise of the slide rule within five years." With the value of 20-20 hindsight we can laugh at such naiveté, but the key question remains: Will we be able to see the naiveté in our own reactions to the technological changes affecting our own organizations and industries?*

What used to work, doesn't anymore. Our final answer to the creativity question is one that may ring especially true in your personal experience. The ever-increasing complexity of the world is leading to a new type of organizational frustration. Anecdotal evidence from frustrated managers in many

---

*For a more extensive discussion of how customers, competitors, and technologies drive the need for continuous innovation, see von Hipple (1988).

industries attests to the fact that solutions to problems that have worked in the past are no longer effective. Perhaps you can relate to one or more of the vignettes in the box entitled "What Used To Work, Doesn't Anymore."

Critical readers might argue that each of the issues outlined in the vignettes already has a new solution; the person in the anecdote needs knowledge, not creativity. The insurance company manager and the purchasing director simply need a thorough grounding in the latest thinking from quality management about process analysis and supplier management.

What Used to Work, Doesn't Anymore

We used to be able to clear out backlogs in claims processing by just hiring more clerks, but it's gotten so complicated that hiring more clerks seems to make the claims backlog grow instead of shrink. I don't fully understand what is going on, but my intuition tells me we need to scrap the whole claims system and redesign it from the ground up.

—A manager in an insurance company

In the past, when we got stung by a raw material supplier, we would drop them and find a new source. Recently, this policy has gotten us into trouble. For example, we recently switched sugar suppliers—something as simple as sugar—and ended up making batches of bad product. Something in the combination of ingredients didn't click chemically. We're still trying to figure it out. It's clear to me that I can't continue with my past purchasing policies. I'm going to have to approach this differently next time around.

—A purchasing director for a food processing company

Sitting people in classrooms and giving them materials and exercises just doesn't get it anymore. The catch-22 is that with downsizing and restructuring, the need to acquire new skills is greater than ever before. With downsizing and restructuring, who has time to attend seminars and classes delivered in the usual way? Heck, who has time to even read a book?!

—A corporate trainer

Likewise, the trainer seems unaware of recent advances in distance learning and other techniques.

While such an analysis has a logical appeal, it fails to recognize three key points. First, the new solutions were themselves the result of a creative process. Granted, it was someone else's creative process, but creativity was needed to bring the new solutions about in the first place. Second, the past tells us that every new solution will eventually become a solution that no longer works. Another cycle of innovation will eventually be needed. Again, I suppose it could be argued that one can simply wait until someone else creatively figures it out.

The third point lays waste to the hope that one can simply leave the creative thinking to someone else. The point involves Nadler and Hibino's (1994) uniqueness principle, which states that, in the complex systems we live in today, each problem and situation we encounter will necessarily be unique. As problems, situations, and organizations become increasingly complex and interconnected, and as the effects of these interconnections become more dominant, the likelihood that the situation in your organization is exactly the same as it is elsewhere becomes very small.*

The uniqueness principle explains the puzzling phenomenon of the failure of clearly logical, but canned ideas. For example, a training program that is phenomenally successful in one organization is a dismal failure in another. Some great ideas brought back from a benchmarking visit are flops when we implement them in our organization. The logical concepts of TQM or reengineering do not bring about an equal measure of success in all the organizations that embrace them.

The uniqueness principle makes a fool of anyone who believes that creativity and innovation can be left to others. Today and into the future, organizations will need to acquire the capacity for internal creativity, or they will find themselves eternally frustrated with wave after wave of "great ideas that just don't seem to work in our organization." It is already happening today—and its going to get worse, not better, on its own.

---

*For more on the dynamics of complex systems, see Senge 1990 and Ackoff 1978.

Two Key Challenges on the Road to Innovation

Having established the need for organizational creativity, let me now describe two key challenges we might face in bringing it about: the challenge of success, and the challenge of know-how.

The challenge of success. One of the most surprising conclusions from the research on innovation is that successful organizations face the greatest challenge in trying to be innovative. This observation is counterintuitive because it would seem that highly successful organizations would be more likely to have the resources needed to stimulate innovation. Further, successful organizations are likely to have become that way through some past innovation of their own. Therefore, you would expect innovation to be in their blood, part of their organizational culture; it should be easy for successful organizations to innovate. This is not necessarily so, according to the research.

Bower and Christensen's (1995) research on cycles of innovation in the hard disk drive manufacturing industry provides a good illustration. This is a good industry to study because the cycles of innovation have come at such a dramatic pace. Between 1976 and 1992, the physical size of 100 megabytes (MB) of storage shrunk from 5400 to 8 cubic inches, while the cost per MB fell from $560 to $5. Bower and Christensen estimate that about half of this improvement came from radical innovations and half from incremental improvement within a technology. Their key finding, however, was that

> No single disk drive manufacturer has been able to dominate the industry for more than a few years. A series of companies have entered the business and risen to prominence, only to be toppled by newcomers. (p. 45)

Why can't leaders who have introduced one cycle of innovation establish a pattern of innovation that carries them through the subsequent cycles? In the case of Seagate Technologies, the company that lost its leadership in the transition from 5.25-inch disk drives to 3.5-inch drives, the explanations were that its customers did not seem to want 3.5-inch drives and the financials did not seem worth pursuing. In other words, *standard business analysis in this successful company argued against innovation.*

At the time of Seagate's leadership, its main customers were making AT-class personal computers where small physical size was not an important attribute. Standard customer needs analysis indicated that Seagate's customers desired more storage capacity, rather than smaller physical size. As a result, Seagate's marketing and financial analysts estimated that the total market for 3.5-inch disk drives was less than $50 million, at a time when the market for 5.25-inch drives was at $300 million annually. In other words, analysis at Seagate showed conclusively that customers did not want 3.5-inch disk drives and that the potential sales and profits were not worth the investment.

Around the time of this analysis, former employees of Seagate and other 5.25-inch drive manufacturers were forming a new company, Conner Peripherals, to explore the potential of the innovative 3.5-inch drive technology. While a $50 million total market is a throwaway to a successful company in an existing $300 million annual sales market, $50 million looked like a great opportunity to a start-up venture. Further, Conner was talking to a new customer, Compaq Computers. Compaq was itself in the process of innovating and establishing a position within the emerging portable and zero-footprint (that is, small size) computer market. As a result, Compaq was very interested in 3.5-inch disk drives. Seagate had never sold to Compaq, and so did not consider this in its customer needs analysis.

In hindsight, we can say that Seagate was successful in one segment of the industry, while Conner was innovating in another segment. Of course, this is only clear now in hindsight. I am sure that Seagate, the successful company, believed that it *was* the industry. If a start-up wanted to pursue an innovation in a small, unprofitable niche, so be it.

Having established itself in this new segment of the computer industry, Conner introduced incremental innovations within the 3.5-inch drive technology that dramatically increased the storage capacity to a level comparable to that of 5.25-inch technology. When the established computer makers, Seagate's traditional customers, saw that they could get the storage capacity they wanted in a smaller package and at no extra cost, they liked the innovation and began shifting business to Conner and Quantum Corporation (another pioneer in 3.5-inch drives). Suddenly, Seagate, the industry leader, was on the defensive and scrambling to introduce its own me-too product in the 3.5-inch technology. The $300 million annual market for 5.25-inch drives—the market that made the investment in the innovative technology look unprofitable in the earlier analysis—shifted over to the innovative product. (In 1994, Conner and Quantum's combined revenues exceeded $5 billion.)

Bower and Christensen (1995) summarize the story.

> *Seagate's poor timing typifies the responses of many established companies to the emergence of disruptive technologies. Seagate was willing to enter the market for 3.5-inch drives only when it had become large enough to satisfy the company's financial requirements—that is, only when existing customers wanted the new technology. (p. 49)*

The experience of Seagate is not an isolated occurrence. Foster (1986), von Hipple (1988), and Utterbeck (1994) summarize scores of similar cases spanning a 100-year period and covering industries as diverse as refrigeration, power distribution, plastics, photography, and semiconductor processing equipment. Utterbeck (1994, xxi) summarizes the research this way: "An unhappy by-product of success in one generation of technology is a narrowing of focus and vulnerability to competitors championing the next technology generation."

Foster (1986) codifies the sad experience of many successful companies in a principle of innovation that he calls the attacker's advantage. The principle of the attacker's advantage asserts that the attacker (the new entrant or the firm that is not the industry leader) has the advantage over the successful firms in innovating. This advantage is a result of two factors. First, it almost always turns out that traditional customers are poor at evaluating a potential innovation, but quick to jump ship once they see it in practice. Ironically, in the case of innovation, staying very close to your customers may be exactly the *wrong* thing to do. The second reason, related to the first, is that it is nearly impossible to accurately predict the financial return from an innovation. Industry leaders will tend to underestimate dramatically (witness Seagate), while new entrants may tend to overestimate (witness the number of great-idea companies that never live up to the initial promises made to investors).

Even if a company has become an industry leader by means of past innovation, the pressure to remain successful by sticking with what has worked in the past is enormous. Couple that pressure with the results of analyses that say that "customers don't really want this specific innovation and it doesn't look profitable anyway," and one is easily led to a logical decision to reject the innovation. Even if one believes, in general, that customers want innovation or that innovation is inevitable, the data in any specific case seems always to say "but not this one."

I do not mean to suggest that successful companies never innovate again. Coca-Cola is constantly experimenting with new advertising campaigns and new company images. AT&T, Bell Labs, and Corning understood the limits of copper cable technology and were the first to develop fiber optic cable in the 1960s; even though the telephone company had an enormous investment in copper cable plant and the new technology was unproved. Charles Schwab & Company (the discount stockbroker) continues to introduce a stream of innovative services that make investing easier for more people.

Success does not dictate the end of innovation in an organization, but the experience of many companies shows that *success raises the barriers to innovation.* Innovation can be done in successful companies, but, paradoxically, it is hard work.

The challenge of know-how. The second major challenge to overcome, once we understand the factors driving the need for continuous innovation, is the challenge of figuring out exactly what to do. When I ask seminar participants to list techniques that they use for generating creative ideas, "brainstorming" is overwhelmingly the most frequent response. For many people, brainstorming is the only tool they can name. A few people can cite other specific techniques like the ones we will cover in this book—these responses usually elicit curious looks from the other participants. The rest of the responses follow a predictable pattern represented by these examples.

- Sleep on it.
- Take a walk in the woods.
- Discuss it with someone who knows nothing about it.
- Keep a pad and pencil at bedside for jotting down ideas that come to you in the middle of the night.
- Think about it while showering, brushing teeth, shaving, putting on make-up, or driving to work.

Such responses support the popular notion of creativity as a zap from the blue; a relatively passive activity where we just have to wait for a good idea to come along. This notion is wrong. We can direct ourselves to generate creative thoughts. We can do better than simple brainstorming.

Why Practitioners of Quality Management Should Be Interested in Creativity and Innovation

I have made the case for a purposeful, organizational focus on creativity, and outlined two key challenges. What has this got to do with the pursuit of quality? I hope that you have already seen a variety of answers to that question. Let me now clarify the important points.

Why Should Practitioners of Quality Management Be Interested in Creativity and Innovation?

- The fundamental goal is organizational success.

- The customers want innovation.

- The traditional quality management maxim of "listening to the voice of the customer" may lead an organization to exactly the wrong conclusion in the face of innovation.

- The traditional, analytical techniques of quality management may not be adequate for all situations.

- It will bring more joy in work.

The fundamental goal is organizational success. We have seen that a purposeful focus on creativity and innovation is an essential ingredient in the formula for long-term business success today. Note that I have not suggested that a focus on creativity and innovation is the exclusive ingredient in success. The question of whether an organization should focus on quality management or creative thinking (or cultural diversity or reengineering or whatever) is the wrong question. More to the point, *or* is the wrong conjunction.

Organizations today are challenged to focus on quality, *and* creativity, *and* diversity, and the like, all at once.

The industrial progress that has brought us the wonders of our modern world—products and services that were unimaginable to our grandparents—has also brought with it complexity. We can argue about whether innovation is a by-product of a focus on quality, or whether true quality will only occur if we somehow focus on innovation, but the argument is silly. The two foci are interconnected, along with many other things, in a systems web that organizations must learn to navigate if they are to be successful. Quality management practitioners, who understand processes and systems, should be among the first to recognize the folly of focusing only on the pieces of the whole.

Practitioners of quality management should be interested in learning more about creativity and innovation because creativity and innovation contribute to organizational success. And that is what we should all be focused on.

The customers want innovation. We know that customers desire innovation, both for its own sake and because it sometimes satisfies them in a surprising way. If quality is about exceeding customers' expectations, then quality management must also be about the business of innovation. If the customers want innovation, how can the practitioners of quality management ethically refuse to learn more about the techniques that can help bring it about?

The traditional quality management maxim of listening to the voice of the customer may lead an organization to exactly the wrong conclusion in the face of innovation. The story of Seagate Technologies, and others like it, should be deeply troubling to anyone actively engaged in quality management. Listening to the voice of the customer is a fundamental tenet in the pursuit of quality. But, as Bower and Christensen point out, listening to their customers was exactly what the leaders of Seagate were doing when they lost the company's leadership in its industry. To be sure, it is easy in hindsight to assert that they misused the techniques of customer needs analysis. Seagate should have talked to all its potential customers, not just its current ones. A rookie quality manager knows that. Unfortunately, such clarity is only possible through the eyes of hindsight.

How will a rookie quality manager, or a well-seasoned quality manager for that matter, know which customers to listen to and how to listen to them if he or she does not understand how to think creatively beyond the current reality? We will all know what should have been done once the story is told and the damage has occurred. The missteps will be logically apparent in hindsight. But will we know what to do when *we* are the characters in the story ourselves?

The traditional, analytical techniques of quality management may not be adequate for all situations. The case of the late medications told in the prologue is an allegory for events that take place daily in organizations in all industries—good analysis leading to stuck thinking.

I am a firm believer in the power of the analytical methods of quality management. I have personally seen hundreds of improvement projects and design efforts achieve magnificent results with simple tools such as flowcharts, histograms, control charts, failure mode effects analysis tables, and designed experiments. While these methods work, I have also been troubled by their occasional apparent failure. Some problems seem to elude improvement. The product or service that we designed so painstakingly sometimes fails to really excite customers.

More troubling is the observation that these apparent failures of analytical methods are occurring more frequently than before. There is no way to know for sure, but I wonder if our success in using the techniques of process analysis have left us with an unwelcome by-product: *The pool of unsolved problems now contains a higher proportion of problems that are not amenable to solution by analytical methods.* We've done the easy ones (and they weren't that easy!). What's left is really going to be tough.

The reengineering literature lends some support to this theory. Several studies, and a number of anecdotal reports, cite failure rates of 50 percent to 80 percent in reengineering projects. (See, for example, Hall et al. 1993; or Hammer and Stanton 1995.) In this context, *failure* is defined as a project that falls short of the performance expectations of its sponsors. In other words, the organizations in question did achieve something, they just could not get as far as they had hoped. (This is basically the same situation faced by the medication error team in the prologue.) In commenting on these failures, reengineering guru Michael Hammer (1995, 19–21) cites "spending a lot of time in analysis" as one of his "top ten ways to fail at reengineering." Calling analysis a potential "tar pit," Hammer asserts that analysis "can cripple the imagination." It seems that the reported gap between actual and expected results in these projects is not for want of more analysis, but for more imagination.

Hammer cites nine other ways to fail at reengineering. The failure of reengineering projects to meet their objectives is in no way a proof that we are reaching the limits of analytical methods. I hope that future organizational research will shed more light on the frequency of this troubling phenomenon. For now, I am content to leave it to the personal experience of readers—have you ever been frustrated by the apparent failure of analytical methods to bring about the result you anticipated in a quality project? If so, you have already proven to yourself that it might be useful to explore a complementary set of techniques for creative thinking.

Remember that this is not an *or* issue. It is an *and* issue. It would be useful to master both analytical *and* creative thinking methods.

It will bring more joy in work. Our final answer to the question "Why should practitioners of quality management be interested in creativity?" references the late quality guru W. Edwards Deming's (1993) repeated call for more "joy in work." Deming asserted that we all have the fundamental right to enjoy what we do. Importantly, he suggested that joy in work was linked to intrinsic motivation, and that intrinsic motivation was essential for achieving high levels of individual and organizational performance. In other words, joy in work is interconnected to the quality of the output of an organization.*

Coming up with creative ideas is just plain fun. It is exhilarating when the solution to a nagging problems comes into focus in a way that you had not imagined before. Creative thinking is intrinsically rewarding, and it might even be extrinsically rewarding if the idea saves the company money or opens up a new market.

Creative thinking is not the only way to bring more joy in work, but it is one way. Being able to introduce directed creativity into a group or department that has become frustrated by its stuck thinking is one way to help raise the quality of the output of that group.

---

*For more on this topic, see Kohn 1990, 1992, and 1993.

The invitation to add new tools to the kit of quality management will not be taken as threatening by those who understand the history of the field. Quality management is an eclectic discipline. Its history is rich with acquisitions of methods from the fields of statistics, engineering, operations research, organizational development, market research, psychology, and others. For example, affinity diagrams were developed by an anthropologist, and Joseph Juran borrowed ideas from the field of economics when he described the Pareto principle. The field of quality management has a strong heritage of using techniques that work, regardless of their origins. The theory, tools, and methods of creative thinking will add to the history of the field of quality management, and help us to be even more effective in the future.

PART II

Some Essential Theory for Directed Creativity

CHAPTER 2

Definitions and the Theory of the Mechanics of Mind

⌣ ⌐ ☺ ☽

Achieving clarity on definitions of terms is essential to making progress in a field of endeavor.

Thomas Kuhn

No theory, no learning.

W. Edwards Deming

Some people claim not to be interested in the logic of creativity and are impatient to get on with the practical techniques. This is a mistake, because you will not use the tools effectively unless you know what lies behind the design of the tool.

Edward de Bono

Having made the case for adding creative thinking to the field of quality management, we now face the issue of how. In this chapter, I will begin to lay out the essential elements of a theory of creativity that has emerged from the cognitive sciences over the past 50 years.

Understanding the theory behind creativity and innovation is key in directing oneself to be creative on demand. While a full review of the theoretical literature from the field of creative thinking is beyond the scope of this book, a little theory is essential for three reasons. First, recent research has debunked some common myths that often block creative thinking. Second, understanding the theory enables us to see what we are trying to accomplish when we use various creative-thinking techniques. And third, as Deming (1993) and others have pointed out, simply applying techniques without understanding how they work is of marginal value because we have no mechanism for learning and growing from our experiences. It is simply not productive to proceed without a good grounding in theory.

Creativity and Innovation Defined

It seems appropriate to begin our exploration of theory by defining what we mean by creativity and innovation. Unfortunately, the literature does not provide a single, generally accepted definition of these terms. This should not trouble us; quality management literature does not provide a single, generally accepted definition of *quality,* and we have still managed to make great progress. Just as the various definitions of *quality* inform us about the richness of that concept, the various definitions of *creativity* and *innovation* each provide useful insight. But, also like *quality,* there is enough commonalty among these definitions to give us a working level consensus about what people generally mean when they refer to creativity and innovation.

What do we mean by creativity? In 1964, creativity researcher Joseph McPherson cited 28 definitions of *creativity* (Taylor 1964). I have collected another 10 to 15 definitions to add to McPherson's list from writings appearing after that time. (It is hard to be exact; some of the new definitions are quite close to ones identified by McPherson.) Shifting through these definitions of creativity, I have identified several underlying themes that comprise what we commonly mean when we say "creative."* These themes are captured in what I propose as a consensus definition of *creativity:*

> *Creativity is the connecting and rearranging of knowledge—in the minds of people who will allow themselves to think flexibly—to generate new, often surprising ideas that others judge to be useful.*

---

*A working paper providing a more comprehensive review of the definitions of creativity is available from the author.

The recent development of a glue to replace stitches as a way of closing surgical incisions is a good illustration of the definition of creativity. Using adhesive to close an incision is a new, useful idea. You may have smiled or expressed pleasant surprise when you first heard it. In hindsight, we can see that this idea is simply a logical connection of existing knowledge—adhesive as a way of holding things together, and the need to repair the skin following surgery. It makes perfect sense now that we hear it, but coming up with the idea required the mental flexibility and courage to step out of the current paradigm of how surgical incisions should be closed. The Zip-lock storage bag—the useful, and at first surprising, combination of a zipper and a plastic bag—is another classic illustration. Similarly, quality function deployment (QFD) was a creative idea in quality management because it took several existing concepts such as customer-needs analysis, competitor analysis, process flowcharting, and matrices, and combined these in a new and surprisingly useful way.

Practical implications from the definition of creativity. Understanding what we mean by *creative* is a big step toward directed creativity. Now we know what to direct our thinking toward. That is, when we wish to be creative, we should try to come up with an original idea by making novel associations among what we already know. As a first step, it may be helpful to explicitly list what we already know to aid this mental association process. It also may be helpful to learn about new concepts simply for the purpose of having them available in the mind for later creative connection. Several creative-thinking tools are based on these notions.

Having called to mind what we know, the next practical step suggested by the definition is to search for new connections and be attentive to surprises. This idea of searching for surprising patterns explains why some creativity techniques suggest that we select concepts at random and try our best to combine them into something useful.

The definition of creativity also provides the practical suggestion that we should cultivate personality characteristics like flexibility and spontaneity in our thinking. If you want to be more creative, purposefully move out of your comfort zone in many small ways on a regular basis. Vary your morning routine, take some paperwork and go sit in the lobby or in a park to work on it, try new restaurants . . . anything that will help you prove to yourself that doing something new is not so bad after all.

Finally, the definition of creativity suggests that we must work hard to develop the practical value of our ideas; creativity is not just about flexible thinking and mental free-association. Our analytical- and logical-thinking abilities are also needed. The ability to practically shape and develop an idea is just as important as the ability to imagine the idea in the first place. Imagination and analysis are equal partners in creativity.

What do we mean by innovation, and how is it different from creativity? Having defined creativity, we can now define the related, but different, term *innovation*. Again, various authors in the literature provide various definitions of this term. (See, for example, Schumpter 1939; Foster 1986; von Hipple 1988; and Higgins 1994.) The consensus definition that I propose for our use here is:

> *Innovation is the first, practical, concrete implementation of an idea done in a way that brings broad-based, extrinsic recognition to an individual or organization.*

An innovation is a step beyond a creative idea. While creativity is about the production of ideas, innovation is about the practical implementation of those ideas. Further, while both creativity and innovation are in the eye of the beholder, innovation involves the significant, formal recognition by others of the value of the idea. This extrinsic recognition might take the form of money (sales of product or service), a prize (the Nobel, a patent), or notoriety (widespread acknowledgment by others). Csikszentmihlyi (1988) points out that this widespread recognition for a concrete action is the key distinction between a true innovation and an idea that is merely novel, statistically improbable, or bizarre.

It is also important to note that the innovator is not necessarily the first person to have the creative idea. For example, Charles Darwin is credited as the innovative thinker who brought us the theory of evolution, even though the basic ideas were first published in an obscure paper by Thomas Malthus several years earlier. Similarly, while Ray Kroc (of McDonalds fame) is widely thought of as the innovator who brought the concept of fast food into the world, it is highly likely that others before him had experimented with the creative idea of a limited menu served quickly. The point is that Kroc's implementation of the idea fundamentally impacted the world in a way that the world recognized.

I stress this point because it is essential to realize that one can be creative, but fail to be innovative. The difference lies in the hard work of implementing our ideas and holding them up to public critique.

The practical implications of this distinction for organizations are clear. Many people in many organizations have had original, creative ideas for process, product, and service innovations. Being averse to risk, the organization failed to act on these ideas. (For example, the graphical user interface for which Apple Computers became famous was actually first conceived at Xerox's Palo Alto Research Center.) Such organizations have missed the competitive advantage that the innovator enjoys while the followers are working to catch up. Successful organizations and individuals must go beyond the mere production of creative ideas. Real success only comes with the implementation of an idea. Real success only comes with innovation.

The practical implications from the definitions of creativity and innovation. The practical implications drawn from the definitions of *creativity* and *innovation* provide our first, theory-directed glimpse of directed creativity. These implications are summarized in the following box. Similar boxes will appear throughout this chapter to keep us focused on practical matters as we cover the various aspects of the theory of creativity.

**Practical Advice for Creative Thinking:
The Definitions of Creativity and Innovation**

- Try to come up with an original idea by making novel associations among what you already know.

- Be attentive to surprises.

- When you feel yourself laughing or smiling at an idea, pause on the thought and work with it.

- Deliberately cultivate personality characteristics like flexibility and spontaneity in your thinking.

- Work hard to shape your ideas so that others can readily see the value in them.

- Do not be content with merely generating creative ideas. Remember, the rewards of innovation come to the one who takes action on the ideas.

What does all this have to do with quality management? Plenty. If, as I pointed out in chapter 1, customers demand innovation, then practitioners of quality management should be out front helping their organizations be more innovative. And if, as our definitions have made clear, innovation requires a balance of creative, analytical, conceptual, and concrete thought, then quality managers already have important skills to bring to the table. We have a rich tradition of analysis. Further, we understand the need for action—we understand that *do, study,* and *act* follow *plan* in the Shewhart/Deming PDSA cycle. Finally, we bring hard-earned experience in the management of organizational change. We simply need to balance our traditional strengths with some new tools for creative thinking.

Some Theory of the Mechanics of Mind

While the definitions of creativity and innovation provide general guidance for thinking, we must still acknowledge that creative thoughts are relatively rare. Why? Because it is simply not natural to think creatively. We are only now beginning to understand why this is so.

During the past 50 years, the fields of the cognitive sciences have advanced our understanding of the details of thinking and the mechanics of the mind. Cognitive science is the multidisciplinary study of thinking that crosses the fields of philosophy, psychology, linguistics, artificial intelligence, anthropology, and neuroscience.* While we remain a long way from a complete understanding of the workings of the mind, research into cognitive processes in general, and creative thinking specifically, has led to two broad conclusions of interest to us here. First, our normal thought processes are not optimized for creative thinking and, second, despite this suboptimization, we can purposefully take mental actions that lead to creative thoughts.

Figure 2.1 presents a high-level, but useful, model of the mind based on the research from the cognitive sciences. The four major components depicted in the model are based roughly on the organization of Osherson and Smith's (1990) collection of papers in the reference work *An Invitation to Cognitive Science, Volume 3: Thinking.* While the title sounds imposing, this collection of research summaries from 10 prominent authors is surprisingly

---

*For a history and overview of the field of cognitive science see Gardner 1985.

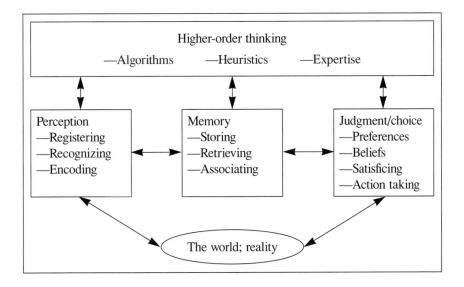

Figure 2.1. A high-level model of the mechanics of mind.

accessible. Readers interested in going beyond the overview of key points that I will present here will find this book fascinating.

As Figure 2.1 indicates, the reality of the world is happening all around us at all times. We experience this reality through our senses and the mental subsystem of perception. We are able to make sense out of all of this input through the interaction of the mental subsystems of perception and memory. Deciding what to do about it involves the mental subsystem of judgment and choice. Finally, the actions we take change the reality of the world.

The overarching controllers of the mind are the processes of higher-order thinking. This subsystem controls the flow of information among the other subsystems. Higher-order thinking processes direct attention, make memory searches efficient, and retain veto power over judgment and choice.

As a simple illustration of the operation of the system depicted in Figure 2.1, consider the everyday reality of driving down the road in your car. Up ahead the traffic light switches to red. The photons of light leaving the traffic signal strike your eyes and register as electrical impulses in the optic nerve leading to the brain. These impulses and those from other sensory inputs (for example, the sound of the radio, the light from other objects in your field of view, and the tactile feel of the steering wheel in your hands) are sent to the memory subsystems to see if any of them are familiar. The red-traffic-light impulse is found in memory and associated with the thought "slow down and come to a stop." In similar fashion, the sound impulse from the radio might be associated in memory with the thought "my favorite song" and the tactile input from the steering wheel might be associated with the thought "cold." The higher-order thinking process of expertise, specifically, the expertise of "driving," kicks in and prioritizes these memory retrievals such that dealing with "slow down and come to stop" takes precedence over "the steering wheel is cold." (Later, when you've come to a stop and have nothing better to do, "the steering wheel is cold" may become the focus of your thoughts.) At this point, the subsystem of judgment and choice takes over and activates the muscles of your leg to take action to apply steady pressure to the brake. Note, of course, that the subsystem of judgment and choice is situation-dependent. While red-light photons from a traffic signal will always activate the memory pattern that says "slow down and come to a stop," if you believe that you will be late for work and your judgment and expertise say that you can make the light, your mind might chose to send a signal to the leg muscles to press hard on the accelerator rather than steadily on the brake. Regardless of the action you take, the reality of the world will go on to its next scene and the mental processes of perception, memory, judgment, and higher-order thinking will be activated for another cycle. The wonder of the mechanics of mind is that all of this happens quite automatically and in a split second. Our minds are optimized to deal efficiently with such normal, mundane realities of everyday life.

So far, we have not said anything about the mechanics of mind that helps us understand creativity better. You can confirm what we have covered so far about the theory of mind just on the basis of your own everyday thinking. Naming the mental subprocesses and describing their functions in mundane life is not terribly enlightening.

The theory of mind has advanced well beyond the simple description of thought just outlined. We now know a great deal more about the details of the various subsystems. More importantly, we can also describe how and why these subsystems are suboptimal for nonmundane thinking such as directed creativity. Understanding the suboptimizations inherent in these mental systems helps us devise strategies to work around the problematic features. If we develop these strategies fully, we can then store them as new higher-order thinking patterns to provide us with a new expertise: that of creative thinking.

The Role of Perception in Creative Thinking

Thinking begins with perception. Perception involves the basic mental processes of registering information from our senses, recognizing meaningful patterns, and encoding that meaning in a simpler form. For example, your eyes might register the image of a woman coming into your office. You recognize the woman by accessing a pattern in memory labeled "Susan," and you encode (summarize) the scene as "Susan is coming to see me." Your perception process appears to be working automatically until you are told that the woman is, in fact, Susan's younger sister Libby, whom you have never met. This new information leads to another perception process (initiated by the higher-order thinking subsystems) where you register and recognize new details such as Libby's younger skin, slightly higher cheekbones, and green rather than brown eyes. This will all be encoded into a new memory pattern, which you will label "Libby."

Sensory stimulus comes to us with a great deal of detailed information; for example, all the details of Libby's face, her style of dress, walk, and so on. Sperling (1960) and Neisser (1967) show that we register all of this visual information and hold it in a special portion of memory, called the iconic memory, for about 200 milliseconds while we process it. (Full verbal information is available for about 2 seconds, decaying slowly over the 30 seconds that follow.) We then selectively encode this information; that is, we use only those bits of the scene that seem to provide a satisfactory match with an existing pattern in memory (in this case "Susan") and discard the rest.*

All of this is good for everyday thinking because it is efficient. It hinders creative thinking, however, because it virtually guarantees that when we look at a familiar situation (for example, from the case in the prologue, nurses are forgetting to give medications on time) we will only see and encode what we have always seen and encoded (they need a log sheet to remind them).

In other words, our everyday perception processes tend to oversummarize the information in a situation, leaving us blind to most of what is happening. While this summarization process provides focus (which is good), it also means that most of the information that comes to our senses is quickly discarded as not being relevant to the matter at hand. This discarding process is bad for creativity because—by definition—creative ideas are surprising.

---

*For a full description of these phenomena, see Potter 1990 and Sternberg 1988.

We would be surprised (that is, have the opportunity to be creative) if a seemingly irrelevant detail provided the key to getting unstuck in our thinking. If left unchecked, the everyday processes of perception virtually guarantee that we will never get to the point of creative surprise because the very information we need is discarded quickly before we get much of a chance to think about it. In short, we miss most of what goes on around us. While this may be helpful in avoiding information overload in dealing with the mundane matters of life, if we fail to perceive fully, it is difficult to make the novel mental associations that are fundamental to creative thinking.

Of course, we are capable of perceiving in fresh ways. We just need to make the effort. The longer we pause to really look at Libby's face, as well as use our other senses to gather information, the more details we will recognize and encode to help us distinguish her from her sister Susan. Similarly, the more we make it a habit to purposely pause and notice things in a work situation, the better our chances of identifying something that will unstick our thinking. Referring back to the alarm clock example and the thought processes outlined in the prologue, the first steps in directed creative thinking often involve making the effort to perceive the situation freshly—to notice things that we have not noticed before. Clarifying the issue and stopping to notice things are key actions we can take to avoid racing ahead toward a collision with that same old brick wall in our thoughts.

These facts from the cognitive sciences are the basis for a variety of creative-thinking techniques in the literature that might seem ridiculous at first. For example, Adams (1974) suggests drawing a detailed picture or diagram of a situation because this will force a closer look. For similar reasons, Fritz (1991) emphasizes spending a great deal of time defining the current reality; von Oech (1986, 49) suggests "explain the problem to an audience and listen to yourself;" Ray and Myers (1986) recommend the use of visualization techniques from Eastern meditative philosophy; and Wonder and Donovan (1984) suggest generating slow-motion mental movies of a situation to aid in noticing details.

These techniques make perfect sense, indeed we can see them as essential, when we understand that our everyday perception processes are not optimized to support creative thinking. Importantly, an understanding of the mechanics of the mind helps us understand what benefit we are supposed to derive from using such techniques. These techniques do not, of themselves,

---

Practical Advice for Creative Thinking: Tuning Your Perception

- Recognize when your thinking is stuck.

- Make it a habit to purposely pause and notice things; what works and why.

- To perceive freshly when you are stuck, try simply pausing to notice something, defining the current reality, drawing a picture, making a slow-motion mental movie, or explaining it to someone and listening to yourself.

---

lead directly to a creative idea. That is not their purpose. The point is simply for us to notice something we have not noticed before. Once something is noticed, then it is available as a bit of knowledge for the subsequent creative process of mental association.

The Role of Memory in Creative Thinking

The second set of fundamental cognitive processes depicted in Figure 2.1 is those associated with memory. I have found the understanding of the mechanics of information storage in memory to be among the most powerful insights I have gathered in my review of the literature on creative thinking.

While it was once believed that each unique memory (for example, Susan's face) occupied a specific place in our brain, modern theory suggests that memories are widely distributed and intricately interconnected in the brain. These modern theories, the connectionist model and the spreading activation theory, trace their roots back to concepts first introduced in 1893 by Spanish neuroanatomist Santiago Ramon y Cajal and mechanisms suggested in 1949 by Canadian psychologist Donald Hebb. de Bono (1969, 1990) provides several delightful, layperson's models of these theories of memory under the umbrella concept he calls the "self-organizing system of mind."*

---

*For a complete description of these phenomena, see Johnson 1991, Hebb 1949, McClelland and Rumelhart 1986, Quillian 1986, Anderson 1983, Churchland 1990, Restak 1991, and Johnson-Laird 1983.

The gist of these theories is that a given concept in memory (for example, "Susan") corresponds to a particular pattern of activity among billions of interconnected brain cells, called neurons. This is depicted in Figure 2.2. A virtually infinite number of mental concepts can be represented over this network of neurons, just as pixels on a finite television screen can be turned on and off selectively to represent an infinite variety of distinct images. Thinking proceeds as activation in one part of the network (for example, the neurons associated with the labels "brown hair," "oval face," and "dark skin") spreads electrically and chemically over time to connected parts of the network (for example, the label "Susan"). The key features of this mechanism are that the direction of the spread from one concept to another is a function of the number of neurons that are shared between the concepts and the frequency with which we have retrieved the pattern in the past.

This memory mechanism explains what we commonly call a stream of thought. For example, returning to the alarm clock idea from the prologue, "forgetfulness" leads to "reminding;" which in the context of "hospital" leads the head nurse to think "log sheet." This occurs because the neural network

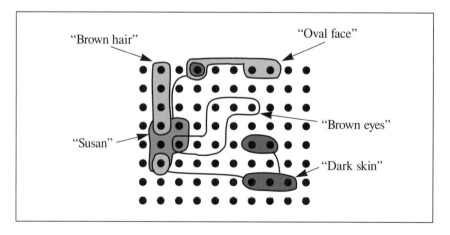

Figure 2.2. Here is a simple graphical depiction of the connectionist model and spreading activation theory. Each dot represents a neuron in the brain. Sets of neurons form memory patterns that give us what we call concepts. Here, when the memory patterns for brown hair, oval face, brown eyes, and dark skin fire simultaneously, their energy spreads to another memory pattern labeled "Susan."

patterns for these concepts in the nurse's mind share many neurons, with strong connections reinforced by having accessed the pattern so often in the past. It is, therefore, easy for the electrical and chemical action of her brain to flow naturally across these connections from one concept to the next.

It is important to recognize that these neural patterns and the strengths of their linkages are highly individualized and learned over time. A nurse in another hospital might naturally flow from the concept of "reminding" into the concept of "chalkboard" rather than "log sheet," simply because that is how they do it in his organization. Similarly, a child, a computer scientist, and a television addict might each have very different ideas that flow naturally from the concept of "reminding."

The concepts of mental flow and streams of thought lead to the alternative depiction of the connectionist model and the spreading activation theory shown in Figure 2.3. This is de Bono's (1969) river and topography model of the mechanism of mind. While it is more abstract than the graphic in Figure 2.2, I find this model just as helpful and easier to work with in explaining the mental actions of creative thinking.

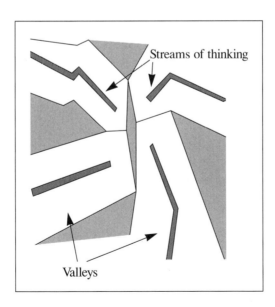

Figure 2.3. de Bono's river and topography model of the mechanism of mind.

de Bono suggests that we think of the mind as a landscape consisting of high ground (shaded areas in Figure 2.3), valleys formed between the high ground, and streams where the run-off water collects at the low points of the valleys. In this model, the flow of thought through the spreading activation in memory is analogous to the flow of water. The valleys represent the processes of perception. The perception process of "registering" creates a mental impulse that we can depict on this model as a drop of falling rainwater. As we saw in the previous section, perception is channeled toward existing patterns in memory in the same way that a drop of rainwater falling anywhere in a valley is channeled into the stream at the bottom of that valley.

de Bono's model is appealing because it corresponds directly to common phrases for mental activity such as "stream of thought" and "mental ruts." In this model, memory is a mental rut. When we learn, we carve another rut (valley) into our mental landscape. The more frequently we access the memory, the deeper the rut (like soil erosion). The deeper the rut, the steeper the walls of the valley, the more quickly we access that stream of thought, and the more automatic is our thinking. This explains why habits are so hard to break. Habits lead to frequent access of the same mental patterns; deep ruts and steep valleys that are difficult to escape.

Before reading on, practice using this model of mind by considering the following questions. (Suggested responses appear at the end of the chapter, but don't peek without trying it on your own.)

1. What does traditional schooling do to the landscape of the mind?

2. Why do actors rehearse their parts before opening night?

3. How would you depict prejudice and stereotyping on this model?

4. Describe the difference between the mental landscape of someone who is a novice in a particular area versus someone who is an expert?

5. How would you describe the process of creative thinking on this model?

So, what are the implications of all this for those who want to engage in creative thinking? First, it is important to recognize that your streams of thought are not inherently correct or incorrect, they are simply what you think at this time, based primarily on what you have learned in the past. Astute readers will recognize the connection between what I am saying here and the notion of paradigms.* A paradigm in science is simply the accepted belief of the day. While practitioners brought up in the current paradigm tend to hold on to it as the only way, every paradigm is destined to be overturned someday by another way. This new way will itself become accepted; that is, the mental activation will spread naturally to it, after repeated use over time. It will become a new mental valley, while the old valley fills in with silt due to lack of flow. Acceptance of these facts—no way of doing things is inherently correct or incorrect, all current ways will someday be replaced, and the new way will eventually seem as natural to us as the current way does now—provides us with the mental freedom to purposely explore other ways of doing things. This understanding of the mechanics of memory forms the basis for creative-thinking techniques like brainstorming that ask us to free-associate, suspend judgment, hitchhike on others' ideas, and aim for quantity.

A second implication for creative thinking lies in the realization that thought patterns are highly individualized and based on past experience. Therefore, when you are stuck in your thinking, try asking someone who is different from you to think along with you. The purpose is not to argue, nor to explain why what he or she is saying will not work (this is a common pitfall). Rather, you should listen for and take advantage of the different mental associations (different mental valleys and ruts) that others hold in their memories. This is the basic, cognitive-systems explanation for why benchmarking—visiting other places and other industries—often yields breakthrough ideas. Other people in other industries have other mental associations and streams of thought. We often say that these other people see things differently. Of course, we know that they see (register) exactly the same photons of light that we see. What we mean is that their mental valleys are in different places than ours, so they encode what they see differently from us.

Finally, an understanding of memory mechanics leads directly to techniques that we can use to stimulate creative thinking. The model leads to the understanding that stuck thinking results from activation that keeps spreading quickly over the same old patterns in our memory network—rainwater that keeps running into the same valley and stream. So try slowing down or backing up in your thinking (that is, deliberately tracing the flow from one idea to the next) to identify the intermediate concepts that make up the

---

*For more on the topic of paradigms, see Kuhn 1962, Scheffler 1967, and Barker 1992.

stream of thought. For example, deliberately backing up from the concept of "log sheet" in the medication error example leads us to the linked concept of "reminding" in our neural network of ideas. Now, because we have identified the concept explicitly instead of simply rushing by it as we normally would, we can purposely link to other associated concepts in memory. "Reminding" might be linked to various other concepts such as "alarm clock," "egg timer," "your mother will tell you when," and so on. Further development of one of these linked concepts might lead to a useful creative idea. Try it yourself. Before reading on, come up with a practical idea for the medication error team using the concept "reminder: your mother will tell you when."*

Another approach would be to open a book, select a word at random, and then deliberately try to connect the situation of interest to that word. The theory behind this technique is that the mental effort required to link to a randomly selected word will force our minds to traverse different streams of thought. Visualize this on the topography model as randomly selecting a raindrop in San Francisco and asking it to make its way to Pittsburgh. It would have to visit a lot of other interesting places along the way. This mental journey may result in surprising, novel associations, if we are attentive to them. Again, try it yourself. Using the words *signature* and *gutter* as mental triggers, make a list of thoughts that apply to the medication error situation.

These techniques, and others, all appear in the popular literature on creative thinking. Each technique seems a bit crazy when you first hear it, but each makes perfect sense when you understand modern theories of the mechanics of memory. Learning to interrupt, step slowly through, and redirect your train of thought in a search for novel associations is a productive skill you can develop to support directed creativity.

The Role of Judgment in Creative Thinking

Judgment is the third set of cognitive processes depicted in Figure 2.1. Judgment is the link between memory and action. We must decide—choose a stream of thinking and follow it to its conclusion—before we can do anything.

---

*Idea: Give someone in the hospital all of the log sheets and have them call the nurses' stations when it is time to administer a medication to a patient.

Practical Advice for Creative Thinking:
Using Your Memory

- Use your perception process to create a store of ideas and concepts in memory.

- Try to come up with an original idea by making novel associations among what you already know.

- Search for patterns in memory and be attentive to surprises.

- Recognize that your trains of thought are not inherently correct or incorrect, they are simply what you think now based primarily on what you have learned in the past.

- Look for different mental associations by listening to other's trains of thought.

- Slow down, or back up, in your thinking to identify the intermediate concepts that make up your train of thought.

- Select a random word and connect it somehow to the situation of interest, being attentive to novel concepts.

- Practice interrupting, stepping slowly through, and redirecting your trains of thought in search of novel associations.

The mental processes of judgment and choice are inherently emotional and belief-laden. Researchers have documented repeatedly that we often make choices that are irrational; that is, our choices do not always stand up to rigorous, logical examination.*

For example, in one classic experiment Tversky and Kahneman (1981) gave students brief descriptions of people and then asked them to rank statements about the person from most probable to least probable. One such vignette described Linda as follows:

> *Linda is 31 years old, single, outspoken, and very bright.*
> *She majored in philosophy. As a student she was deeply con-*

---

*For a full description of these phenomena, see Osherson 1990, Stich 1990, Tversky and Kahneman 1973, and Wason and Johnson-Laird 1970.

> *cerned with issues of discrimination and social justice, and
> also participated in antinuclear demonstrations.*

Based on this description, more than 80 percent of the subjects ranked
the statement "Linda is a bank teller and is active in the feminist movement"
as more probable than the statement "Linda is a bank teller." This ranking is
clearly irrational because it violates the elementary laws of probability. The
probability of teller *and* feminist cannot be greater than the probability of
teller alone. The subjects in the experiments were graduate students in medicine, psychology, education, and decision sciences who could clearly demonstrate their knowledge of the basic laws of probability in independent tests.
They readily admitted the irrationality of their choice when the logical fal-
lacy was pointed out. It seems that their beliefs and stereotypes about bank
tellers and members of the feminist movement clearly overwhelmed rationality and logic in their choice. This and similar experiments have been repli-
cated many times with different subjects, different wordings of the choices,
and different vignettes. The effect is generalizable.*

The irrationality of judgment does not mean that humans are hopelessly
prejudiced, stupid, or dishonest. Rather, we are simply limited in our capacity
to process all of the information needed for purely rational thought and,
therefore, must settle for a limited rationality, augmented by intuition and
emotion. Cherniak (1986) illustrated this point by showing that trying to
make purely rational decisions in a world with only 138 logically independent propositions would yield so many combinations that a super-fast computer, operating since the dawn of time, would not be able to evaluate all the
options. Clearly, the real world presents us with more than 138 logically
independent propositions on even our most routine days. And, clearly, computers are much faster than the human mind at repeated evaluations of truth
tables. If the super computer is overwhelmed in its attempt to live by pure
logic in such a simple world, then our human minds haven't a chance of living solely by logic in the real world.

While pure rationality is impossible, the other extreme, complete irrationality, is also unlikely. Stich (1990, 181) points out, "It is widely con-
ceded . . . that any system of mental representation must exhibit some

---

*See Osherson 1990 for a thorough review of this literature.

degree of rationality." Mass murderers can explain their actions in ways that make sense, at least to themselves. Likewise, your colleagues, family members, and friends usually have internally understandable explanations for their own behaviors and choices. Most of the time, we act in ways that make some sense, if only to ourselves.

We can summarize the large body of research into the mental processes of judgment and choice by saying that it is clear that we do not use pure logic in deciding what to do in response to the various situations we encounter in the world around us. Instead, we make choices based on our personal preferences and beliefs, how the options are presented to us, and our estimates of how easy it will be to justify our choice if challenged by others. Cognitive scientists call these mental processes belief preservation, choice framing, and justification, respectively.

Simon (1981) coined the term *satisficing* to describe the human approach to choice making. Satisficing is the mental activity associated with making reasonably good, but not necessarily optimum, choices in response to the challenges of life. For example, we are engaging in satisficing when we do this year's budget the same way we did last year's, even though we know that the process was far from perfect. We are engaging in satisficing when we use some of the elements from the old process in the design of a new process, rather than completely rethinking the design from the ground up. Satisficing is pragmatic. Again, this is efficient for everyday thinking because it allows us to get on with it, but it works against us when we need creative thinking.

In the medication error case, the quality improvement team engaged in satisficing when it chose an idea (a log sheet to remind the nurses), convinced itself that this should work (that is, engaged in justification and belief preservation), and then simply stopped generating alternative approaches. The team was sure that the idea would work, or at least it should work if everyone would cooperate. When the idea failed and the team was asked to think again, it ended up simply returning to the original idea, pointing out that it should have worked, rejustifying its choice, and concluded that either there is simply no way to resolve the difficulty (errors are inevitable) or that nurses are hopelessly uncooperative (they just would not look at the log sheet). While cognitive researchers do not fully understand the neural mechanics behind these seemingly emotional processes of satisficing and justification, the fact that we all do it naturally is indisputable.

These findings about the cognitive processes of judgment provide the theory behind the oft-repeated creative thinking maxim that we should suspend judgment. A full appreciation of the role of judgment in thinking enhances our understanding of this maxim. Not only should we avoid prematurely judging others' ideas, we should also avoid prematurely concluding that our own ideas are sufficient. Perkins (1981) and Simon (1981) point out that good thinkers search longer and deeper; they avoid early satisficing.

The cognitive processes of judgment may also explain why setting a matter aside and coming back to it later sometimes yields a creative breakthrough. It is commonly presumed that this incubation phenomenon is a result of subconscious thought processes mysteriously at work behind the scenes during the intervening time. Perkins (1981) suggests that it might simply be that the strength of our emotions, justifications, and beliefs subsides over time, enabling us to see the issue free from the blinders of satisficing and justification. In any event, and perhaps for a variety of other reasons, setting something aside and coming back to it later is another thing that the mechanics of mind suggests we can do to support directed creative thinking.

Another potential antidote to the problem of satisficing is to deliberately set a quota for the number of ideas that you will fully develop before making a final choice. This technique is commonly employed in product or service innovation where multiple design teams are asked to work independently on the development of the same product. (See, for example, Tracy Kidder's (1981) *Soul of the New Machine.*)

Understanding that there is some degree of rationality in all points of view, but that no one is perfectly rational, suggests another action we can take to support directed creativity: we should seek advice and critical analysis from others. As in seeking others' ideas because they may have different associations in memory, the key here is to focus on listening to the other person's stream of thought and internal rationality, not on arguing or rejustifying your choice.

Finally, since complete rationality is impossible, we must recognize that complete suspension of judgment is also impossible. We cannot avoid making choices based on beliefs and preferences, but we can explicitly recognize our beliefs and preferences as such and be willing to modify them if the idea does not work out.

So, an understanding of the cognitive processes of judgment and an awareness of the natural mental tendency toward satisficing leads to a variety of specific actions that we can take to support directed creativity. It also explains the seeming paradox in the creativity literature where, on the one hand, we are counseled to suspend judgment and, on the other, we are reminded to develop practical ideas. The judgment that we should suspend is that which prematurely rejects a concept before it is developed or that shuts down the generation of options because we are satisfied with the one we have. The judgment to use is that which forces us to take a hard look at our goals and the details of exactly how we will implement a given concept. Clearly, judgment plays an important—and positive—role in creative thinking.

**Practical Advice for Creative Thinking:
Using Your Judgment**

- Be aware of the danger of both premature judgment and satisficing.

- Never think that you have arrived at the end of your thinking on a matter; as practical, push yourself to generate more than one good option.

- Try avoiding the blinders of emotion, judgment, and satisficing by setting the issue aside for a while and coming back to it later.

- Actively seek out the rationality in other's points of view.

Higher-Order Mental Processes

The final element in the system of cognitive processes depicted in Figure 2.1 is generically labeled *higher-order thinking*. Simply put, higher-order thinking is the mental management of repeated acts of perception, memory, and judgment, directed over time toward some goal. Directing our creative thoughts in order to solve a nagging problem or generate a breakthrough idea is an example of higher-order thinking.*

---

*Again, for a complete description, see Osherson and Smith 1990 and Sternberg 1988.

Research indicates that heuristics are key to higher order thinking.* Perkins (1981, 192) defines a heuristic as "a rule of thumb that often helps in solving a certain class of problems, but makes no guarantees." An example of a heuristic in quality management is Juran's (1964) advice to "look for the vital few." This is useful advice in that it points us in a potentially productive direction; although it does not guarantee that we will always be successful. Of course, heuristics are not necessarily always right. The advice "if it ain't broke, don't fix it" is an example of a heuristic of dubious value. Contrast these heuristics with an algorithm, for example the method for doing long division. An algorithm is an exact procedure that guarantees a solution; if we follow the steps of long division, we will always get the correct answer. A heuristic is simply a rule of thumb that is based on the accumulated experiences of many people.

A variety of researchers have demonstrated that experts in a given area do more effective higher-order thinking primarily because they have better heuristics than novices.† This is understandable in light of the previous discussion about the impossibility of completely rational judgment. In other words, since the number of detailed criteria we should ideally evaluate in making a practical decision is immense, there is no way to specify an exact algorithm that will cover every conceivable situation. Rather, we must rely on some rules of thumb about what is important and then make our best choices consistent with those heuristics.

For creative thinking, the implications of this are that we should concentrate on the development and application of heuristics that improve the likelihood of getting beyond incidents of stuck thinking. Throughout this chapter, I have attempted to do just that by offering the heuristic advice in the various boxes describing how we might overcome the suboptimization inherent in our normal cognitive processes. This is the best we can do for now. When we understand enough about the workings of the mind to reduce creative thinking to an algorithm, then we can simply program computers to do all of our thinking for us. We are a long way from that point (and what a boring world it will be if we ever get there!).

---

*The concept of heuristics is further described in Wallas 1926, Newell and Simon 1972, Schoenfeld 1979, Polya 1957, Langley and Jones 1988, and Holyoak 1990.

†For example, see Holyoak 1990, De Groot 1965, Larkin et al. 1980, Chi et al. 1982, and Lesgold 1988.

Summary of the Theory and Its Implications for Directed Creativity

Understanding the definitions of creativity and innovation, and the mechanics of mind, is an essential part of learning how to be creative. Since we all have the same basic mental equipment, we all possess the capacity for creative thought. We now know that our minds are simply not optimized for creative thought. We can also now see what we may need to do when we want novel ideas. Knowing how your mind usually works—perception is channeled toward existing patterns, concepts in memory are tied together based on past frequency of connection, judgment is biased toward the status quo and satisficing—puts one in the best position to purposefully effect a shift in thinking. Now that we know something about the processes of thinking, we can begin to improve them.

Answers to Questions in Section on Memory

1. Traditional schooling is about digging ruts and creating valleys to form streams of thought (memories of facts and procedures).

2. Rehearsal makes the mental valleys deeper and thereby makes the associated streams of thought (in this case, the lines of the play) more automatic.

3. Prejudice and stereotyping can be depicted as very wide valleys. All incoming information is channeled into a single stream of thought.

4. The mental landscape of a novice would have relatively few valleys, and those that do appear would be rather shallow. The expert would have numerous and deeper valleys, with an elaborate network of flows and interconnections between them.

5. The process of creative thinking can be depicted as digging channels or tunnels to connect stream of thinking that are not normally connected. Alternatively, creative thinking can be a helicopter that picks up water in one valley and deposits it in another valley. Either way, creative thinking is about linking mental valleys that are not normally linked; combining existing concepts to form new ideas.

CHAPTER 3

Heuristics and Models: Attitudes, Approaches, and Actions That Support Creative Thinking

ξ ᵭᵭᵭᵖ ⋀⋀ ⦚⦚

It sounded an excellent plan, no doubt, and very neatly and simply arranged. The only difficulty was, she had not the smallest idea how to set about it.

Lewis Carrol, of Alice in *Alice in Wonderland*

When your logic fails, try a hunch.

James T. Kirk, *Star Trek*

The theory of the mechanics of mind is a theory about the workings of the piece parts of the processes of creativity. Building on our understanding of these elements, we will now step back to examine these creative processes as a larger whole. In this chapter, we will look at heuristics and models for creative thinking. These are the essential mental attitudes, methods of approach, and concrete actions that will underlie our use of directed creativity.

Heuristics from the Creativity Literature

When we approach a new field, like creativity, one of the most important things to learn are the heuristics of that field. Unfortunately, as with quality management, there are many proposed heuristics for creative thinking and no generally accepted, single list that we can reference. Some of the proposed heuristics of creative thinking are based on research studies, while others are simply statements of experience-based principle. Whatever their origins, the various rules of thumb that have emerged in the literature during the past 50 years form an implicit theory about ways to boost creative output and organizational innovation. Our study of heuristics for creative thinking will, therefore, further lay the theoretical foundation for the tools and applications we will discuss in subsequent chapters.

Let's begin our quick review of the literature with a basic set of heuristics to show how simple rules of thumb emerge naturally from our understanding of the mechanics of mind. Teresa Amabile (1989), an influential creativity researcher, offers the following simple set of heuristics to parents and children in her book *Growing Up Creative: Nurturing a Life of Creativity.*

1. Break set: break out of your old patterns of doing something.

2. Keep options open as long as possible.

3. Suspend judgment.

4. Think broadly: try to see as many relationships as possible between different ideas.

5. Break out of scripts: break out of well-worn habits of doing things.

6. Perceive freshly: try to see things differently from the way you and other people normally see them.

7. Use tricks or little rules of thumb that can make you think of new ideas: for example, "make the familiar strange and the strange familiar," "play with ideas," "investigate paradoxes."

Amabile's list of basic heuristics is clearly tied to the model of mind we examined in the previous chapter. Item 6 is advice for our mental subsystem of perception. Items 1, 4, and 5 are an appeal to the mental valleys and associative thinking processes of memory. Items 2 and 3 are aimed at the subsystems of judgment and choice. Finally, item 7 suggests overall direction for higher-order thinking.

These items are not dissimilar to the practical advice in the various boxes scattered throughout the previous chapter. From what you now know, you could have generated a similar list of basic heuristics yourself. Once we understand some theory about the workings of the mind, we are no longer constrained to view creative thinking as a mysterious gift that only other people know how to use.

While Amabile's advice is (for the most part) directed to specific mental subsystems, other heuristics in the creativity literature speak more to the complex interactions among these subsystems. For example, in his book *The Mind's Best Work,* Harvard educator David Perkins (1981) offers 10 heuristics for boosting creative output. Items on Perkins' list include the following:

- Try to be original (that is, do not be content with merely copying what others have done).

- Find the problem (that is, experiment with various ways of defining an issue to see what insights you gain).

- Practice in a context (that is, concentrate your creative energy on some area of work or life that you care deeply about).

Rather than directing advice to specific subsystems of mind, Perkins' heuristics require coordinated effort among the subsystems. For example, to follow Perkins' advice to try to be original, we must focus our perception processes on finding new things in our environment, deliberately search for highly unusual mental associations in memory, and self-judge our ideas relative to the criterion of originality. This is a much more complex set of mental gymnastics than Amabile's more direct advice to keep options open, suspend judgment, and perceive freshly.

The contrast between these two lists illustrates the challenge inherent in offering heuristic advice. The first list is so focused on mental subsystems that it might seem trivial to you now, while the second gives advice at such a high level that it might seem difficult to implement. Perkins (1981, 195) summarizes it this way: "All in all, heuristic advice seems damned both ways, for being either too obvious to bother with or too vague to actually follow."

It is useful, therefore, to consider heuristic advice at various levels, such as basic, intermediate, or advanced. In such a scheme, Amabile's advice is at the basic level. Once these basic thinking patterns have become second nature to us—the valleys in memory have become deep and wide and the mental scripts automatic—we might be ready to move on to the intermediate level of Perkins' list.

In the end, you will have to decide what level and what specific heuristic advice is right for you. You will have to choose and adapt the available advice to fit your needs. Further, the heuristics you find most helpful will change over time as your expertise grows and your situation changes.

Eight Heuristics for Directed Creativity

With this brief introduction to the heuristics in the classic creativity literature, let me now offer the list of heuristics for directed creativity that we will use in this book (see Figure 3.1). This list is compiled both from the advice of experts like Amabile, Perkins, and others, and from my own experience. I have purposefully kept the list short so that you can commit the heuristics to memory and practice these new mental behaviors regularly.

Heuristic 1: Make it a habit to purposefully pause and notice things. The importance of learning to perceive the world in a fresh way is clearly a part of the generally accepted theory of creative thinking. Nearly every expert

---

1. Make it a habit to purposefully pause and notice things.

2. Focus your creative energies on just a few topic areas that you genuinely care about and work on these purposefully for several weeks or months.

3. Avoid being too narrow in the way you define your problem or topic area; purposefully try broader definitions and see what insights you gain.

4. Try to come up with original and useful ideas by making novel associations among what you already know.

5. When you need creative ideas, remember: attention, escape, and movement.

6. Pause and carefully examine ideas that make you laugh the first time you hear them.

7. Recognize that your streams of thought and patterns of judgment are not inherently right or wrong; they are just what you think now based primarily on patterns from your past.

8. Make a deliberate effort to harvest, develop, and implement at least a few of the ideas you generate.

Figure 3.1. Basic heuristics for getting started in directed creativity.

includes advice to this effect. For example, Perkins (1981, 217) suggests that we "make use of noticing;" McGartland (1994, 91) asserts that the creative person is capable of "receiving new information and seeing new distinctions;" and Fritz (1991, 299) advises us to "practice objectively observing current reality."

But why pause and notice? What is the point of this seemingly passive activity? If creative thinking is the novel association of existing concepts in memory, then it follows naturally that it is useful to create a storehouse of concepts. This is the purpose of pausing and noticing. You are not looking for anything in particular. You do not need to know how you are going to use the information. You are simply storing up concepts (de Bono 1992).

One way to implement this advice is to condition yourself to stop and reflect whenever you notice something new around you. For example, I travel frequently on Delta Airlines. Recently I noticed that on some flights Delta has instituted a new, carry-on-yourself, deli-snack meal service. As you enter the jetway to board the airplane, you can pick up a sack containing a sandwich and other items. Now that's something new.

Pausing to notice means thinking for just a moment about the positives, negatives, and concepts represented in a new experience. Positively speaking, Delta's new system offers passengers a choice and the ability to decide when they want to eat—something you do not get with traditional airline meal service. It is probably less expensive for the airline, and it eliminates a hassle for the flight attendants. On the negative side, some customers might see it as cheap, there are more paper wastes to deal with, and there is the need for a process to accommodate passengers who fail to pick up a bag but want a meal later during the flight.

The final act of noticing is to extract concepts. A potentially useful concept that I can extract from this experience is the idea of offering more choice and personal customization at a lower cost.

On our mental landscape model, everything we notice in this way creates a new valley in memory. The concepts in these mental valleys are now available for future linking to issues that need creative thought. I do not know how or when I will use this particular observation, but I am sure that one day it will serve as a good analogy to help me solve a problem or redesign a process.

To get started using this heuristic, set a goal of purposefully noticing one new thing each day. Start a notebook as a concrete way of reinforcing this habit and maintaining your new mental valleys (or carry a small tape recorder or use your laptop computer, or call your own voice mail and leave yourself a message). Record the essence of the situation you noticed, along with a quick analysis. At a minimum, this analysis should include positives, negatives, and extracted concepts. Do not be constrained by this; record any thoughts you have. The point is to pay enough attention to the situation to cause a mental groove to form for later use. After a while, you will find yourself noticing many things every day. You will be surprised at your new ability to creatively link your experiences to topics that arise in your work and life.

So, pausing and noticing is more than just passive observation. Activating the judgment system through analysis provides the so what? of noticing. We quickly forget most of what we notice primarily because we do not analyze it (activate judgment processes). We do not pause long enough to give the event meaning and to interconnect it to other concepts. The theory of the mechanics of mind suggests that purposeful pausing and noticing will enhance our ability to produce future creative outputs.

Finally, let me also point out how this heuristic can be very helpful in the pursuit of quality in our organizations. First, good noticers are better problem solvers. This is because people who notice more have more analogies and metaphors that they can apply to problems at hand (Sternberg and Lubart 1995). Second, many successful designs for products and services that uniquely meet customers' needs were based on noticing. For example, George de Mestral, the inventor of Velcro, noticed the mechanism by which sticker burrs attached themselves to his pants leg when he walked through the woods. Similarly, stock brokerage firms began offering electronic trading services when they noticed that many of the people who have money to invest are also computer users. Third, noticing is already the basis of the quality management tool of benchmarking. The purpose of a benchmarking visit is to notice something that can be applied analogously to the issues in your company. In essence, we can interpret this first heuristic of directed creativity as a call for continuous benchmarking as we go through our daily lives. Finally, noticing can play an important part in improving our organizations' strategic planning. Spotting the beginning of a trend before your competitors do enables you to be out front in capturing a new market or customer need.

Practice your noticing as you read through the remainder of this chapter. What do you notice about these heuristics of creativity that can be applied to the issues you and your organization face in the pursuit of quality?

Heuristic 2: Focus your creative energies on just a few topic areas that you genuinely care about and work on these purposefully for several weeks or months. While some popular books seem to suggest that we should apply creative thinking anywhere and everywhere, research shows that we will be most productive if we engage in sustained efforts over time on a few topics. The study of creative lives clearly shows that great creators in business, science, and the arts focus and work intensively on their creations over time.*

Focus and time serve many purposes. Focus on a particular topic over time means that our mental valleys associated with that topic will become richer and more complex. We can explore more novel linkages with other concepts. We are less likely to satisfice because there is no pressure to come up with an idea in the next 10 minutes. Focus on an issue over time also increases the odds that noticing will yield a new insight. As Louis Pasteur pointed out, "Chance favors the prepared mind." Finally, focus on a topic over time increases the likelihood that we will have the motivation to implement some of our creative ideas on the topic. In other words, focus helps us go beyond creative thinking to innovation.

In order to focus, we must care about the topic. And in order to care, we must have some intrinsic motivation. Amabile (1983), Torrence (1987), and others have demonstrated the critical link between intrinsic motivation and creative output in both children in school and adults in work situations. To summarize, this research suggests that if you want creative ideas about something, find someone who really cares about the topic, provide them some tools for stimulating creative thoughts, and promise them that you will do something with their ideas. This might explain why organizations do not generate more innovations. Often people are not assigned work that they really care about, they do not have the training to be creative, and they do not believe that anyone would support them even if they had a good idea. As practitioners of quality management, we should be active in our organizations in helping to establish more favorable conditions for innovation.

---

*For fascinating biographical studies of the lives of great creators like Albert Einstein, Martha Graham, Charles Darwin, Watson and Crick, Steven Jobs, and others, see Gardner 1993, Wallace and Gruber 1989, Weisberg 1993, Shekerjian 1990, Ray and Myers 1986, Ghislen 1952, and Torrence 1987.

Of course, the focus heuristic brings with it a big potential pitfall: stuck thinking. If we are not careful, intense focus can lock us into a specific way of thinking about a topic. If we think about something long enough, we might convince ourselves that we have thought about it in every possible way. Other heuristics on our list will help us to avoid the trap of stuck thinking that can come from too intense a focus. Just remember to keep multiple options open, constantly identify and question your assumptions, and never stop looking and listening for new insights.

Practically speaking then, this heuristic suggests that we should have only a few (one to three) topic areas as the primary focus of our creative energies at any given time. This is consistent with the project-by-project approach to quality management advocated by Juran (1989). We need not avoid using short bursts of creative thought directed at other topics, but the theory suggests that if all we are doing is scatter-shot creativity, we should not expect to make significant creative breakthroughs. We should also set aside time to regularly work on our focused topic areas, in much the same way that we set aside time to work on a quality improvement project.

Between work sessions, let noticing do its work (heuristic 1). You will be amazed at how fluid your mind becomes at relating daily experiences back to your focused topics. This occurs because focus has deepened the mental valleys associated with the topic and thereby increased the probability that new perceptions will be channeled toward it. The emotion associated with caring further heightens this effect.

The focus-over-time heuristic also implies the need for a predetermined end time. Short-term deadlines of only a few minutes, hours, or days can work against creativity by heightening the urge to satisfice. Amabile, DeJong, and Lepper (1976) have shown experimentally that externally imposed deadlines decrease creativity. So it is important that our predetermined end time be self-set, subject to revision, and extended in time at least a few weeks or months. But it is dangerous to proceed without an end time. While there is always the possibility of one more idea, recall that creative ideas have no value unless we act upon them. End times are helpful in bringing closure to one cycle of creative thinking and preparing us for the next. Predetermined end times also help avoid premature closure. Resist the urge to abandon further creative search just because a seemingly great idea has occurred to you early on. Pursue the implementation of that great idea, but keep up your active efforts to explore other possibilities throughout the time period you have set for yourself.

This notion of focus should feel comfortable to practitioners of quality management. We are accustomed to working on projects with defined objectives and time frames. We can practice this heuristic of directed creativity within the context of our existing focused efforts, or we can use our organization's project infrastructure to commission specific innovation efforts.

Heuristic 3: Avoid being too narrow in the way you define your problem or topic area; purposefully try broader definitions and see what insights you gain. In their review of the literature, Tardif and Sternberg (1988, 431) cite "constant redefinition of problems" as a consistent theme in creative thinking. Getzels and Csikszentmihalyi (1976) and Weisberg (1993) present biographical and experimental evidence that creative individuals are not only good problem solvers, but good problem finders.

From a heuristic standpoint, the important piece of advice here is to think in the direction of *broader* definitions of the topic. Adams (1986, 115) warns that "more specific problem statements lead to quicker solutions, but less conceptual creativity than more general statements."

Nadler and Hibino (1994) give a concrete illustration of this heuristic in their "case of the slippery packing crates." The case involves a national manufacturer of consumer goods that was about to make a multimillion dollar investment in loading dock automation to eliminate the problem of damaged crates. A young staff engineer saved the company a great deal of money and effort by suggesting a broader view of the topic. While the immediate need seemed to be for creative ideas in the narrowly focused area of eliminating damage to crates, a broader statement of the issue was to find creative ways to distribute the company's goods to the marketplace undamaged. This broader statement of the creative focus lead to major restructuring of the company's warehousing network. This creative approach reduced the number of handling points, both reducing shipping damage and lowering costs.

The define-topics-broadly heuristic was also one of the keys behind the creative approach in the late medications case in the prologue. Redefining the topic as "ways to remind busy people that a certain time has come" leads immediately to a host of new ideas.

As with the other heuristics, there is also a potential pitfall here. As systems thinkers have pointed out, every process is part of a larger system, and every system is part of an even larger system (Senge 1990; Ackoff 1978). Therefore, no matter how we eventually define the issue, there is always a larger definition. For example, in the damaged crates example, we could work on restructuring our product line to reduce the number of things we ship. In the medication errors case we could restate the issue as one of getting doctors to order fewer medications, or we could search for creative ways to help people live healthier lives and avoid hospital stays altogether. The pitfall is that this need to address bigger issues can keep us from taking any action at all.

An unhealthy understanding of systems thinking can lead to a form of resistance called *trumping*. If someone would rather stay with the status quo, a good way to stall action is to suggest that no real change can occur unless we address a larger system. Often, the person making such a suggestion knows full well that we lack the resources or clout to deal with the larger system. He or she has trumped our attempt to take action by playing a larger system card.

As with all of the heuristics of directed creativity, the key lies in balancing thoughtfulness and action. Before diving into an issue, the define-topics-broadly heuristic suggests that we take the time to examine multiple definitions of the issue. Look for an opportunity to seize on an expression of the topic that provides room for novel approaches. Before you begin, set a time limit on this issue exploration (perhaps a few hours, days, or weeks). When the time limit is up, pick a statement of the issue that you think provides room for creative thought, but that also seems like something you can do something about over a reasonable period of time. Then get on with it! Remember that the rewards of innovation come only to the true innovator—the one who takes a new idea and actually puts it into action. There is nothing wrong with initiating a parallel effort to work on the issue at a higher level over a longer time frame. Just don't allow others to trump you into doing nothing while you wait.

The define-topics-broadly heuristic is clearly applicable to many situations we face in quality management. Whether we are involved in problem solving, design, customer needs analysis, or planning, it is always a good idea to take the time to explore multiple definitions of an issue before diving into activity.

Heuristic 4: Try to come up with original and useful ideas by making novel associations among what you already know. As we saw in the preceding chapter, this heuristic is a central theme in creativity. It is the main process for generating creative ideas. Furthermore, it is the basis for the assertion that everyone is capable of creative thought. Everyone has concepts stored away in memory. If there is any trick to creative thought, it is simply making the effort to explore associations among those concepts.

Various tools and methods for directed creativity support this heuristic. The medication errors case in the prologue illustrated this idea of association when we explored various ways of "reminding" and applied these to the hospital situation. In chapter 2, I briefly mentioned the random-word technique. Here, we interject randomly selected words and purposefully try to associate them with our topic of interest. Another technique that supports this heuristic involves bringing in a collection of objects, distributing these to team members, and asking each person to come up with thoughts about how the objects might relate to the issue at hand. While these techniques seem silly at first, I find that people are more willing to try them and are more productive when they understand that the point is to stimulate novel conceptual associations in the mind.

This heuristic is more than simply the basis for some methods and tools. It represents an essential attitude for the creative person. The creative person knows that there are an infinite number of ideas out there, because there are so many possible permutations among known concepts. The creative person never feels defeated or at the end of the road of ideas. There is always another idea to be had by combining something that has not been combined before. All that is required is flexibility and the perseverance to keep on trying.

Of course, the potential pitfall in this heuristic is another form of trumping. Because there is always the possibility of one more idea from an association that has not yet been tried, one can easily get stuck in the generation of ideas. Again, setting an end time is helpful. Generate many alternatives, but at some point commit to take action with the best ideas you have. There will be time in the future to think again and try something else.

Heuristic 5: When you need creative ideas, remember: attention, escape, and movement. The principles of attention, escape, and movement are behind all of the tools of directed creative thinking. When you need to be creative, pay attention to things in new ways, escape your current mental patterns associated with the topic, and keep moving in your thinking to avoid premature judgment and satisficing.

Chapter 4 is devoted to this heuristic and its role in helping us understand the diversity of methods that have been proposed in the literature for stimulating creativity. We will explore this heuristic more completely there.

Heuristic 6: Pause and carefully examine ideas that make you laugh the first time you hear them. People often express a delighted surprise the first time they hear a creative idea. Further, many scholars of creativity assert that humor is one of the purest forms of creativity. *Therefore, laughter may be the most reliable clue that we are on to something creative.**

Consider the mental mechanics of processing a joke. My favorite comic, Steven Wright, tells marvelous three- and four-line jokes that lend themselves easily to such analysis. For example, Wright says in his trademark deadpan voice,

> *I used to work in the factory where they make fire hydrants.*

He pauses—like a good comic always does—to let your mind settle in a mental valley. What mental images do you have of a factory where they make fire hydrants? Big, a little dirty, furnaces to cast the iron, employees in soiled work clothes, and so on. Your mind only needs a millisecond or two to retrieve the patterns. It is automatic.

Wright continues:

> *But I quit.*

Again, the classic comedian's pause. Your mind again fills the pause with thoughts that logically connect with the "factory" patterns that were activated by the previous line. Our minds are always searching for comfortable mental valleys to settle into. Let's see, what are all the reasons why someone might quit their job at the fire hydrant factory: hard labor, workplace safety concerns, outdated personnel practices, low pay, and so on.

---

*For more on humor as a pure form of creativity, see de Bono 1969, Koestler 1964, Perkins 1981, Adams 1974, and von Oech 1983.

Wright delivers the punch line:

They wouldn't let you park anywhere near the place!

The audience reaction? Laughter.

A good joke depends on the mind's natural tendency to try to make sense of things by retrieving past patterns (mental valleys). The comic's sense of timing in telling a joke is all about giving your mind the split second it needs to settle into a mental valley. The joke is dependent on the audience sharing a common, logical understanding of the set-up situation. The joke is not funny if you do not know what a fire hydrant is, or if you do not have any concept of why someone might logically quit their job at a factory that makes them. In fact, if you do not know anything about fire hydrants and factories, you could take the joke as a simple statement of fact. I'd quit too if they wouldn't let me park anywhere near the place. What's so funny about that?

The punch line of a joke is the key creative feature. After letting your mind settle into a comfortable mental valley, the comedian links you with another, surprising valley. The joke is funny because of the association between fire hydrants and parking restrictions. The punch line is funny because it takes something that is logically true in one context (you cannot park near a fire hydrant on a city street) and applies it to another context (employee parking at the fire hydrant factory).

The point of all this is that humor depends on the same connecting and rearranging of knowledge that is characteristic of all creative thought. This classic observation from the creativity literature leads me to a hypothesis. Although I know of no research that confirms this, I theorize that laughter is actually a biological response to the connection of neurons in the brain that do not usually get connected. In other words, laughter is the body's way of signaling a novel, creative connection in the mind.

Therefore, this heuristic supports directed creativity by sensitizing our perception processes to notice laughter and to take it as a signal that a novel mental connection has occurred. We should laugh along, but then stop and say, "Wait a minute, let's explore that . . . how could we use that idea?" In my experience, this is almost always useful.

I recently conducted a seminar for the National Health Service in London where I asked participants to think like bankers in order to come up with creative ways to enhance patients' perceptions of the quality of service when they visit a health clinic. I noticed one of the participants say something that made the person next to him smile. During the debriefing of the exercise, I asked him to input his idea. He seemed a little embarrassed and said it was nothing really. I remained poised with the easel pen to record his idea and gently insisted. "Well," he said, "banks are always advertising about their 'personal bankers,' so I thought we should advertise our 'personal clinic receptionists.'" There was laughter in the room, but I recorded the idea on the easel pad anyway.

I then said, "Let's play with this one for a bit. What makes a banker a 'personal' banker and how might we apply that to a clinic receptionist?" After a minute of group discussion we had the following creative ideas.

- Develop a database of photographs of all our patients. Tie it to the appointment schedule, so the receptionist has photos on his or her computer screen of the next four to six people who are scheduled. When someone walks in, it's easy for the receptionist to greet him or her by name.

- Combine this with the idea of using valet parking. Valet needs to get patient's name anyway for parking slip. The valet could radio name and brief description to receptionist, who then greets patient by name. Receptionist could also have already pulled up all patient's records and so forth to further reduce waiting time.

These are good, implementable, creative ideas for service improvement. All I had to do as a facilitator was to not allow the group to rush past the original comment simply because it brought out laughter.

I find it helpful to write laughable suggestions up on an easel, board, or overhead. The writing does three things. It allows the laughter to continue for a moment. It indicates that someone (me) has taken the suggestion seriously. And, importantly, it provides a pause that the mind will automatically use to search for a productive valley to connect to.

The pitfall in using this heuristic is that, typically, laughter is considered out of place in work settings. Therefore, you may have to coax people into expressing their initially outrageous or humorous ideas. I know, you're thinking, "I can name several people that won't need any coaxing." That's great. The trick is to make everyone comfortable with it. In fact, the biggest challenge may be in making yourself comfortable with it!

I have two suggestions for overcoming this pitfall. First, whenever you ask individuals or groups to generate ideas, always ask them to purposefully generate at least one totally outrageous idea along with their other ones. Then, at some point in the processing, specifically ask for the outrageous ideas. The initial instruction gives people the permission to come up with a far-out idea and the calling out gives the facilitator the chance to get ready to explore. Second, use the notion that laughter might be a physiological reaction to novel connections in the mind to make laughter in the workplace seem not only welcome, but essential to innovation. Serious, straight-laced people often believe that humor is an unproductive waste of time. Providing a little theoretically based background to suggest that laughter can be used to further the goals of the organization can lower the barriers.

Heuristic 7: Recognize that your streams of thought and patterns of judgment are not inherently right or wrong; they are just what you think now based primarily on patterns from your past. This heuristic captures the essence of the flexible thinking that is associated with creativity. It is also the heuristic that requires the most fundamental, internal change for most of us. It is, therefore, a natural barrier to individual and group creativity.

This heuristic from the creativity literature has already been brought into quality management through the concept of the theory of knowledge in Deming's system of profound knowledge. In his challengingly cryptic way, Deming (1993) captures the essence of this heuristic when he says

> *The theory of knowledge teaches us that a statement, if it conveys knowledge, predicts future outcome, with risk of being wrong, and that it fits without failure observations of the past. (p. 105)*

While Deming's language may be hard to grasp, we have already seen several examples of what he is talking about. The medication errors improvement team in the prologue predicted that a log sheet would bring about the future outcome of more medications delivered on time. Why did they predict this? Primarily because their observations of the past indicated that it had worked before. Of course, the team and its leader were not as analytical about it as I might be seeming to suggest. Rather, there is evidence that they thought that their approach was more than a mere prediction. They thought that they were *right*. This is evident in the way the leader presented the issue:

"Maybe we should just give up on this" and "We put in the log sheet, but they didn't use it." When you have the "right" answer but it still doesn't work, the only choices you seem to have are to give up or place the blame elsewhere. Similarly, successful companies and managers always have the data of the past to prove that they are right. You do not need creative ideas if you already have right ideas.*

But the innovations that our organizations need to meet the challenges of the future cannot come about through blind adherence to today's right answers. If customers are demanding innovation and competitors are delivering it, we must somehow give up what we have come to believe is right.

Before I go on, I want to be very clear about what I am not saying. *I am not saying that there are no ethical, moral, or theological absolute truths.* Personally, I have very strong religious and moral beliefs, but we are not talking about cosmic, theological belief systems here. We are talking about whether a log sheet is the only way to remind nurses to deliver medications. Whether one hard disk drive technology is the only way to go. Whether a computer has to have a keyboard. Whether a bank has to have a building. The vast majority of what we do in business and daily work has nothing to do with absolute truth, but so many of us act as if it does!

The practical implication of this heuristic is that we should be continuous learners and innovators. If you desire creativity and innovation, abandon the notion of "the only right way" to do something. This does not mean that you must discredit the past ways. It is okay to feel that something was the right or best way *in its time and place.* Simply realize that with every passing second we come to a new time and place. The rules, assumptions, background, and criteria of success are ever-changing.

Since different people have different ways of thinking and no one way is the right way, when you want creative ideas, consider asking someone else. When you do, listen to them intently. Forget trying to explain why you are right and they are wrong. It doesn't matter, because there is no absolute right and wrong in most of the areas of business and daily work.

This heuristic also contains some implications specifically for practitioners of quality management. When forming groups to problem solve, design,

---

*For a delightful exploration of this topic, see Edward de Bono's (1990) *I Am Right You Are Wrong.*

or reengineer, select group members on the basis of diversity if you want creative approaches. I am not strictly talking about cultural diversity here. Rather, I am talking about diversity in points of view and background. For example, ask a secretary in the accounting department to serve on a product design team. When you do, establish the ground rule that the secretary has been purposefully placed on the team to ask questions, challenge the traditional ways, and provide a different point of view. Don't stop there. Seek out the opinions and ideas of children. Bring spouses into a group. Hire school teachers during summer vacation. Start an exchange program with the quality managers of other companies in your town who are in different industries than your own.*

Whatever action you take to implement this heuristic, realize that the most important action is internal and unseen. The mechanics of bringing diversity into groups will do little good if the others in the group believe that "I am right and you are wrong." The creative key lies in internalizing the thought patterns of others to enrich the possibilities of concept connection. While outward action is helpful, this heuristic is primarily an inward attitude.

A second challenge that this heuristic brings to practitioners of quality management has to do with our notions of conformance and standards. While some might disagree, I see no reason why creativity and conformance to standards cannot coexist in our pursuit of quality. This no-inherently-right-way heuristic does not prohibit us from declaring something to be the best way for the moment. The issue here is about permanence and exclusivity. We can standardize on the best way for the moment, but still be open to the purposeful pursuit of another best way for the future. McDonalds, Coca-Cola, and AT&T are examples of highly successful companies that believe both in innovation and standardization.

Heuristic 8: Make a deliberate effort to harvest, develop, and implement at least a few of the ideas you generate. This is another creative heuristic that is already somewhat a part of the tradition of quality management. You may recognize it as the do-study-act portion of the Shewhart PDSA cycle. (Shewhart 1939; Deming 1986).

---

*Clay Carr (1994) explores the pros and cons of the linkage between workplace diversity and creativity in chapter 4 of his book *The Competitive Power of Constant Creativity.*

While the mind is magnificent in its ability to imagine how something will turn out, it is not perfect. Often, we need to see a concrete representation of our idea in order to develop it creatively. In their videotape research on art students, Getzels and Csikszentmihalyi (1976) found that the most creative students seemed to plan less than their less creative counterparts. The students were placed in a room with a collection of objects and asked to compose a photograph by creatively arranging the objects on a table. Consistently, those works that were independently judged as the most creative grew out of a process in which the student quickly began arranging the objects upon entering the room. Those students who spent longer just thinking, or who did a lot of thinking between manipulations of objects, consistently produced works judged as less creative.

Our understanding of the mechanics of mind suggests a generalizable explanation for the phenomenon observed with these students. Our judgment processes tend to channel our thoughts toward existing patterns in memory. The more we just think about it, the more opportunity we give ourselves to settle into a comfortable (that is, existing) mental valley. On the other hand, putting our ideas into concrete form activates our perception processes and creates a new, albeit shallow, mental valley. Now we can incrementally build on that new valley. A concrete implementation of an idea generates the possibility of a new, creative starting point for our thinking.

Using this heuristic requires a precommitment to action. The implementation might be only a prototype of a new product or pilot of a new process. The point is about concreteness, not necessarily permanence. This precommitment to action builds on our understanding of the difference between creativity and innovation. As we have already pointed out, creative ideas mean nothing until will make them real.

Summary of heuristics for directed creativity. Here, in abbreviated form, are the eight basic heuristics that will get us started in directed creativity (refer to Figure 3.1 for the full text).

1. Pause and notice.

2. Focus in a few areas.

3. Define topics broadly.

4. Try for original ideas by novel associations.

5. Practice attention, escape, and movement.

6. Examine ideas that make you laugh.

7. Remember, there is no inherent right or wrong.

8. Implement a few ideas.

I have tried to convey a sense that these heuristics are more than just one person's prescription for creative thinking. Rather, there is a great deal of broad-based experience and some good scientific research behind this advice. I encourage you to read the references cited throughout this chapter to form you own convictions about how to boost your creative output. I also suggest that you develop your own list of heuristics over time as you gain experience. If you understand some theory of mind, your rules of thumb are just as likely to work as the next person's.

Models for the Processes of Creative Thinking and Innovation

Let us now turn our attention to a special type of heuristic: the model. In contrast to heuristic statements that provide a focused gem of wise advice, models strive to capture the whole of something in a overall, integrated fashion. Models also typically show sequence, interconnection, pattern, flow, and organization. Models are critically important to mental functioning because they allow us to anticipate future actions, needs, and steps.

We can illustrate the value that models add over heuristic statements in the familiar territory of quality management. We have noted that the Pareto principle is a heuristic statement: When faced with multiple things, search for the vital few. This is a good piece of advice. It can be applied at a point in time, but it also describes a specific habit that we should want to cultivate through repeated use over time. By itself, however, it does not capture the whole of problem solving.

In contrast, the Shewhart/Deming PDSA cycle is a model. It provides an overview of the entire scheme of problem solving and scientifically based learning. Importantly, this model allows us to look ahead to next steps. Part of our plan must include how we will check later. When we do (implement a plan) we should do so in a way that will make it easier to act (make permanent) later on. Of course, the PDSA model does not tell us how to plan or check effectively. We need specific heuristics to help us do that. So models and heuristic statements work together to provide scripts to guide higher-order thinking.

A review of creative-thinking models in the literature. Analogous to the various models of quality improvement, planning, and reengineering in the quality management literature, there are also several models for the process of creative thinking. Arieti (1976) has catalogued eight such models that were proposed during the period 1908 to 1964. I have collected several additional models that have been proposed since. As with the definitions and heuristics of creativity, analysis of the various models reveals some consistent patterns.*

- The creative process involves purposeful analysis, imaginative idea generation, and critical evaluation—the total creative process is a balance of imagination and analysis.

- Older models tend to imply that creative ideas result from subconscious processes, largely outside the control of the thinker. Modern models tend to imply purposeful generation of new ideas, under the direct control of the thinker.

- The total creative process requires a drive to action and the implementation of ideas; in other words, innovation versus creativity alone.

These insights from a review of the many models of creative thinking should be encouraging to us. As practitioners of quality management, we have strong skills in practical, scientific, concrete, and analytical thinking that will serve us well as we engage the creative process. Contrary to popular belief, the modern theory of creativity does not require that we discard these skills. What we do need to do, however, is acquire some new thinking skills to support the generation of novel insights and ideas. Importantly, we also need to acquire the mental scripts to balance and direct these new creative thinking skills in concert with our traditional analytical skills. If we can meet this challenge, we stand well-equipped to help lead our organizations to competitive advantage through innovation.

---

*A working paper that reviews the models and illustrates these patterns is available from the author.

A synthesis model of the creative process. Figure 3.2 presents the model of creative thinking that we will use as a framework for the remainder of this book. It is a synthesis of the concepts behind the various models proposed during the last 50 years.

Let me walk you through it, beginning at the nine o'clock position on the circle. We live every day in the same world as everyone else, but creative thinking begins with careful observation of that world coupled with thoughtful analysis of how things work and fail. These mental processes create a store of concepts in our memories. Using this store, we generate novel ideas to meet specific needs by actively searching for associations among concepts. Seeking the balance between satisficing and premature judgment, we then harvest and further enhance our ideas before we subject them to a final, practical evaluation. But it is not enough just to have creative thoughts; ideas have no value until we put in the work to implement them. Every new idea that is put into practice (every innovation) changes the world we live in, which restarts the cycle of observation and analysis. Directed creativity simply means that we make purposeful mental movements to avoid the pitfalls associated with our cognitive mechanisms at each step of this process.

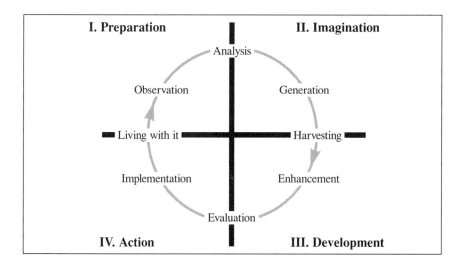

Figure 3.2. A model for the process of directed creativity.

For purposes of explanation, we can further divide this model into four phases. We will use these four phases of preparation, imagination, development, and action to organize our tools of directed creativity in part III of this book.

Note that this model continues in the tradition of others in asserting that creativity is a balance of imagination and analysis. The model also purposefully avoids taking a stand on the controversy of whether imagination is a conscious or subconscious mental ability. While I personally believe that imagination is a conscious, nonmagical mental action, the activity of generation in the model welcomes creative ideas regardless of their source. Finally, notice that this model clearly supports the notion that innovation is a step beyond the simple generation of creative ideas. The action phase of the model makes it clear that creative ideas have value only when they are implemented in the real world.

Summary of Some Essential Theory for Directed Creativity

In these two chapters, I have tried to boil down for you the essential theory that will underlie the methods for directed creativity that we will study next. You should now understand that creative thought is a capability that anyone with a functioning mind possesses. If you can think, you can think creatively—provided you put forth the effort to do so.

The other reason for exploring some theory before jumping headlong into methods is that applying techniques without understanding how they work is of marginal value. Without an underpinning of theory, there is no mechanism for learning (Lewis 1929; Deming 1993). You will see the theory playing itself out in the methods that we will explore in subsequent chapters. Further, you are now in a position to invent your own methods to fit the unique situations you face. Theory is powerful knowledge in a world that demands more adaptation than rote copying.

As you work to help make your organization more innovative, do not underestimate the power of knowing some theory of creativity. Without an understanding of the theory, the tools can seem silly or pointless. You will find it difficult to overcome the natural tendencies toward analysis and logic that are present in most organizations unless you share some of the theory behind the methods of creativity. I have also found that just a little bit of theory is enough to get even some of the most analytical thinkers I know to give directed creativity a try.

Finally, let me point out that the title for this part of the book is *Some Essential Theory of Directed Creativity*. There is much more that could be said. I have liberally supplied footnotes and additional references to guide your further study. I encourage you to become a student of the field of creativity and innovation. The background that I have given you in these two chapters is sufficient for you to pick up nearly any material from the field of creativity and understand it.

PART III

Methods and Tools for Directed Creativity

CHAPTER 4

Three Basic Principles Behind the Tools of Directed Creativity

Give me a lever long enough and a place to stand, and I will move the world.

Archimedes

If all you have is a hammer, everything begins to look like a nail.

Anonymous

Just as there are tools that bring the theory of quality management into practical application, there are also tools that help us direct our thoughts in creative endeavors. In fact, there are hundreds of such tools in the literature. Unfortunately, this variety leaves the impression that no one really knows how to stimulate creativity and it is all just a hit-or-miss game. Rather than being an indication of chaos in the field, the variety of methods is really an indication of just how easy it is to develop your own creative-thinking tools.

I will begin this chapter by describing four very diverse tools for creative thinking. I have purposely chosen such diverse methods in order to build the central point of the chapter—despite the apparent diversity of tools to support creative thinking, all such tools are based on three simple principles: attention, escape, and movement.

Examples of Tools That Support Creative Thinking

There are many tools for creative thinking in the literature. Edward de Bono (1992) describes 13 tools, McGartland (1994) has 25 tips and techniques, VanGundy (1992) covers 29 tools, Michalko (1991) describes 34 techniques, von Oech (1983) has 64 methods in his *Creative Whack Pack,* Koberg and Bagnall (1981) give guidance on 67 tools, and Higgins (1994) tops them all with his book *101 Creative Problem Solving Techniques.* While there is some overlap among these compilations, there are at least 250 unique tools in these seven books. And these are only a few of the references available on the topic of creative thinking!

It certainly makes sense that we would need different tools to accomplish the different purposes implied by the steps of the directed-creativity model, but even tools that have the same stated purpose can be radically different. Let me illustrate this type of diversity by briefly describing four methods for generating new ideas (the imagination phase in our model).

Trans-disciplinary analogy (TDA). VanGundy (1992) describes a tool for idea generation that he attributes to Henry Andersen, a marketing manager at Mitsubishi Heavy Industries America, Inc. Despite the deep-sounding name, the tool is easy to explain and use.

After defining a topic for creative thinking, form a group of at least five people. The group members should come from a variety of occupations. Each group member selects a discipline or activity of special interest. The selection could be an academic discipline (for example, history), a professional pursuit (for example, investing), a hobby (for example, beekeeping), or a simple but uncommon activity of daily life (for example, tree pruning). The selection does not have to be the person's occupation, but it should be an area in which he or she has some expert knowledge. Next, each person selects some central concept from that discipline or activity (for example, history—that history repeats itself; investing—buy low and sell high). Finally, these disciplines and central concepts are listed on an easel sheet along with a statement of the topic requiring creative thinking.

After all the disciplines and concepts are recorded, the group selects one that sounds interesting and the person who listed it gives a detailed description of the concept. For example, the history buff might cite three detailed examples of history repeating itself, while the investor might describe the patterns that stock market technical analysts look for on charts of daily high-low-close prices. The point is to tell the other members of the group something intricate that they don't already know.

The group members listen carefully to the explanation and then use it as stimulation for ideas on the session's topic. For example, consider a quality improvement team in a clothing manufacturer with the topic, "We need creative ideas to reduce complaints of split seams." After hearing the details of "history repeats itself," the group might suggest researching sewing practices and thread strengths from 20 years ago for clues to solve today's problems. After generating a few such ideas from one concept, the group repeats the process with another concept from the list. For example, the image of fluctuating stock market prices on a graph might lead to the suggestion to experiment with staggered, rather than straight, stitching. This process can go on for as long as the group desires.

TDA is a sensible technique when one considers the mechanics of mind and the theory of creativity. It relies on novel associations between the focused topic and the memory streams that are stimulated by the inputs from group members about detailed concepts in other fields.

Stepping-stones. Roger von Oech (1983) suggests that we can generate useful ideas by starting from an outrageous, impractical idea. (Other authors describe similar tools.) Accepting the outrageous idea causes us to temporarily suspend our judgment subprocesses, while the idea itself sends us exploring potentially useful valleys in memory. The stepping-stone technique can be used by groups or individuals.

von Oech illustrates this simple tool with the story of a chemical company that was looking for innovative product design ideas to ease its customers' task of stripping old paint from houses. One engineer posed an outrageous, stepping-stone suggestion: Put gunpowder in the house paint and then blow it off when the time came! (Such a suggestion should now trigger your directed-creativity heuristic to examine ideas that make you laugh when you first hear them.) To turn an outrageous idea into a stepping-stone, we extract some concept from the idea and pose a question to stimulate thinking. What other ways are there to create a chemical reaction that would help remove old house paint? This question led to the suggestion of putting an additive into house paint that would be inert until another chemical was applied to the old paint at a later date. The resulting chemical reaction makes the paint easy to strip.

Dreamscape. Michael Michalko (1991) describes a third tool for idea generation. This one is primarily an individual technique and involves the use of dreams.

Michalko suggests forming a question about a creative challenge and repeating that question to yourself several times just before going to bed. When you wake the next morning, quickly record any dreams that you had. (Michalko has several suggestions for doing this and for increasing the odds that you will remember your dreams.) Repeat this process for several nights. (Vivid dreamers report that some dreams play out in a series over several sessions of sleep.) After you have recorded several dreams, analyze each one by answering questions such as: How might the people, places, and events in this dream relate to my topic? Does the dream suggest a change in the nature of the topic? What associations does the dream conjure up that might help me with my topic? Michalko cites several historical and anecdotal examples to illustrate the use of this tool.

Personally, I am not a fan of this technique. First, the use of dreams perpetuates the stereotype of creative thinking as a magical process. Also, I have a great deal of trouble recalling my dreams, so this technique is hard work for me. Nevertheless, it is an example of the kinds of techniques commonly found in the literature. Many people report that such techniques work well for them.

The dreamscape tool relies on the fact that dreams consist of memory streams that are somewhat randomly stimulated and linked together while we sleep. The analysis process that follows the dream experience is a purposeful attempt to link these memory streams with our focused topic.*

Manipulative verbs. The fourth and final tool I will describe here is a classic from one of the pioneers in the field of creative thinking, Alex Osborn. Osborn was an advertising executive who developed the tool of brainstorming in the late 1940s. As part of his system of brainstorming, Osborn developed several specific methods for idea generation. One such method is his list of manipulative verbs.

---

*For more about the use of directed dreaming, see Morris 1992.

Osborn (1953) suggests that we generate creative ideas by visualizing the subject in new or unique ways. His verbs suggest manipulating the subject in some way, such as changing its size, function, or position. Osborn's list of verbs is *magnify, minify, rearrange, alter, adapt, modify, substitute, reverse,* and *combine.*

For example, consider a group in a food processing company looking for innovative ways to increase sales of packaged food. Creative ideas stimulated by the manipulative verbs might include the following:

Magnify Convert more products to giant-sized packages. Create a store display that is a giant replica of the food product (this might attract children). Make the printed directions on the package large and market this feature to senior citizens.

Minify Convert more products to single-serving packages and market this feature to people who cook only for themselves. Reduce the portions in packages of snack foods and market this feature to weak-willed dieters who just can't stop eating until the package is empty. Market a line of food products that is sold only through small, mom-and-pop grocery stores and generate interest through a nostalgic advertising campaign.

And so on with the other verbs.

Osborn's technique stimulates the imagination by using the mind's ability to visualize things that do not yet exist. It also relies on the fact that our memory patterns for words can have a large number of associative links to other concepts.

The diversity in methods. These four methods illustrate diversity in several dimensions. First, the tools differ according to whether they are intended to be used by groups or individuals. TDA clearly relies on group input, while stepping-stones and manipulative verbs could be used by either a group or an individual working alone. While the dreamscape tool is clearly individual-based on the front end, individuals could come together to share their dreams and answer the analysis questions.

The four methods also differ in the amount of prework required. TDA is very ad hoc. No particular preparation is needed beforehand. Just come as you are and we'll see what happens. The manipulative verbs tools is also ad hoc in its use, but relies on a previously prepared list of verbs. The dreamscape tool requires some advance preparation—concentrating on the topic just before going to sleep and arranging to record the dreams the moment you wake up. The stepping-stones tool can go either way. You could make it ad hoc by quickly preparing a list of outrageous ideas and going to work on these stepping-stones immediately. Or you could generate the outrageous ideas in a preparatory thinking session and then use them as inputs to another session.

While all four methods rely on stimulation of novel memory streams, the mechanisms for this stimulation also differ greatly. TDA uses expert knowledge in one person's mind to temporarily create new mental patterns in the minds of others in the group. The stepping-stones tool uses memory patterns that were purposefully selected for the attribute of outrageousness. This means that there is a low probability that these memory streams have been applied to the issue in the past (that is, a higher probability that a novel association will occur). Dreamscapes uses memory patterns selected by the subconscious processes associated with dreaming, while the manipulative verbs are basically prepackaged patterns.

Finally, these four tools differ enormously in the degree to which one could expect immediate acceptance in the typical work environment. The manipulative verbs tools is probably the least far out of the four methods. It would not be hard to talk colleagues into experimenting with this method. It comes across as almost an analytical method. The stepping-stones tool is a little bit more risky. It requires the use of humor, which is not always readily accepted in all work settings. I find that a quick example, like the house paint additive story, is usually enough to break through this barrier because it implies that serious analysis will follow shortly after the lightheartedness. TDA can face significant social barriers. Without some ice-breaking, people can sometimes be reluctant to get into the spirit of sharing some special, uncommon knowledge with the group. Others miss the point of this tool and seem to be consciously trying to select a discipline or concept that will clearly link to the focused topic. This, of course, defeats the purpose of making novel connections and leads to failure, which further raises the social barriers against it. The dreamscape tool would clearly be the most far out tool of these four. At best, you could probably only suggest it to some of the people you know.

The diversity suggested by these four methods only partially illustrates the variety one finds in reading through the descriptions of the more than 250 tools in the creative-thinking literature. As a mostly analytical thinker, I must confess that I was turned off by what I first interpreted as a complete lack of rigor in this field. Of course, we must admit that the tools of quality management are not totally rigorous either. There are a variety of ways to construct a cause-effect diagram, display data graphically, or set up the matrices of QFD. In quality management, however, this variation is clearly a variation on a relatively small number of themes. One can recognize a cause-effect diagram even when it is in a different format. Someone who has used QFD can usually recognize another person's QFD matrices, even if they do not contain the exact row and column headings that one is used to.

In contrast, it is not obvious how the vastly different tools suggested for creative thinking could all be leading in a common direction. As it turns out, there is a structure. Importantly, knowing this structure unlocks a world of possibilities for the further development of useful methods for continuous, on-demand, directed creativity.

Three Basic Principles Behind All Methods for Creative Thinking

While the various tools for creative thinking were created without explicit reference to any structure, I believe that all such tools are variations on the themes of mental attention, escape, and movement. This structure is loosely based on ideas that I first encountered in Edward de Bono's 1992 book *Serious Creativity*. de Bono uses the three terms independently to describe the specific mental action required by certain tools he presents in his book. I am expanding on de Bono's ideas and suggesting that these three mental actions form an integrated framework that underlies all methods for creative thinking.

Attention. Creativity requires that we first focus our attention on something—typically something that we have not focused much attention on before. The primary innovation of the Apple Macintosh computer in the early 1980s was that its designers focused not on raw computing power, but on the user interface. By focusing attention on things that are normally taken for granted (in this case, the command line interface predominant in the early 1980s), creative-thinking techniques prepare our minds for break-throughs (here, the graphical user interface).

All methods for creative thinking require that we do something to focus attention. For example, in the TDA tool, we first focus attention on the topic at hand by writing down a statement of it, and then we turn our attention to some obscure facts from another field. Creative ideas come from the inter-section of these two attention fields. In the stepping-stones tool, our attention is directed to a central concept in an otherwise outrageous suggestion. In the dreamscape tool, we first intensely focus mental attention on the topic at hand by repeating it several times to ourselves before going to bed. After we have recorded our dreams, we then pay close attention to the elements con-tained in those dreams. In using the manipulative verbs tool, we pay attention to the topic at hand and then to the mental pictures formed when we imagine various manipulations of the elements in the topic.

Other tools also illustrate this theme of attention-setting. For example, Wonder and Donovan (1984) propose that we construct a mental, slow-motion movie of a situation and look for aspects that we have previously overlooked. Similarly, Nadler and Hibino (1994) suggest that we spend time writing alternative statements of an issue and placing them in what they call a purpose hierarchy, rather than simply diving into the issue. In other words, as we noted in heuristic 3, they suggest that it is fruitful to pay attention to the very definition of the issue itself.

Escape. Having focused our attention on the way things are currently done, the second principle behind all creative-thinking methods calls us to men-tally escape our current patterns of thinking.

In TDA, the detailed thought patterns from other disciplines provide a mental escape from the thought patterns we would typically bring to the topic under discussion. An outrageous suggestion, a good night's sleep, and specific manipulative directions provide the means of mental escape in the other three tools.

Again, other tools employ this same mental action. For example, de Bono (1992) suggests that we use the *po* tool to signal our intention to make a statement of mental escape. To a group working to decrease the time that customers wait to receive a service, we might say, "Po, they have passed a law making it illegal for customers to wait more than 30 seconds; what are we going to do now?" The statement invites us to escape our current paradigm about customer flow and, for a moment, imagine a very different world.

The principle of escape explains why a simple walk in the woods can bring about creative thoughts. When we walk in the woods, we escape the confines of the current ways, both mentally and physically. Similarly, staring at yourself in the mirror while you shave or put on make-up provides a momentary mental escape that may allow a novel mental connection about a work problem to emerge. I am not suggesting the use of these relatively passive techniques in the active pursuit of directed creativity. We can do better. To the extent that simple distraction works in creative thinking, however, it works because it is a means of mental escape.

Movement. Simply paying attention to something and escaping current thinking on it is not always sufficient to generate creative ideas. Unfortunately, the natural mental processes of judgment tends to reject new thoughts as not productive or too ridiculous to dwell on. Movement—the third underlying principle behind the diverse tools of creative thinking—calls us to keep exploring and connecting our thoughts.

Notice the prominent role of this principle in the four tools we have used for illustration in this chapter. After hearing the TDAs, we invite the group to mentally move and actively search for useful connections between what they have just learned and the topic of interest. The stepping-stone and manipulative verb techniques require a similar free association and mental movement. The analysis questions in the dreamscape tool also encourage this action.

Movement is a key principle behind the classic creative-thinking technique of brainstorming. The ground rules of brainstorming are to generate as many ideas as you can, with no criticism, building on the ideas of others. In other words, keep moving. Similarly, asking a group to come up with a sketch that illustrates their vision of the company's future is also a movement technique. You can't simply state the vision and be done with it; your mind must dwell on it long enough to complete the sketch. During that time, the mind—which is never idle—generates new connections and ideas that might expand the basic concept.

The value of understanding the three principles. The benefit of this simple, three-part structure is that it opens the way to the development of an infinite number of methods for directed creativity. You can now develop your own techniques. Importantly, you can develop techniques that are specifically suited to the issues you are dealing with, to your own personality and preferences, or to the subtle dynamics of a particular group. As long as your new technique contains elements that focus attention, provide escape from the mental patterns normally associated with the topic, and encourage a high level of flexible mental movement, you can be reasonably assured that it stands as good a chance of working as any other technique you may have read about. If your technique doesn't bring you success initially, you can modify the means or mixture of attention, escape, and movement and try again. There is no magic in the methods written down in books—at least no magic that you cannot duplicate on your own.

Figure 4.1 captures the three basic principles and provides a quick checklist of things to consider in constructing your own tools for directed creativity.

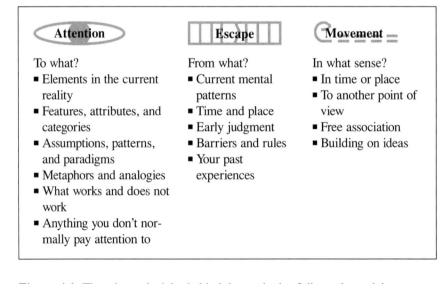

Attention	Escape	Movement
To what?	From what?	In what sense?
▪ Elements in the current reality	▪ Current mental patterns	▪ In time or place
▪ Features, attributes, and categories	▪ Time and place	▪ To another point of view
▪ Assumptions, patterns, and paradigms	▪ Early judgment	▪ Free association
▪ Metaphors and analogies	▪ Barriers and rules	▪ Building on ideas
▪ What works and does not work	▪ Your past experiences	
▪ Anything you don't normally pay attention to		

Figure 4.1. Three key principles behind the methods of directed creativity.

Inventing Your Own Methods for Directed Creativity: An Example

Steven Ross is the quality manager for the accounting firm of Smith, Jones, and Duzkiwitz (SJ&D). The firm has 63 accountants and is one of the largest and most respected firms in the city. With its size and respectability, SJ&D has also developed a reputation for being somewhat stuffy. The size, prestige, and tradition of the firm has worked in its favor in the past when most of the local economy revolved around similarly conservative, large employers, but that has changed over the years. Corporate downsizing has shifted the center of the local business community. A much greater percentage of the local economy is now based on small, entrepreneurial businesses started by those caught up in the downsizing trend.

These new business leaders need SJ&D's accounting and financial services, but wood-paneled offices, country club lunches, and formal relationships mean little to them. Many of the firm's clients—small business owners who are quickly becoming millionaires—show up at meetings in denim jeans and pullover shirts. (Much to the dismay of the firm's partners who wouldn't think of conducting business in anything other than a well-tailored suit.) Finance is important to these new business leaders, but so are lots of other operational and developmental details of their business. What they want are innovative services tailored to their needs and lifestyles—and that is exactly what they are starting to get from some of the small accounting firms in the city.

To their credit, the partners in the firm have recognized the need for innovative change and are anxious to do something about it. Mr. Duzkiwitz—none of the junior members of the firm would dare to call him by his first name, Raymond—called Steven Ross to his office a few days ago and asked him to head up an effort to generate some innovative pilot services in the firm. "I figured," Mr. Duzkiwitz explained, "that since this need is primarily driven by the customers, that this was a natural for you and the quality management effort.

"But," Duzkiwitz continued, peering over the top of his reading glasses, "I am not looking for small improvements. And I also don't want the firm being seen as simply copying what other accounting firms are doing. We didn't get to where we are today by following the crowd. The clients we are losing are creative innovators in their own fields. And they expect their accounting firm to be an innovator in its field.

"What we need are some new, fresh ideas," Duzkiwitz continued leaning back in his chair. "Creativity. Service. That's the ticket. A year from now, I want the local business section of the newspaper to feature a story on us hailing the innovative services that we have brought to our clients. Calvin, Herbert (that is, "Mr. Smith and Mr. Jones"), I, and the rest of the partners are behind you on this. We'll personally spearhead the changes, but we need some ideas to run with. We have every confidence in your ability to deliver. We suggest you form a team to begin working on it right away. I'll have Elaine send out a memo stating that you have my full authority to proceed in the exploratory phase of this effort." Duzkiwitz swiveled in his chair to access his calendar on the firm's computer system. "Can we get an initial set of ideas back from your team in, say . . . a month?"

Quite a challenge. Clearly, Steven Ross and his colleagues can use their analytical skills to do some useful background work. Just as clearly, this group is going to need some creative, outside-the-box ideas in customer service. Using the principles of attention, escape, and movement, let's quickly construct a directed creativity plan for Steven's team.

Accounting firms tend to be rule-oriented and paradigm-bound, so it might be good to begin by paying attention to these traditional rules and paradigms. The problem is that it is not clear how open people will be to confronting these traditions head-on. Let's see . . . perhaps we could get at this by asking the design team to list all the ways in which a typical accounting firm is different from other organizations that are known for customer service. This would give us both *escape* and *attention,* so that is good.

Simply generating the list of other organizations that are known for great customer service would focus further attention on what we mean by "great service." So it would be worthwhile to let the group do this. We could heighten the attention even more by actually sending out people to visit these organizations (another means of escape) with the purpose of bringing back at least three new observations about great customer service. Note that the requirement would be that people bring back new insights, not just a rehash of what is already known. You really have to pay attention to discover something new.

Well, so far we have provided plenty of attention and escape. Now we need to plan some mental *movement.* Suppose we took the items on the lists of ways in which an accounting firm is different from other organizations and parceled these out to groups of employees, asking them to come up with five concrete ways in which the firm could narrow the distinction represented by the item. Involving more people and asking for multiple ideas stimulates mental movement. We could further encourage this movement by asking the groups to use the rules of brainstorming. Going further, we should also ask them to submit at least one totally outrageous idea. We could then distribute these on e-mail and ask others to use them as stepping-stones for generating practical ideas. These processes should generate quite a bit of mental movement in the firm over a several-week period.

To continue the creative process, we will ask everyone to submit all their ideas to the original team for harvesting, development, and evaluation. Recall that these are the next steps in the model of the directed-creativity cycle presented in chapter 3. These next steps would involve further creative mental actions to focus attention on the pros and cons of each idea. The group could then actively search for ways to escape the cons that would otherwise result in rejection of the ideas. Further mental movement could occur as pieces of ideas are combined to form new ideas.

This sounds like a good initial plan. We will revisit Steven Ross and the challenge of generating service design innovations in our hypothetical accounting firm throughout the next few chapters. We will use this example to illustrate a variety of methods for directed creativity—methods that will take us well beyond this initial plan.

For now, I hope that you can see from this example how easy it can be to invent your own methods for directing creative thoughts in a specific application. Now that you understand the basic principles, you can develop tools that are just as valid as anyone else's tools. Specifically, you can design methods to accommodate various criteria. How quickly do we need the ideas? How much involvement do we want from others? How much effort do we want to put into it? What will our personalities, both individually and corporately, allow us to do comfortably? How much time do we need to spend in the preparation, imagination, development, and action phases of the creative process in order to bring about some true innovations?

As the example also illustrates, you could develop your own methods or borrow pieces of methods that you have learned about elsewhere. You could plan it all out or guide the process incrementally as you go along. There are many ways to succeed. Just remember: *attention, escape,* and *movement.* Directed creativity is the repeated application of these three simple mental principles as we progress through the creative cycle of preparation, imagination, development, and action.

CHAPTER 5

Tools That Prepare the Mind for Creative Thought

ぅり ーナา ら ⟨

Genius, in truth, means little more than the faculty of perceiving in an unhabitual way.

William James

The obscure we see eventually. The completely obvious, it seems, takes longer.

Edward R. Murrow

You can observe a lot just by watching.

Yogi Berra

The framework of attention, escape, and movement takes the mystery out of the tools of directed creativity. With an understanding of this framework, anyone can create a new tool to suit a given situation—no special gift is needed.

While there is nothing magical about the existing tools of creative thinking, it is, nevertheless, useful to know about them. Seeing what others have done stimulates our thinking about the possibilities for our own creative pursuits. Furthermore, an existing technique might strike you as being just the thing you need for a given situation. There is no value in reinventing the wheel just because you can.

In this chapter we will explore the concepts and tools that support the preparation phase of the directed-creativity cycle (see Figure 5.1). In doing

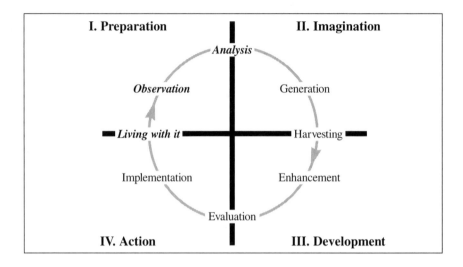

Figure 5.1. Activities in the preparation phase of the directed-creativity cycle.

so, we will address the key question: How can we enhance our powers of observation in order to see more creative possibilities?

I believe that lack of preparation is one of the main reasons why creative ideas are so rare. I am amazed that people expect to be able to walk into a room with a brainstorming group and emerge an hour later with break-through ideas for meeting long-standing challenges. I am amazed, but not surprised. It was not long ago that I had the same naive view of creativity. The study of creative lives shows that this is simply not how it works. While there are occasional instances of ah-ha moments, most true innovations are the product of much thought over an extended period of time (Sternberg and Lubart 1995). The quality of creative ideas depends on the quality of the preparation that went into them.

Key Concepts in the Preparation Phase of the Directed-Creativity Cycle

Creative preparation is primarily about the principle of attention. During this phase of the creative cycle, we seek to pay attention to something in an uncommon way, for the purpose of extracting useful concepts.

In chapter 3, we examined several heuristics that can direct our attention during the preparation phase. For instance, the pause-and-notice heuristic suggests that we stop from time to time and purposefully observe in order to store up concepts in the mind for later use.

In many ways, the pause-and-notice heuristic is just a restatement of the activities in the preparation phase of the directed-creative cycle depicted in Figure 5.1. "Living in the world," the first activity, is unavoidable. The world is always there. It goes on. It happens. The creative thinker fully engages the world, observes it with an ever-fresh curiosity, and analyzes it thoughtfully to gain new insights. Despite the common presumption, it is not necessary for the creative thinker to live in a zany, artificial, or illusionary world of his or her own. To be creative, the only lifestyle change required is that we simply pause more and notice more. Creative preparation, then, is primarily an on-going activity that we engage in as we go about our daily lives in the world.

The world that I am talking about here exists in your workplace and your personal life. Try as we might to separate these domains of life, the world is continuous. The compartments that we try to fit it into are artificial. In the preparation phase of the creative cycle, we learn to be open to the possibility that chance events in our personal life might be the key to solving a problem or generating a breakthrough idea in our work life.

Let me give you a quick example of this. Several years ago, a colleague, Dr. Glenn Laffel, and I were conducting workshops on quality management at a hospital in Vancouver. During one of these sessions, someone identified a process problem in getting physicians' orders to the hospital's laboratory in a timely manner. The process goes something like this. The physician orders tests for the patient by writing in the patient's chart, a nurse pulls the orders by transcribing the information onto a lab order sheet, the order sheet is delivered to the lab, the lab arranges to collect a sample, and, finally, the lab conducts the tests. It's all very complex. We had some quick discussion about flowcharts, cause-effect diagrams, and potential delays in the process, but then moved on in the seminar without really resolving the issues.

Later that evening, Glenn and I went out for dinner. We happened into a small, crowded Chinese restaurant and began looking over the dizzying array of choices on the menu. The server eventually came over to our table, smiled, and said that she was ready to take our order. "Won ton soup . . . beef with broccoli . . . fried rice instead of white rice." I began. As I was speaking, the server pulled out a small, handheld device and began punching buttons. "What is that?" Glenn asked. "Oh," she said, "I am entering your order. See the screen over by the cook?" She pointed to direct our attention. "I press the buttons, what you want appears on the screen, and the cook is already beginning to get your meal ready. It's like a radio-computer thing," she said, shrugging her shoulders to indicate to us that we shouldn't expect much more of a technical explanation out of her.

Glenn and I couldn't help laughing after she left. The hospital down the street can't figure out how to get laboratory orders entered in a timely manner, and this little, hole-in-the-wall Chinese restaurant is using a technology that could provide the answer! Since that episode, I have noticed many similar situations where technology we come across in our everyday lives, and in many cases take for granted, could be adapted to generate a breakthrough idea for a company. Pause for a minute now and try it yourself. Consider the everyday technology of the automated teller machine (ATM). What innovative capabilities and services could your company develop if it had a partnership with a bank? How might the existing ATM network be used as a way to interact with customers?

During the preparation phase of the directed-creativity cycle we should be attentive to chance events that occur around us—Glenn and I just happened into that restaurant; all we were looking for was a meal, not a solution to a business problem. But we should also be deliberate in our pausing to notice. Again, let me illustrate this point with an example.

I am writing this chapter on a beautiful spring day in Raleigh, North Carolina. It is late afternoon. I am here working with a client, but we finished early and I returned to my hotel. The hotel has an enclosed, nicely landscaped courtyard where guests can sit and enjoy days like today. I am behind schedule on this book manuscript, so here I sit under a gazebo writing. I've just decided to deliberately pause and notice.

What I notice is how nice it feels to be here right now. The concept of "rewarding" comes to mind, along with the concept of "working." In essence, I notice that although I am working hard, I am also rewarding myself at the same time. I'll now store away in my mind the concept of linking rewards and work. While we normally think of rewarding someone *for* their work, I extract from this pause-and-notice episode the concept of rewarding someone *while* they work.

That's it. I do not have to go any further at this point. I will simply store this away in my mind (and in a little notebook I carry). Someday, one of my clients will ask me to help them design a process or solve a problem having to do with reward systems for quality. I will now be prepared to trigger their imaginations by retelling this story and asking the provocative question, "What are some ways that we could give people the feeling that they were being rewarded while they work?" (Notice how preparation leads naturally into the imagination phase of the creative cycle.)

These two examples illustrate the essence of preparation for directed-creative thinking. Live in the world and go about your daily activities. Just stop every so often and ask yourself questions like, "What is going on right now?" or "What is that over there?" Then dwell on it long enough to find a new mental concept to store away. It only has to take a minute. There is no need to act on your observations right away.

If you are really starting to get this mental mechanics stuff, you may have noticed something working behind the scenes in the example I just gave. Why did I just happen to extract the concept of "rewarding while you work" as I sit here on this lovely spring day in Raleigh? There are literally hundreds of things going on around me as I write this. Why this particular concept?

What we tend to notice during the preparation phase is influenced by the patterning mechanics of mind. I am a consultant in quality management and have just finished a day's work with a client. Some of the deepest valleys in my mental landscape have to do with quality management and the needs of organizations. Reflecting on it now, I am not at all surprised that my purposeful creative observations got channeled toward this deep valley. The situation was similar in the Chinese restaurant, and it is okay. In fact, this patterning mechanism is quite useful.

The automatic channeling phenomenon in my mind is a by-product of the focus and broad-topics heuristics that we examined in chapter 3. I have a focus for my innovations, but one that is not too narrow. I care a lot about innovating around the topic of quality management and its application in organizations. Because I care and the mental valleys are deep, when I direct myself to pause and notice, my mind automatically adds the implied focus in a sort of mental parentheses. I say to myself, "pause and notice," but my mind says, "pause and notice (something that might at least obliquely relate to the things that organizations engaged in quality management are interested in)."

So, the focus and broad-topics heuristics of directed creativity also contribute to the preparation phase. They subtly direct our attention to things in the world around us that we are more likely to use later as raw materials for creative imagination.

Having drawn your attention to this mental phenomenon, I will now warn you that I find it best not to think about it too much. For me, it is harder to notice something creatively useful when I explicitly say to myself, "pause and notice something that relates to quality management;" rather than simply saying, "pause and notice." Being too explicit activates the quality management mental patterns so strongly that it impedes my ability to see anything really novel. It is analogous to the advice we give kids who are learning to pitch a baseball: "Don't try to aim it, just throw it."

So, the preparation phase of the directed-creative cycle is primarily a continual activity that goes on in the background as we go about our daily lives. As we will see as we get into the tools, we can also supplement this with specific activities. Think of creative preparation as providing the raw materials for innovation—concepts stored up in memory, with novel linkages to other concepts, that our imaginations can rearrange later. The keys to directed creative preparation are captured in the five mental actions of paying attention, pausing, noticing, extracting meaning, and storing up for later use.

Therefore, the tools we need are tools that support these activities. In the remainder of this chapter, we will look at some examples of tools from the creativity literature. Anything that helps us accomplish one or more of these five mental activities will help us build a mind that is better prepared for creative thought.

A Loose Classification of Tools for Preparation in Directed Creativity

I have compiled a list of more than 60 tools that support creative preparation from my review of the literature. I think it is fair to say that nearly all authors in the field of creativity and innovation consider preparation important enough to offer some concrete suggestions on how to go about it.

To bring some order to this seemingly chaotic array of methods, I suggest the loose classification scheme depicted in Figure 5.2. The headings at

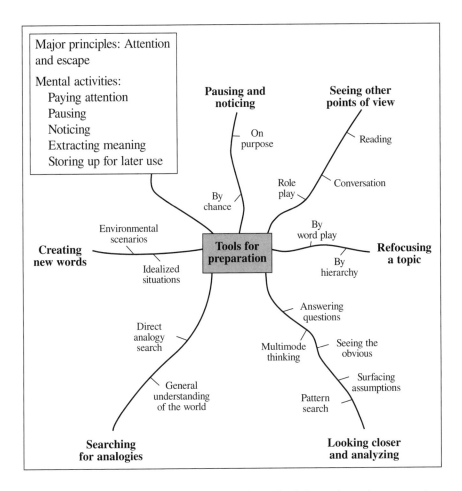

Figure 5.2. A loose classification scheme for the tools of directed-creative preparation.

the end of each spine on the diagram describe major categories of tools. The items coming off the spines represent subsets of tools under each category. Refer often to Figure 5.2 as you read through this chapter. This will create a mental valley that will later enable you to select tools for specific applications by simply looking over the figure.

I want to stress that Figure 5.2 is a *loose* classification scheme. Our judgment and perception systems have a strong tendency to lock onto classification schemes. This leads to a strong and automatic desire to make all future input conform to the scheme. I emphatically do not want that to happen here. Figure 5.2 is merely a device to enable me to present the tools in an orderly manner.

Pausing and Noticing

I introduced this topic as heuristic 1 in chapter 3, and I gave the two examples of my Chinese restaurant and courtyard episodes earlier in this chapter. To reiterate, the key activities are to stop, reflect, and extract meaning from the things that go on around you. As indicated in Figure 5.2, you might stop because something has occurred by chance (my Chinese restaurant story) or because you have just decided that it is time to stop (my courtyard story). In either case, the key is to deliberately assign some meaning to what you observe.

Consider the extracted meaning to be whatever pops into your mind. Do not agonize over it. It does not have to be immediately useful (although it is certainly okay if it is). Do not spend more than a minute or two on it; time brings analysis which often drives you back into an existing mental valley.

Make sure to store the meaning. You can aid this storage process by verbalizing the meaning. Repeat the episode and its meaning to yourself or others several times over the next few hours following the observation. Better yet, develop a more permanent storage system such as a notebook, tape recorder, or computer file.

Set a goal of recording at least one episode-meaning paragraph each day. Put the notebook or recorder on your desk and then when it happens to catch your eye during the day, take that as a signal that it is time to pause and notice something. Another technique would be to set your watch alarm, or computer's alarm clock, to go off at a random time. It does not matter how you do it, but find something that works for you. Most people report that they only need this crutch of a reminder for a short period of time (a few weeks). It soon becomes a habit.*

If Steven Ross and several of his colleagues at the accounting firm had the habit of recording episode-meanings, one of the first things they might do

---

*For more on the use of reminders in developing good habits for quality, see Roberts and Sergesketter 1993.

for creative preparation is simply review their various notebooks for relevant concepts. I return frequently to my notebooks and am routinely surprised to see what jumps out at me. Past observations often yield surprising creative thoughts when juxtaposed against a specific problem.

Even if Steven is just getting started with directed creativity and does not have a rich notebook yet, he can still pause and notice examples of good service prospectively. He can do this by himself or with several colleagues. He might even get his spouse, children, or others into the act!

When using tools that help you pause and notice, remember:

- Explicitly assign a meaning to an episode.
- Don't try too hard.
- For now, just store concepts.
- Record your thoughts so you won't forget them.

Seeing Other Points of View

The pause-and-notice tools just described help you store your own new mental valleys based on things that happen in your world. Another way to store up new mental valleys is to borrow them from someone else's mind.

Books are mental valleys committed to paper. Reading, therefore, is one way to appropriate someone else's mental valleys. Of course, you also get the author's biases, but since we are just storing up concepts, this need not bother us. As an example of a preparation phase tool that uses reading, Higgins (1994) describes an "opportunity search" where an individual or group purposefully reads science fiction books or trade journals in other fields looking for things that trigger creative thoughts.

So read anything and everything. Especially read things that seem to have little to do with your field or your company's business. Read science fiction novels, romance novels, murder mysteries, history, political commentary, physics, biology, house building . . . anything. The purpose is not to master a topic, but rather to store up new mental patterns. With this in mind, short summary articles like the ones in *Scientific American* or *Reader's Digest* are just as good as whole books on a topic.

Of course, in today's world, books are not the only medium by which mental valleys are transmitted. Movies, presentations, television programs, Internet pages, and so forth serve the same purpose. So the next time you have surfed through all 68 cable channels on your television set without finding anything to watch, punch in a random number and watch whatever you get. Consider it a creative pause. Tell yourself that there has got to be something there to notice. Extract some concepts and record them for later use.

Michalko (1991) describes talking to strangers as another way to appropriate the mental valleys of others. Simply ask people what they do for work or hobbies, and then really get in to it. Listen, ask questions, seek to understand something that they understand. Focus the conversation on the other person, not on yourself. Do not try to show off what you know—that defeats the purpose.

It is also okay if the conversation is directly focused on topics that you are pursuing. Just be sure to place prime importance on listening, rather than debating the matter or establishing your own credibility. Michalko (1991) points out that Frank Perdue took a job as a meat clerk in a supermarket in order to learn more about how shoppers select chicken. By listening, Perdue learned that shoppers choose chickens by color and absence of unplucked feathers—themes that he then brought into his innovative research, operations, and marketing plans. In a similar story, a hotel executive profited by installing pizza ovens in his hotel after listening to the garbage collectors tell about the large number of pizza boxes they routinely picked up from hotel dumpsters. Talking to people outside your usual social circle is great preparation for creative thinking.

A final set of creative preparation tools that I will group under this loose heading are ones that involve some type of role play. Many authors suggest various tools that employ the basic idea that we be someone else. "How does the customer think about our product or service?" is a familiar example of this technique that most quality management practitioners have used. We can extend this in several other directions. Our accountant Steven Ross might ask himself, "What would 'service' mean to me if I were a fast food restaurant manager? a small child? a bus driver? a consumer electronics salesperson? the owner of a printing business? a horse?"

Be anyone. It does not matter. There is no way to know which role play will bring about the best creative insights. Try several. As we noted in the examine-ideas-that-make-you-laugh heuristic, the more outrageous and disconnected the role play seems to you at first, the more likely it is that you will get a truly novel idea out of the exploration. If you have no idea what someone else might think, read or have a conversation in order to find out. Remember, we are just exploring and preparing at this stage. Do not force final ideas too soon. Just enjoy for the moment thinking like another person and see where it takes you.

When using tools that help you see other points of view, remember:

- Read and absorb material from many different field and genres.

- Talk to strangers.

- Listen intently; seek to understand the other person's mental valleys.

- Purposely try to think like someone else.

- Even outrageous role plays can yield creative insights.

- The purpose of preparation is mental storage; you do not have to agree with or use the new knowledge immediately.

- Record your thoughts so you won't forget them.

Refocusing a Topic

The preparation methods for directed creativity described thus far are general methods for storing up mental patterns. In addition to these non–topic-specific methods, creative preparation can also employ tools to explore specific areas.

In our discussion of the focus and broad-topics heuristics, we noted that it was useful to pay attention to how we define the issue that is the target of our creative efforts. We discussed the importance of widening our viewpoint but also warned against never-ending redefinition (the pitfall of trumping). Therefore, we need some tools to employ in the preparation phase of the directed-creativity cycle that will help us expand our thinking on the definition of the topic, but that will keep us from going on forever.

Koberg and Bagnall (1981) describe the key word distillery tool as a method for refocusing a topic before diving in. Alone or in a group, write a statement that describes the topic as you see it now. The statement can contain multiple sentences; whatever it takes to capture it. Now go through the statement circling words and phrases that seem to you more essential than the others. Rearranging these words and phrases, craft another statement of the topic. The struggle required to get a coherent statement of the topic often yields insight into what is really important about the challenge you are facing. I like to combine this technique with VanGundy's (1992) two-words method. VanGundy suggests selecting key words from your original statement of the issue and either consulting a thesaurus for substitutes or putting the words together in random combinations.

Let me partially illustrate these tools using Steven Ross' challenge to "develop innovative pilot services that would please the customers of an accounting firm." Key words to circle in this topic statement would be

Develop	Innovative	Pilot
Services	Please	Customers
Accounting	Firm	

Some interesting, randomly selected word pairs constructed from this list would be

Pilot–firm

Please–innovate

Innovate–develop

Pilot–accounting

Steven could simply type up a list of such word pairs as preparation for a future idea generation session. "Pilot–firm" leads to the creative idea of setting up a separate subsidiary to experiment with innovative ways to practice accounting, in much the same way that General Motors set up Saturn as a "new kind of car company." "Please–innovate" makes me think of asking every employee of the firm to submit a small innovation in their work area every month. Another idea that comes from this is to establish a monthly newsletter for our clients in which we ask them to rate three proposed new service ideas on the criteria of how pleased they might be if we implemented them. The newsletter deadline would give us healthy pressure to come up with ideas. Even if we never implemented anything, we would at least be communicating something other than our traditional, stodgy image.

By using synonyms, we can change "pilot–accounting" into "novice–bookkeeping" (or any number of other things) and add these new pairs also to the list. "Novice–bookkeeping" stimulates my imagination to suggest a innovative service where we partner up with accounting schools at universities around the country via the Internet. The firm's customers could designate a school that they would like to help; usually their alma mater. We would then contact that school to form teams of students who would work under our supervision to provide the bookkeeping, accounting, and tax preparation services that the customer requests. The accounting firm gets some free labor, the universities and students get real-world situations to aid learning, and the firm's customers get the satisfaction of helping their old schools. They might also be very pleased by the psychic reward of being recognized by their alma mater as a successful businessperson. (I once noticed at a class reunion that many people have a very strong, often irrational, desire to look good to their old teachers and classmates.)

Synonyms could also be used to generate multiple statements of the topic that could be explored later in the imagination phase of the directed-creativity cycle. For example, playing with the original topic statement and synonyms for various key words, Steven could restate the challenge as "We want to . . ."

- Induce new value into our customers' businesses.

- Develop a new line of innovative business services that will surprise our customers by becoming a club or network (rather than the firm that we are today).

- Propagate new, valuable ideas among our customers; be a clearinghouse or laboratory to share business ideas.

I could go on, but I think you get the idea. The main point here is that such tools help us refocus the topic during creative preparation through the use of word play.

Nadler and Hibino (1994) suggest the purpose hierarchy tool as another way to direct our attention when refocusing our topic. This tool directly supports the broad-topics heuristic—purposefully try broader definitions and see what insights you gain. To construct a purpose hierarchy, write a concise statement of the topic as you now see it on a card or Post-it note. Now ask: What are other, more broadly stated purposes for wanting creative thinking on this topic? Why do I care about this? What am I really trying to accomplish? Continuing with our accounting firm example, "We want to . . ."

- Enhance the reputation of the firm.

- Enhance the reputation of the firm as an innovator.

- Stop the loss of business.

- Get good press.

- Show our customers that we are like them.

- Show our customers that we are like what they perceive themselves to be.

- Generate more revenues.

Write each restatement on a card or Post-it. Now notice that these purposes vary in scope. For example, "get good press" is a smaller purpose (less noble, more crass, more short-term thinking, and so on) than the original statement "develop innovative services to please customers." These various statements can therefore be arranged as a progression from small to large, or short-term to long-range, or major to minor, or noble to crass. The specific criteria used for the ordering is not so important; just pick something that seems relevant to your situation. This ranked list is called a purpose hierarchy.

The value of this tool lies in the exploration of the many ways to view the topic. Later, in the imagination phase of the directed-creativity cycle, we can generate ideas at several levels of this hierarchy. For example, we might say: Give me creative ideas to get good press for the firm. Now give me creative ideas that would show our customers that we are like them. Now give me ideas for services that are simply innovative in their own right, and so on. Each restatement of the issue starts the mind at a slightly different mental valley and, therefore, enhances the chances for novel connections.

At the beginning of this section, I said we needed tools that would help us expand our thinking, but that would also keep us from going on forever. Certainly, we have demonstrated the expansive value of these tools, but how do we know when to stop? Unfortunately, we can never know for sure. There is always one more word pair, one more synonym, one more statement of purpose. The best approach is to set a time limit, or an item-count limit, and simply move on when we reach that limit. For example, we could generate a page of word pairs and then select 13 of them to pass on to the imagination phase. Or, we could decide beforehand that we are going to have seven items in our purpose hierarchy. Simply pick a reasonable number and stop. If your subsequent imagination and development efforts fail to turn up any really good ideas, you can always return to your original list and develop more items. But committing yourself to words on a page by a certain date will keep you from endless preparatory thinking.

When using tools that help you refocus a topic, remember:

- There is value in exploring several different statements of the topic.
- Pick out key words in your current topic statement, and then randomly pair them or substitute synonyms to see what creative insights you get.
- Explore broad restatements of your topic with a purpose hierarchy.
- Set a time or count limit, and then stop when you reach it.
- Save your notes for later use in the imagination phase.

Looking Closer and Analyzing

In describing models for the creative process in chapter 3, I stressed repeatedly that creative thinking is a balance of both analytical and generative thought. So it makes sense that we should also have some analytical tools available to us during the preparation phase of the directed-creativity cycle. Several generic types of analysis aids are listed under this category in Figure 5.2.

Kepner and Tregoe (1963, 1981) provide the most well-known set of issue analysis questions in their 5Ws and an H list: *who, what, where, when, why,* and *how.* These simple questions can be quite powerful in creative preparation—if we resist the urge to answer them too quickly. For example, in our accounting firm, the quick answer to the who question is: our customers. But what about businesses that are not our current customers? businesses that do not even exist yet? families and individuals? teenagers who are just getting their first jobs? retirees? people who have just lost their jobs? More ideas for innovative services emerge if we expand our list of who we think we are offering the services for. The quick answer to the where question is: We offer our services in the offices of SJ&D. But what services can we bring directly to the clients' home or business? what services can we offer over the telephone? via the Internet? in a shopping mall? in partnership with a quick-copy center? in partnership with a bank via its ATM network? over a cable TV channel?

As these examples illustrate, while traditional analysis is typically concerned with finding the right answers, analysis in directed creativity is more concerned with asking expansive questions. In the preparation phase of the creative cycle, we ask questions and begin exploring to open our eyes to possibilities. We do not need to decide anything yet; we are simply storing away possibilities for later imaginative combination.

Edward de Bono's (1985, 1992) Six Thinking Hats is another useful device for creative analysis because they encourage multimode thinking. de Bono suggests that we direct our thinking in specific directions by means of the metaphor of putting on and taking off colored thinking caps. de Bono's six hats* are

White	Think about data, facts, and information.
Yellow	Think about positives, benefits, good things.
Black (or purple)	Think about negatives, warnings, pitfalls.
Green	Think about creative possibilities and new ideas.
Red	Think about feelings and intuitions.
Blue	Exert control or direction over thinking.

The beauty of the six hats is that they are an easy-to-remember, but reasonably comprehensive, outline of the various thinking modes we need to apply to a topic. While I have introduced them here in this chapter on preparation, the six hats have a variety of uses throughout the creative thinking cycle.

To use the six hats in creative preparation, someone in the group figuratively puts on the blue hat as the leader of the thinking session. This person

---

*de Bono gives the negative thinking hat the color black. Have you ever noticed how socialized we are in the United States to associate the color black with negative or bad things? I guess this would be okay in isolation, but we also strongly associate the word *black* with an ethnic group in our society. Taken together, I worry about the mental linkages that subtly cause us to think of black people in negative ways. To avoid encouraging this mental linkage, and with apologies to Edward de Bono, I prefer to assign the color purple to the negative-thinking hat. I will use this convention throughout this book.

might then say, "Let's start with yellow-hat thinking. What are all the positive things we can say about the current situation or about what we envision from our topic statement about our future situation?" For a few minutes, everyone in the group must be positive as we list thoughts. The blue-hat leader then says, "Now, let's put on the purple hat and list negatives and cautions." This is repeated with all the hats to yield a fairly comprehensive list of thoughts at this early stage of the creative cycle.

The hat metaphor gives each mode of thinking its time and place. It helps us avoid premature negative thinking. It also makes everyone equal—negative people must think positively when the yellow hat is in use, both analytical and intuitive people must practice the opposite mode of thinking when the white and red hats are on, and so on. This is useful because it stimulates mental pathways that might be otherwise underutilized.

The six hats are equally useful even when you are working alone. They serve as a reminder to exercise all of your thinking modes. As with a group, simply use the hats one at a time and compile your thoughts.

While Kepner and Tregoe's analysis questions and de Bono's six hats provide general frameworks, it is also important to have some tools that zero in on specific issues related to analysis in creative preparation. For example, von Oech (1986, 35) advises "don't overlook the obvious" in your creative analysis. As an illustration, he describes the evolution in the size of the front wheel of the bicycle during the 1860s and 1870s. In those days, the pedals were attached directly to the front wheel, so the only way to get the bicycle to go faster was to make the front wheel larger. Of course, as designers introduced ever larger front wheels, bicycles became increasingly unsafe. No one had yet thought of using gears and a drive chain as a way of getting more out of each revolution of the pedal. The curious thing, von Oech points out, was that bicycles were manufactured on equipment that used drive chains! One day, H. J. Lawson looked up, made the obvious connection, and changed the bicycle forever through the innovation of drive chain technology.

The bottom line is that in the preparation phase we should ask ourselves: What resources, technologies, ideas, and concepts are right in front of me? Make a one-page inventory of such things. The more obvious and taken-for-granted the better. Steven Ross' list of obvious things at an accounting firm might include computers, word processing software, a front door, a back door, a parking lot, a reception area, and the clothes we wear. Again, there does not have to be a reason for writing something down. You do not have to see just yet what your imagination might do with the item later on. We are simply paying attention now.

To illustrate that there are creative possibilities from this list of obvious, trivial things, consider the following ideas. From "the clothes we wear" we might think of establishing a database on our clients regarding how casually or formally they dress so that we can dress accordingly at our appointments with them. From this same item, I thought that perhaps many of our clients might have their own softball or other recreation teams. We could get their T-shirts and make a display to put in our reception area. It would advertise the clients and give us a more casual, with-it appearance. From the "parking lot" item we might establish a drop-off box or kiosk in our parking lot. Our entrepreneurial clients might appreciate the convenience of being able to get receipts or other financial information to us at any time of the day or night without getting out of their cars. Try it yourself. Take an item from the list of obvious things in an accounting firm and generate an innovative idea. I hope that you are seeing how easy it can be to generate innovative ideas if we simply take some time in preparation.

Related to the seeing-the-obvious tool are the methods that many creativity authors supply for calling our attention to assumptions, paradigms, and other rules we take for granted. While some authors provide elaborate instructions, table formats, and diagrams to support this, I prefer to simply take our a clean sheet of paper, write the words *assumptions, paradigms,* and *rules* at the top, and start listing things until the page is full. Again, the more obvious and fundamental these items, the better.

A final type of tool under this loose category of looking closer and analyzing are tools that help us see patterns. Because creativity has to do with associations among concepts, multidimensional grids often aid our creative pattern search. For example, Michalko (1991) describes the FCB grid tool, developed in 1978 by Richard Vaughn, research director of the advertising agency of Foote, Cone, and Belding. The basic grid has four quadrants, as illustrated in Figure 5.3.

Unfortunately, the terms are from the language of marketing and advertising and may seem a little foreign to some readers. *High involvement* means expensive products and services, *low involvement* means less costly. *Think* represents verbal, numerical, analytical, cognitive products and services that are strongly coupled to facts and information. *Feel* represents products and services that appeal to customers' emotional needs and desires. The typical accounting firm would be in the first quadrant—relatively expensive and strongly coupled with facts and information. A fine jewelry store would be in quadrant 2 (expensive and appealing to emotions) while the jewelry counter in a discount store would be in quadrant 4 (less costly, but appealing to emotion).

Regardless of the terms used, the point of any such grid is to search for creative patterns and possibilities. Figure 5.3 indicates that our hypothetical accounting firm of SJ&D is currently in the high involvement–think quadrant. Many competitors are also in this quadrant with us, but they are closer to the feel side because they too are small, entrepreneurial firms, like their customers. There are also some low involvement–think competitors; discount accounting services offered by people working out of home offices. The creative insight in the analysis here is that the feel quadrants are unoccupied.

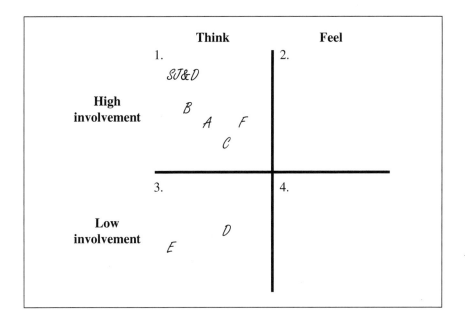

Figure 5.3. An FCB grid analyzing the competitive positions of various accounting firms.

What innovative services could we offer that would fall into these quadrants? Perhaps we could offer a finance seminar at a nice resort exclusively for owners of small start-up businesses and their guests. Or how about this . . . the word *feel* makes me think of the synonym *intuition*. Business owners want to have a good intuitive feel for the state of their business finances. Typical balance sheets and accounting reports may not be supplying this to them. How could we modify our financial reporting to convey a better feel for the numbers? Maybe we could offer simulation and modeling tools that clients could play with, like the flight simulators advocated by systems thinkers and learning organization proponents (see for example, Senge 1990). (As an aside, do you see the subtle role of reading as preparation for creative thought? Reading stores up concepts while flexible mental movement makes the creative associations to the situations we face.)

The FCB grid supports innovation by helping us identify areas where no one has gone before. Creative thinking in these uncharted waters might yield what Kano et al. (1984) call "quality that surprises the customer."

While the FCB grid uses high-cost/low-cost and thinking/feeling as scales, we could try other variables to see what patterns emerge. Centralized/decentralized, low-speed/high-speed, and standardized/customized are a few alternative choices. Whatever scales you use, the goal is to find directions for innovation and to boldly go where no one has gone before!

When using tools that help you look closer and analyze, remember:

- Ask: who, what, when, where, why and how—but resist the urge to answer too quickly.

- Analysis in directed creativity is not about finding the right answers; it is about asking expansive questions.

- Practice multimode thinking (for example, Six Thinking Hats).

- Don't overlook the obvious; list what is right in front of you.

- Make a list of assumptions, paradigms, and rules.

- Grids can help you see patterns in an industry and spot opportunities for innovation.

- Save your notes for later use in the imagination phase.

Searching for Analogies

Much of creative thinking revolves around the application of analogies. Koestler (1964, 200) notes that "some writers identify the creative act in its entirety with the unearthing of hidden analogies."

As an example of the use of analogy, Rice (1984) notes that the idea for Pringles potato chips came about through a search for an analogy to solve the problem of broken chips. Someone asked, "What naturally occurring object is similar to a potato chip?" One suggestion was dried leaves. Exploration of this analogy led to a discussion about pressed leaves in a scrapbook or collection. This, in turn, led to the insight that the leaves must be pressed flat for storage while they are still moist; leaves will crumble if you wait until they are already dried. This idea became the basis for Pringles' innovative manufacturing and packaging process for its potato chips.

The dictionary defines analogy as the inference that if two or more things agree with one another in some respects, they will probably agree in others. When Robert Camp (1989) of Xerox performed the first benchmarking visits to L.L. Bean to study its warehousing operations, he was using creative analogy. While Xerox and L.L. Bean are very different companies, they are similar in the sense that they both do warehousing. Camp's innovation was to suggest that Xerox could learn something useful by exploring the common area between the two companies—warehousing—while temporarily setting aside the differences.

Of course, noticing an analogy or similarity is only half the story. Seasoned benchmarkers know that only rarely can processes and solutions be copied directly from one company into another. Adapting the processes and solutions observed in the analogous company back into your own organization is key to the successful use of benchmarking. This need for adaptation is a generic challenge whenever we use an analogy. For now, however, we will postpone this challenge of adaptation until the imagination or development phases of the directed-creativity cycle.

Pausing and noticing and seeing other points of view (two types of tools that we have already examined in this chapter) are nonspecific means for creating analogies. The more we notice and understand about the world in general, the more analogies we can create when facing a future specific challenge.

We can also seek out analogies specifically for our topic of interest. Several authors suggest techniques for direct-analogy search. For example,

Higgins (1994) suggests that we "take an excursion." After gaining a general understanding of your focused topic, take a trip (literally or imaginatively) to a zoo, a museum, a shopping mall, a school, or your own factory or other places of business. You will be amazed at how much you will see that you can relate back to your topic of interest. In a related technique, Mattimore (1991) describes sending people out with cameras on a "photo excursion" to bring back pictures of potential analogies that they can present to a group at a later idea generation session. Plsek (1995) describes the use of excursions to generate creative analogies in the case of a health care organization sending team members to visit the Mall of America in Minneapolis looking for customer service and communications ideas.

Gordon (1961) developed a comprehensive tool for creative thinking, called Synectics, that relies heavily on the use of analogies. At the risk of oversimplifying this powerful methodology, let me describe it briefly. A trained Synectics facilitator works with a group to get a topic statement and to extract key words (like the key word distillery tool described earlier). The facilitator selects a key word and asks the group to think about an example of that key word in a world that is very distant from the participants' world. Participants then silently jot down concepts, images, and associations from that distant world. After this period of preparatory thinking, the facilitator asks participants to develop absurd ideas on the original topic by using material from their images of the distant world. The group then uses these absurd ideas as stepping-stones to develop more realistic ideas.

The Synectics method spans the entire directed-creativity cycle and involves attention, escape, and movement. My intent in introducing it here is merely to point out that the identification of analogous, distant worlds and absurd ideas can be a useful creative preparation.*

Returning to our friend Steven Ross, let's go right to the heart of it all and ask, what are some direct analogies for accounting? Here is what comes to mind for me.

- All present and accounted for; that is, what methods does the army use for roll call?

---

*For more on Synectics, you can read comprehensive works such as Gordon 1961 or Prince 1970. Good, short (three- to five-page) summaries of the method are given in Adams 1974, 1986; Koberg and Bagnall 1981; and LeBoeuf 1980.

- Accounting for victims following a disaster; that is, what can we learn about accounting from organizations like the police or the National Transportation Safety Board that investigate disasters?

- How do computer operating systems keep track of transactions—what is the latest thinking in this field, and what insights might that give us into better ways of doing financial accounting?

Again, we do not have to know now if these analogies are good ones. We do not have to know how we are going to use them. The point is that it would be useful creative preparation to identify six to 10 potential analogies and do some research (reading, conversations, visits) prior to idea generation. Every new mental valley we can create is one more possibility for the imagination.

When using tools that help you search for analogies, remember:

- An analogy does not have to be perfect to be useful.

- Expect to work hard in the imagination and development phases generating creative thoughts from an analogy.

- When using analogies, focus on the common areas between the proposed analogy and your topic; don't let the differences excite premature judgment that rejects the analogy.

- Use literal and imaginative excursions to identify analogies.

- Laughable thoughts often contain the seeds of innovation.

Creating New Worlds

A final set of directed-creativity preparation methods from Figure 5.2 is the methods for creating new worlds. The basic approach involves constructing a detailed future or idealized scenario and then thinking about what you would do if such a scenario were true.

Wack (1985) describes how Shell used scenario planning back in the early 1970s to stimulate creative strategic thinking. By imagining a then-unheard-of world with high crude oil prices, low reserves, and constrained distribution channels, Shell planners were able to identify strategically important variables in the petrochemical industry and manage them accordingly. As a result, Shell significantly outperformed its competitors when these unlikely scenarios came true during the oil embargo of 1973–1974.

Senge et al. (1994) outline the steps for creating scenarios. Good scenarios begin with a clear sense of purpose—what we have been calling here a focused, but broad topic. Under the topic, list what you feel are the driving forces in the situation. Divide these forces into two groups: predictable and uncertain. Now create several (two to four) detailed scenario descriptions by combining the predictable forces with several possibilities for the unpredictable forces. These scenarios can then become food for thought in the imagination phase of the directed-creativity cycle.*

For Steven Ross and the accounting firm of SJ&D, a partial list of predictable and uncertain factors driving the accounting business in the community might include the following:

Topic: Innovative accounting services for our clients

Predictable factors	Uncertain factors
Population	Tax laws
Community demographics	Uses for personal computers
Trends toward an economy based on service, high-tech, and small manufacturing businesses	Desire to insource or outsource accounting functions

Using these factors, Ross and a team of colleagues could construct two to four one-page scenarios as a creative preparation exercise. Assuming that the predictable factors go as anticipated, at least for the medium-term future, what would SJ&D do under the following scenarios?

Scenario 1: The government enacts a very simple, flat tax that obviates the need for the tax planning and preparation work that SJ&D currently does for its clients. (Tax-related work is currently 70 percent of our business.) Naturally, the clients start doing their own tax planning and tax filing using their own internal personnel. Clients continue to

---

*For more about scenario planning, see Senge et al. 1994; Senge 1990; de Geus 1988; Ackoff, Finnel, and Gharajedaghi 1984; and Porter 1980.

evolve their computer systems along current trend lines; no major breakthroughs in this area.

Scenario 2: The tax system gets even more complex than it is today. Clients also begin hiring their own accounting personnel and keep more of the work traditionally done by SJ&D. Through the use of the Internet and evolving electronic data interface standards, all businesses and households in the community are linked together on an advanced computer network with capabilities to transmit voice, data, and images.

Each such scenario creates a new world. In the imagination phase of the directed-creativity cycle, we will want to walk around in these new worlds and think about what we would do. What services would we offer? How would we create value for our customers? What new trends will be spawned under these conditions? And so on. The exploration of these virtual worlds will give us innovative ideas that we might be able to adapt to the real world of today. Or, we might decide that a future scenario is so promising that we will proactively work to bring it about sooner.

Creating a new world need not only concern imagining a new environment (as we just did). We can create other types of scenarios to spur the imagination. For example, as the head of Bonneville Power Administration, Peter Johnson (1988) created a "phantom super-competitor"—an outrageously idealized organization that could accomplish anything—and then challenged himself and his organization to keep up with it.

The key ideas behind scenarios are creative escape and the balance of analysis and imagination. We escape time and effort by simply leaping over to a new future or new situation without having to bother with how things got that way. The only question is: What are we going to do now? After some imaginative exploring, we are likely to have several innovative ideas that might help us back in the real world, the here and now. While our scenarios must provide escape, they must also be plausible or they will simply become a silly game. Constructing plausible scenarios that nevertheless escape the current world requires the balance of creative and analytical thought that is the hallmark of the preparation phase.

When using tools that help you create new worlds, remember:

- The basic idea is to construct a detailed picture of a new world and then walk around in it.

- Separate environmental factors into those that you feel are reasonably predictable and those which are uncertain.

- Create environmental scenarios by holding the predictable factors steady and randomly modifying the uncertain factors.

- You can also create idealized competitors, customers, employees, or technologies; anything that provides creative escape will help.

- Scenario construction is an art, there is no way to know which scenarios will generate the most creative ideas; simply go for maximum variety in two to four cases.

- Blend your creative and analytical skills (or assemble a team with a good mix) to generate plausible but imaginative scenarios.

Summary and on to Imagination

The key messages of this chapter are

- Preparation is an essential part of the directed-creativity cycle. It is naive to think that you can just walk into a brainstorming session and emerge with several breakthrough ideas effortlessly.

- Creative preparation is something that should go on all the time as we live our lives in the world. It is immediate—here and now. You never know when something interesting might happen.

- Creative preparation is also deliberate. You can sit down and do it.

- Creative preparation is about expansive thinking. The goal is to have more identified and available mental valleys than when you began.

- Preparation is a blend of both generative and analytical thinking.

- The preparation phase leads naturally into the imagination phase of the directed-creativity cycle, but you do not have to immediately imagine creative ideas as you prepare. It is enough simply to prepare. If you do both the preparation and imagination by yourself, you take away the fun that others can have contributing their own imaginative ideas.

Do not shortchange the preparation phase of the creative cycle. Lack of purposeful preparation is a major reason why innovation is so rare. Using the tools described in this chapter, craft your own methods for preparation. Use Figure 5.2 and the various boxes throughout this chapter as memory joggers to remind you about the variety of approaches you might try.

Purposeful preparation for directed creativity has another, subtle psychological benefit. Walking into a brainstorming group with several, well-thought-out, creative stimulus handouts makes it look like you know what you are doing. This is important. Many people believe that creativity is only about being silly or off-the-wall. As a result, they do not put much effort into creative thinking. Showing that you have prepared, and acting like you seem to know what you are doing, gives others the confidence to give creative thinking another try. You never need to let on that you really have no idea whether any of the things that you have prepared will stimulate a innovation. It is enough simply to be confident and see where you end up.

Over a week's time, Steven Ross and his colleagues at SJ&D could prepare a nice collection of items to stimulate imagination. They could have several pages of notes about things people have noticed, heard, or read about. They could prepare the original topic statement, along with several provocative restatements. Word pairs and synonyms from the key words in the topic statement could also be used in idea generation sessions. Lists of assumptions, rules, paradigms, and things that are right before our eyes could supply direction for creative escape. And, of course, there is the key insight that none of our competitors has yet offered services in the feel dimension of the grid we constructed. We could also ask groups to explore specific analogies and prepared scenarios. Surely, we will do a better job of idea generation based on these predeveloped items than if we had simply put people in rooms and said, "Okay, let's brainstorm for innovative services."

CHAPTER 6

Tools That Stimulate the Imagination for New Ideas

𓀀 〰 ·ʔ· ⸘

Imagination is more important than knowledge.

Albert Einstein

Imagination makes man the paragon of animals.

Shakespeare

I have a microwave fireplace. You can lay down in front of the fire all night . . . in just eight minutes.

Steven Wright

The preparation phase of the directed-creativity cycle leads naturally into the imagination phase. Indeed, as we have seen, it is often difficult to restrain the mind's natural movement into imagination when we pause and notice. Of course, there is no real need for restraint; do not let our model with its artificial phases get in your way!

In this chapter, we will explore the imagination phase of the directed-creativity cycle. The activities of this phase of the cycle are depicted in Figure 6.1. It is here that we transition from mental storage and analysis into mental movement and idea generation. Then, since our definitions of creativity and innovation include the criteria of usefulness and practicality, we will begin to harvest the best ideas from among the many we have generated.

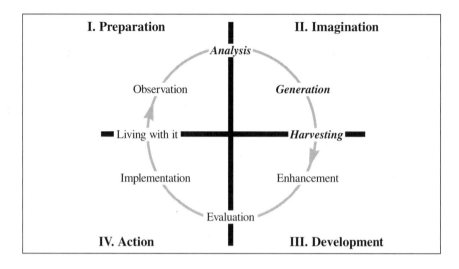

Figure 6.1. Activities in the imagination phase of the directed-creativity cycle.

Activities and Heuristics That Support the Imagination

While the preparation phase was primarily about creative attention and some escape, the imagination phase of the directed-creativity cycle primarily utilizes escape and movement. Our imaginations possess the wonderful ability to escape the confines of our current thinking on a topic. We are all capable of imagining whole new worlds, new rules, and new ways of doing things. If you have ever read a novel, been to a movie, or pretended with children, you have already demonstrated to yourself the reality of imaginative escape.

Equally wonderful is the power of mental movement. Our minds are constantly at work. It is extremely difficult to *not* think. When mental escape breaks the bonds of the current reality, mental movement finds another place to settle. If we direct our mental movement toward novel connections, we end up with creative ideas (heuristic 4). For example, through imagination, the quality manager at a soft drink company can escape current reality and suggest the unlikely scenario of the government outlawing packaged carbonated drinks (the no-bubbly-drinks bill!). What in the world would we do? The mind races and mental movement makes the required creative associations.

Since we are barred from bottling carbonated beverages, what other things do we have stored away in our minds under the concept of "beverages?" Coffee . . . milk . . . water . . . juices. While we are at it, let us also take imaginative advantage of the mental linkage between the concepts of "beverage" and "liquid." There are many liquids that we might package if we could not sell carbonated drinks. How about car antifreeze in two-liter bottles? Going further, our imaginations can ask: What is the opposite of a liquid? A solid, of course. Why not combine a pull-top soft drink can with a solid food like peanuts, chocolates, or peppered nut mix? The creative possibilities brought about by mental movement and association are endless. Importantly, anyone can do it.

While judgment is needed to harvest promising innovations from among the virtually infinite array of possible mental associations, premature judgment is a significant barrier to imagination. The no-inherent-right-or-wrong heuristic encourages us to be flexible in our thinking during the imagination phase. In so many cases in the work world, our notions of what is right or wrong, acceptable or not, sensible or eccentric are just relics of someone else's past judgment. Why are telephone keypads arranged with the digits 1 to 3 on the top row, while calculator keypads have those digits on the bottom row? Why do life insurance agents typically come to your home, while stockbrokers expect you to come to their offices? While I am sure that someone can explain the historical logic behind such things, the truth is that for many things the only reason we still have them as they are today is that it's just the way it has always been.

Learning to view all things as being subject to change is key in unlocking the imagination. The personality trait of flexibility may well be the most important distinction between someone who is viewed by others as naturally creative, and someone who must work at it. (Recall that we included mental flexibility in the definition of creativity in chapter 2.)

I can offer two tips from my own experience that have helped me to be more flexible in my thinking. First, I find it helpful to try to imagine how things might have gotten the way they are. For example, why don't stockbrokers typically come to you? I bet it is because back in the old days the stock ticker (the device that reports the prices of stocks) was a large, mechanical device that had to be attached to a dedicated line hooked up to the stock exchange. It is difficult to imagine a stockbroker moving around with such a device. I find that once I think something through like this, I am much more willing to accept that it is about time for some new thinking on the matter. In other words, for me, it helps to analyze a little before I create.

A second thing that has helped me to be more flexible is the realization that I can always reinstate any rule, convention, or principle that I escape. I consider every trip of imagination a temporary journey only. I always start out with the knowledge that I can return to where I was. Of course, I often find that once I imagine something new, I do not want to return to where I was. Before starting out, however, I (and others) need the mental safety of knowing that I can always return if I want.

I am not sure how generalizable these two tips are. You should do your own thinking about what it will take for you to practice this heuristic. Remember that judgment is never completely rational. If you fail to deal with it proactively and consciously, it will likely interfere with your ability to imagine.

Let me also recall to your attention the examine-ideas-that-make-you-laugh heuristic. Remember that laughter might well be the body's reaction to a novel connection among neurons in the brain. Therefore, during the imagination phase, be prepared to explore thoughts that seem a little nutty the first time you hear them. Prepare groups in advance for this by explaining the theory (see the text associated with heuristic 6 in chapter 3). Do not let your idea generation session degenerate into a joke-telling contest, but do not stifle humor.

As a final reminder, remember the implement-a-few-ideas heuristic. Imagination is boundless and fun. Just remember that idea generation without action is creativity without innovation. Keep telling yourself and your groups that one good idea implemented is better than 10 great ideas still on paper. Set a time limit for the imagination phase and respect it. Move on to development and action, and then begin the directed-creativity cycle again.

Let me end this section with two final pieces of practical advice. When doing the work of imagination

■ *Always generate multiple alternatives.* Idea generation is about making novel mental connections. The more ideas you keep open simultaneously in your mind, the more opportunities there will be for novel associations.

- *Create in short bursts.* Idea generation is hard mental work. When your mind is tired, it will tend to settle into a comfortable thinking pattern—the way it has always been, the status quo, the un-novel. Two hours of idea generation will not be as productive as four 30-minute sessions with breaks in between.

The Tools for Imagination

Figure 6.2 presents a loose classification scheme for the tools that support the imagination phase of the directed-creativity cycle. Again, let me disclaim any rigid adherence to these categories. Many tools in the literature have characteristics that cross the categories. The purpose of the scheme is simply to allow me to present the tools systematically. Use Figure 6.2 as a memory jogger to help you develop your own methods based on the material in this chapter.

Brainstorming: A Popular But Weak Tool for Imagination

Brainstorming is by far the most widely used tool for creative thinking (Placek 1989). Brainstorming is mentioned in most business books that advocate the use of groups and is described in nearly every book on the basic tools of quality management.

The history of brainstorming. Brainstorming was developed in the 1940s and 1950s by advertising executive Alex Osborn. Unknown to Osborn at the time, a similar technique had been practiced by Hindu teachers in India for more than 400 years (LeBoeuf 1980).

Osborn was a friend of psychologist J. P. Guilford. In his research on people who exhibited creative behavior, Guilford (1950) had identified five key traits.

Fluency   the ability to generate many ideas in a set time

Flexibility   the ability to rapidly free associate

Originality   the ability to express uncommon ideas

Awareness   the ability to see beyond the immediate facts

Drive   the willingness to try without fear of failure

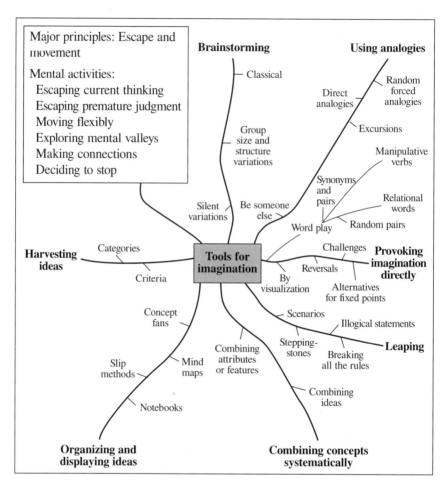

Figure 6.2. A loose classification scheme for the tools of directed-creative imagination.

Since creative thinking was essential in an advertising agency, Osborn sought to develop a method that would bring out these five traits in everyone. Over several years, he developed a model for the creative process and a complete set of tools to support it. Osborn's (1953) model for the creative process comprised seven steps.

1. Orientation: pointing up the problem
2. Preparation: gathering pertinent data
3. Analysis: breaking down the relevant material
4. Ideation: piling up alternatives by way of ideas
5. Incubation: letting up, to invite illumination
6. Synthesis: putting the pieces together
7. Evaluation: judging the resulting ideas

Notice that Osborn's model spans the full cycle of preparation (steps 1–3), imagination (step 4), and development and action (steps 5–7). Osborn called this entire process *brainstorming.*

Unfortunately, what has survived in the business literature today are primarily only the methods and rules associated with Osborn's fourth step, Ideation. With Guilford's five creative traits in mind, Osborn developed a crisp list of four basic rules for ideation sessions.

1. *Criticism is ruled out.* Adverse judgment of ideas must be withheld until later.
2. *Freewheeling is welcomed.* The wilder the idea, the better; it is easier to tame down than to think up.
3. *Quantity is wanted.* The greater the number of ideas, the more the likelihood of winners.
4. *Combination and improvement are sought.* In addition to contributing ideas of their own, participants should suggest how ideas of others can be turned into better ideas, or how two or more ideas can be joined into still another idea.

From what we now know about the mechanics of mind, Osborn's four simple rules are brilliant. They clearly address the key issues of premature judgment and mental movement. They also clearly create an environment that supports Guilford's traits of fluency, flexibility, drive, and—to a lesser extent—originality and awareness.

Osborn (1953) and Clark (1958) describe the complete system of brainstorming, offering detailed advice on group size, preparation before brainstorming, how to record ideas, how to harvest the ideas, and so forth. Clark (1958), LeBoeuf (1980), Tempe (1987), and Higgins (1994) are four of the many authors who have chronicled the numerous success stories of the complete brainstorming system when applied to business issues.

Why brainstorming is a weak tool for imagination. The weakness of the modern practice of brainstorming lies in the fact that the four basic rules that have survived from Osborn's original work do not address the mental subsystem of perception, and they do not give strong guidance on how to be original and aware. To be fair, these issues are addressed somewhat in the other steps and tools in Osborn's original model. Osborn never intended the four rules to be the whole of brainstorming.

Specifically, modern brainstorming is a weak tool for four reasons. First, *while suspension of judgment and going for quantity is necessary for creative thinking, this is not sufficient.* de Bono (1994) likens brainstorming to the situation of a man, tied up with ropes, in a room with a violin. In this condition, the man obviously cannot play the violin. If we cut the ropes, will the man be able to play? Not necessarily. Cutting the ropes removes a constraint, but if the man has no skill or experience with the violin, he is still unable to play.

Second, *as practiced today, brainstorming sessions naively assume that no prior preparation is needed.* Again, this is not Osborn's fault. As we saw in the previous chapter, preparation is important in the directed-creativity cycle. It is naive to assume that brilliant, never-before-thought-of ideas will suddenly burst forth from a group of people assembled to brainstorm for an hour. While this certainly can happen, the question remains: Should we expect it to happen regularly? Of course not.

Third, *brainstorming exhorts us to creativity, but fails to tell us how to achieve it.* The rules of brainstorming tell us to freewheel, go for quantity, and build on the ideas of others, but this tells us nothing about how to get novel ideas in the first place. The situation is reminiscent of Deming's (1986) and Juran's (1989) criticism of the management practice of exhorting others to do quality work without answering the basic question: What should I do different from what I am doing now? With brainstorming, the assumption is that the creative ideas are there already, locked up in the mind—we just need to let them out. Of course, in some cases this assumption is true. Many people report that brainstorming sessions have provided a forum for finally getting serious attention on ideas that people have been thinking about for some time. In this situation, however, it would seem more correct to say that brainstorming is a tool for constructive group discussion rather than a tool for creative idea generation.

Fourth, *as practiced today, brainstorming sessions rarely do an effective job of harvesting the rich set of ideas that are generated.* Again, Osborn supplied follow-up steps and tools for this in his complete system. Today, the usual experience in a brainstorming session is that we fill multiple easel pages with ideas and then vote on or otherwise select only one or two of the ideas to develop. In most brainstorming sessions, nothing is ever done with the many ideas that fail to make the cut. We can do better.

Strengthening your practice of brainstorming. In summary, then, brainstorming is not a bad tool—it is just weak by itself. Despite this, I advise you to keep all those posters you have in conference rooms that list the rules of brainstorming. Further, I suspect that many of your organizational brainstorming norms about group size, recording techniques, room layout, taking turns or not, silent listing before vocalizing or not, and so on are just fine. I would, however, encourage you to think of these as minimal conditions and logistical details only. You can now supplement your practice of brainstorming with more powerful techniques for directly stimulating the imagination.

So, before convening your next brainstorming session, spend time beforehand in preparation. Then use these outputs from the preparation phase as structured inputs to several brainstorming sessions. Plan specific brainstorming sessions to utilize further the concepts that we will cover in this chapter. When you assemble brainstorming groups, review the traditional rules of brainstorming, but then explain specifically how you plan to stimulate the group's imagination during the session (for example, with an analogy, word play, or leap). Finally, do some thoughtful harvesting on every idea generated. We will discuss how to do this later in this chapter, but every idea deserves some attention—even if you end up discarding it.

Variations on classical brainstorming. Several writers have developed modifications to classic brainstorming. These variations are primarily around the logistics and structure of brainstorming sessions. Since these variants also fail to tell us how to come up with new ideas, they share the fundamental weaknesses of classic brainstorming. Nevertheless, knowing about these variants may help you further in developing your own tools for directed creativity.

VanGundy (1987, 1992) describes various methods for *brainwriting*— sessions where participants generate ideas silently, instead of saying them aloud as in classic brainstorming. The basic advantage here is that of equalization. Naturally shy or quiet people, who might freeze up in a group, have just as much chance to express ideas as outspoken people.

Participants might silently write their ideas down as a precursor to sharing them aloud, as in the Mitsubishi brainstorming method (Tatsuno 1990). Or they might put their ideas into a pile in the center of a table, where someone else will later read them aloud to the group, as in the Battelle Institute's brainwriting pool method (VanGundy 1992). Or they might contribute their ideas from a distance without ever meeting face-to-face to compile what John Haefele of Procter & Gamble called a "collective notebook" (Haefele 1962; Pearson 1979). As these variants illustrate, there are many ways to get people to contribute ideas in brainstorming. You can choose methods that fit the personalities of the people you are dealing with and the logistics of your situation.

Other brainstorming variants involve structure and group size considerations (Higgins 1994). For example, in the Phillips 66 method, a large group is broken down into small groups of six. They have six minutes to generate ideas, which are then shared back in the larger group for harvesting. The six-minute brainstorming period can be repeated several times to allow for combinations of ideas. Others have suggested variants involving multiple groups in different locations, the use of multiple groups with slightly different problem statements, musical chairs approaches where participants constantly change groups, five minute periods of silence between idea generation bursts, and so on.

The purpose behind any effective variant of brainstorming must be to create an environment that reduces barriers to free participation and increases the number of ideas generated. The bottom line is, try anything you can think of that does not contradict Osborn's four basic rules and that seems to meet your needs. Just remember that simply removing barriers to participation and exhorting for quantity may not help people come up with novel ideas. The basic assumption behind all brainstorming methods is that the novel ideas are already there; they are just waiting to be invited out. You will need to decide for yourself if that assumption is true for your group and your topic. If not—if you need never-before-thought-of ideas—you should supplement brainstorming with some of the more focused creativity tools described in the remainder of this chapter.

When using brainstorming, remember:

- The classic rules of brainstorming are necessary, but not sufficient, conditions for generating novel ideas.

- Prior preparation and subsequent processing are important, but typically overlooked, parts of brainstorming.

- If you want never-before-thought-of ideas, you will need to supplement your brainstorming sessions with more focused tools for stimulating the imagination.

- There are many useful variants of classic brainstorming; try anything that you can think of that does not contradict Osborn's four rules and that seems to meet your group's needs.

Using Analogies

In the previous chapter, we covered a variety of preparation techniques that involved identifying an analogy. Here in the imagination phase, it is time to actively explore these analogies. We might do this alone, with a few colleagues, or with a larger group. The rules of brainstorming—suspend judgment, free-wheel, go for quantity, build on others' ideas—can help set the stage. Instead of simply opening the floor for ideas, however, we will stimulate the imagination by providing detailed background information on some analogous situation and then invite our minds to make specific creative associations.

Returning to our accountant friends at the firm of SJ&D, Steven Ross might meet for lunch with two friends and discuss what he has learned about how the National Transportation Safety Board accounts for victims following a plane crash. (Recall that this was one of the analogies that we identified in the previous chapter.) In this case, a client's company budget is analogous to a passenger manifest, and the shoe box of receipts that the young entrepreneur brings in at tax time is analogous to the strewn debris at the crash sight.

In addition to preselected, direct analogies, we could also select an analogy at random and simply dive in with little or no preparation. To aid such an effort, Michalko (1991) provides a list of parallel worlds; the list is reproduced as a resource in the appendix. To use the list, simply close your eyes and point to the page. Now use the world that your finger happens to land on as a forced analogy. Do not give up too easily; try to get something out of it, and then repeat the process with several worlds.

Suppose that Steven had randomly selected fishing from the list as an analogous parallel world. What can we take from the world of fishing that we could adapt to the challenge of coming up with innovative accounting services to please our clients? Consider fishing lures. Different lures are needed for different types of fish. This suggests that we should think carefully about which lures to use to please which clients. Fish are attracted to lures because they look like something good to eat; that is, lures attract because they appear to meet a basic need. What are each of our clients' most basic needs, and how can we adapt our relationship with them so that we are offering tailor-made innovative services that are in tune with those needs?

The excursions and be-someone-else tools that we talked about in the last chapter also stimulate imagination by way of analogy. How is an accounting firm like a zoo (excursion)? Or, what would service mean to a fast food restaurant manager (be someone else)? Several questions such as these would make lively provocation for a brainstorming session.

For example, let's apply imagination to our typical process for doing tax returns for small business owners. Our usual process involves the business owner meeting with a senior partner, who collects the input information and gives the owner only a rough estimate of the final tax bill. A junior accountant actually takes the numbers and puts them onto the various tax return forms several days or a week later. Applying the two analogies suggested in the questions above brings to mind several potentially innovative ideas.

■ People like watching the animals at the zoo just to see what they do. Many entrepreneurs are curious people who like to learn more about things.

We could invite the business owner to come in and sit down with the junior accountant who actually processes their return. This might give entrepreneurs a better understanding of their detailed financial situation and help us uncover additional tax breaks for them.

- Fast food restaurants have drive-through windows where you order over an intercom. To save the entrepreneur's valuable time, we could conduct the interview and collect the input information over the telephone, via fax, via computer linkage, or a combination of the above.

Each analogy will typically result in one to 10 ideas. The first one or two ideas might be a struggle, but after that, people typically begin to get the hang of it and become comfortable with the required mental movement. Be prepared to introduce several analogies during the course of a 30-minute idea generation session.

The most important barrier to overcome when using analogies is the mistaken notion that there is a right answer. Perhaps from past experience with puzzles, people seem to think that there is something specific they are supposed to see in the analogy. Simply keep stressing that the purpose of the analogy is idea generation—any ideas that come to mind. There is no need to explain how the ideas relate to the analogy; just express them. For reasons that I do not completely understand, I find that this barrier is less prominent as group size decreases. So I often ask people to form groups of two or three to get started in generating some initial ideas from proposed analogies.

When using analogies, remember:

- We can identify analogies through thoughtful preselection (direct analogies), on-the-spot random selection (forced analogies), imagining other places (excursions), or imagining other people (be someone else).

- People may struggle at first with analogies, but stick with it.

- Analogies are not a puzzle; there is no right answer.

- Analogies seem to work best initially in very small groups; break large groups into pairs to get the ideas flowing.

Provoking Imagination Directly

By far, the most interesting tools for directed creativity are those that provoke the imagination by taking specific advantage of what we now know from modern theories of mind. In introducing directed creativity to groups, I usually start with one of these tools. They are fun, easy to use, and most likely to generate an ah-ha experience for participants.

Imagination by word play. We have already seen the imaginative power of word play. In the last chapter, we took Steven Ross' initial charge statement, distilled the key words, played with combinations and synonyms, and generated several innovative ideas. A brainstorming group could easily spend 30 minutes profitably exploring word pairs and synonyms.

In addition to these word plays on the original topic statement, various authors in the creativity literature have proposed other forms of mental manipulation involving words. For example, Osborn (1953) provided a checklist of manipulative verbs to stimulate imagination in his system of brainstorming. Koberg and Bagnall (1981), Higgins (1994), von Oech (1986), and others have suggested many additions to Osborn's original list. A list of manipulative verbs is provided as a resource in the appendix.

In theory, any verb will do. I like the words in the resource in the appendix because several have multiple meanings, depending on the topic to which they are applied. Just remember that there is no way to know which one will stimulate the best creative ideas, so do not try to be purposeful in your selection. Use several words selected at random and see what comes from them. I generally select the words in the presence of the group to make it clear that I have no preconceived notions or right answers in mind. Let's try some manipulative verbs on Steven Ross' challenge to develop innovative pilot services that would please the customers of an accounting firm.

Stimulus word	*Idea*
minify	Make it easy for small businesses to set up Keogh and 401(k) retirement plans by developing a kit of plans and forms.
combine	Building on this idea, develop a relationship with a discount brokerage firm that could seamlessly handle the

investment side of retirement planning. If we do this well, it could become a product that we offer in partnership with the brokerage firm on a national basis.

reverse   Thinking about getting clients to do our work. . . . We could set up training programs to teach practical accounting to designated employees of the client's company. We would then provide a service of supervising these people. Clients might like it because we would be helping them develop their current employees.

As with the analogy tools, stress to those working with you that every idea is a good one at this point. Further, all our judgments should be positive in nature. In other words, we want to have on both the green (creative) and yellow (positive) hats from de Bono's Six Thinking Hats. We are not looking for a specific response. The manipulative verbs simply suggest a mental valley to start with. Mental movement then takes over and tries to connect that valley with the mental valley associated with our topic. Any associations that occur along the way are potential innovative ideas.

In addition to manipulative verbs, we can also use relational prepositions and conjunctions. A compilation of such words suggested by Crovitz (1970) and VanGundy (1992) also appears as a resource in the appendix. To use these to stimulate imagination, select two major elements associated with the topic of interest. For Steven Ross, potential element pairs might be accountants and clients, tax returns and payroll records, clients and capital formation, and so on. Let's work with the two elements *clients* and *capital formation*. Next, select one of the words at random from the resource list; I just chose *opposite*. Now, explore the image of "clients as the opposite of capital formation." (If it feels a little weird and hard to grasp, you should get excited. This sensation is telling you that this is a highly unusual connection of concepts.)

Here are two ideas that I generated after a few minutes of thinking about "clients as the opposite of capital formation."

- Our clients are often opponents in the competition for a limited capital pool from the banks and venture capitalists in our community. We could set up some sort of cooperative among our clients to share the capital pool better. We would be at the center of the cooperative as a broker–networker.

■ Instead of thinking of our clients as the opposite of investors or venture capitalists, we can encourage them to become venture capitalists themselves. We could help forge relationships among our clients in which they supply capital for each other's businesses around specific projects where there is a mutual benefit.

Again, in a 30-minute idea generation session, we might explore four to six element pairs and relational words. If you have a large group, you could break them into smaller groups, each with different words to explore. There are many ways to mix and match the various tools in this chapter. Do not hesitate to try something.

A final type of word play involves the use of nouns selected at random. (See de Bono 1967, 1969, 1992; von Oech 1983, 1986; or Michalko 1991.) Again, a table of random nouns is provided in the appendix. There is nothing special about the words in this table. You could get the same effect by taking a book, opening to a random page, closing your eyes, and pointing to words until you land on a noun.

However you select the random noun, use the image that it conjures up in your mind as a starting point for mental movement. I just selected the random word *amoebae* from the random word list. (When using the random word list, resist the urge to toss out the selected word in hopes of getting a better one. Again, the more distant sounding the word seems to you at first, the better for creative stimulation.) For our accounting example, the word *amoebae* stimulates the following ideas.

■ Amoebae are microscopic organisms that move around undetected. Using Internet search engine technology, we could develop a software "worm" that could search in the background through files on the client's computer system that are potentially relevant to constructing a comprehensive financial picture of the organization.

■ Microscopic organisms constantly divide and multiply. Teaching clients how to do some of their own accounting internally is one way of dividing and multiplying. We could also develop a focused financial consulting service to help clients spin off portions of their businesses into separate companies or subsidiaries as a way of multiplying their efforts or reducing their risk.

Imagination by visualization. If individual words can stimulate the imagination, and if a picture is worth a thousand words, then visual images are another useful way to provoke the imagination directly. Various authors have proposed techniques for doing this. For example, we could send people out with cameras to take photographs of interesting scenes and then ask people to generate ideas on our focused topic based on whatever comes to mind when they see the photo (Mattimore 1991). VanGundy (1992) suggests a related technique using photographs from highly visual magazines like *National Geographic* or *Life.* Wonder and Donovan (1984) suggest videotaping a scene and watching it in slow motion or backwards to see what creative insights are evoked.

We can also use actual physical objects. This adds the sense of touch to that of sight, which might stimulate even more creative linkages in some people. Mattimore (1991) describes how product development consultant Steve Kange used baskets of exotic fruits to stimulate a group looking for innovative new flavors for candy. The objects need not be directly related to the topic at hand. McGartland (1994) describes the Thunderbolt Show and Tell method where group participants are told to bring a favorite toy from their home or office to a brainstorming session.

We can also draw our own pictures and use them for imagination stimulation. Michalko (1991) describes Leonardo da Vinci's technique of creative doodling. da Vinci would close his eyes and draw random lines and squiggles on a page for a minute or two. When he opened his eyes, he used any patterns that appeared to him in the doodles as a starting point for imagination. Edison used a similar doodling technique. Of course, we need not restrict ourselves to doodles. Ask participants in a brainstorming session to draw a picture of the problem, a picture of a situation that makes a happy customer, a picture of their favorite place, and so forth and then use these to stimulate ideas.

Imagination by reversals. Our thoughts tend to flow in a coherent stream from mental valley to mental valley. Paradigms, unwritten rules, and conventions of the past set a direction for this flow that we take for granted. For instance, we take for granted that when thinking about customer satisfaction, it is only logical to think about what we can do for the customer. Similarly, we naturally want to focus on what we can do to increase satisfaction, decrease costs, and reduce cycle time.

If you have been following our discussion of mental mechanics, you should be anticipating what will come next. Whenever we come across a logical, uni-directional mental flow, *going in the other direction has the potential for stimulating innovative ideas.* Creative reversal methods do just that. (See de Bono 1992; VanGundy 1992; Adams 1974, 1986; and von Oech 1983, 1986.)

To use reversals to stimulate the imagination, identify performance indicators, relationships, assumptions, and process flows in the broad topic area that you typically think of primarily in one direction only. Make a list of ways to purposefully make it go in another direction, scan the list for creative thoughts (typically ones that make you laugh), and use these to trigger ideas back on the original topic.

For example, Steven Ross can use creative reversal by exploring ways that SJ&D can decrease customer satisfaction. We could

Raise our prices.

Make clients wait longer.

Make a lot of errors.

Insult our clients.

Embezzle funds from our clients.

Notice that the first three items are pretty unimaginative, but the last two show some creative thought. This is often the way it goes. Someone suggests something like "insult our clients," and others start getting into the act. Typically, there is hearty laughter. Of course, we now know that laughter is a clue that we are on to something. A humorous, creative reversal might be a link to an innovative new service idea. For example, working with the last two reversal suggestions, consider the following:

■ Now that we think about it, perhaps we inadvertently insult many of our clients with our formal style of dress compared to their casual style. Maybe they think that we don't approve of them (and maybe that is true). How can we counteract this? Perhaps we could start a series of lunchtime seminars where we get a well-known speaker to come and talk about the trend toward casual dress in the workplace (or sports teams at work, or community service at work, and the like). Clients could get valuable information, and our sponsorship would imply that we endorse such efforts.

▪ Now that we think about it, embezzlement is actually a common problem in small, start-up firms. We can offer a special assessment and consulting service to help clients install checks and balances in their evolving financial systems to reduce their exposure to potential embezzlement.

Creative reversals can be a great deal of fun. While we usually begin by laughing at the reversal provocations, we often end up concluding, "Hey, you know, that's not a bad idea!"

Alternatives from fixed points. A final, important tool for directly stimulating the imagination is de Bono's (1992) "alternatives from fixed points" tool. de Bono asserts that all creative ideas are alternatives to something. An idea could be an alternative that replaces what we are currently doing; for example, "instead of always wearing tailored suits, my idea is that we dress casually when we meet our clients." An alternative can also be something that replaces a current vacuum in our approach; for example, "although we have not done so in the past, my idea is that we start offering consulting services on computer and financial systems security to our clients."

Not all alternatives are useful creative ideas. For example, consider this exchange (adapted from de Bono 1992).

I want alternatives to our current financial reports.

How about pasta as an alternative.

When we set out to seek useful alternatives, there is always an implied reference point. We are seeking alternatives with respect to something or with reference to something. Wearing casual clothes is an alternative to wearing suits with respect to "the image we convey to our clients." Offering advice on security is an alternative way to "provide valuable services connected with finance." These are fixed points. They are fixed either by the laws of nature (no matter what we do, we will always be conveying some image to our clients) or by previous decisions (we have decided that our basic mission is to provide services connected with finance).

Although *pasta* is different from *financial reports,* it is not a useful alternative because it does not relate to the implied fixed point of "services connected with finance." But note that "serving pasta" might be considered a useful alternative to "preparing financial reports" if our fixed point was stated as "generate revenue any way we can." The messages here are that fixed points are critically important, and we can better practice directed creativity by making them explicit rather than implied.

To use the alternatives-from-fixed-points tool, focus on something specific within the topic area. Now identify the fixed point(s) by asking: What is the purpose here? What is happening? Where is the value in this?

We may need to be somewhat forceful in asking these questions, but we need not be combative. The key skill here is what de Bono (1992) calls the creative challenge. In a creative challenge there is no need to discredit the current way of doing things, nor to prove that there is anything wrong with it or us. We can generate alternatives just because we want to or just because our customers want us to. So when we ask, What is the purpose of that? or What is the value in that?, we are not looking for an explanation or defense of the current way. This would only lead to an argument, not a creative insight. Rather than an explanation or argument, a creative challenge seeks only to identify a concept from which to generate alternatives. We do not need to decide now whether we will use any of these alternatives; we are merely exploring possibilities.

As illustrated in Figure 6.3, in SJ&D the focus area *reception* has multiple fixed concepts—multiple answers to the questions just raised. We can stimulate the imagination by writing down these fixed concepts and challenging ourselves to generate specific alternatives with respect to these fixed points.

We can now craft several creative ideas from among these alternatives by using flexible mental movement. For example, we could

- Install motion detectors and closed circuit cameras in the hallway. A beep tone would alert the receptionist that someone is coming. By looking at the camera and the computerized appointment schedule, the receptionist could typically figure out who it is that is coming (at least narrow it down) and what meeting room he or she is to be escorted to. The receptionist clicks on the appointment schedule, sending an electronic message to the principal accountant and the back-up person to get ready for the appointment. Meanwhile, the receptionist greets the client at the door and escorts him or her directly to the

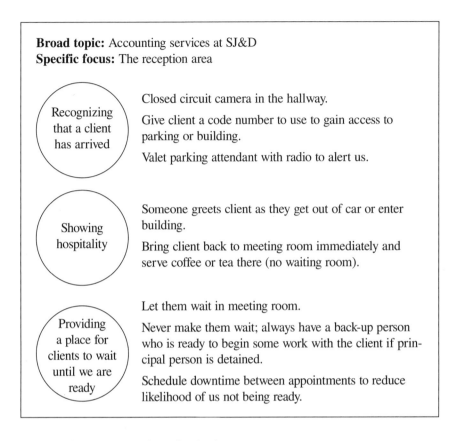

Broad topic: Accounting services at SJ&D
Specific focus: The reception area

Recognizing that a client has arrived

Closed circuit camera in the hallway.

Give client a code number to use to gain access to parking or building.

Valet parking attendant with radio to alert us.

Showing hospitality

Someone greets client as they get out of car or enter building.

Bring client back to meeting room immediately and serve coffee or tea there (no waiting room).

Providing a place for clients to wait until we are ready

Let them wait in meeting room.

Never make them wait; always have a back-up person who is ready to begin some work with the client if principal person is detained.

Schedule downtime between appointments to reduce likelihood of us not being ready.

Figure 6.3. Alternatives from fixed points.

designated meeting room. The receptionist stays with the client, serving coffee or tea, or just chatting, until someone arrives to begin the meeting.

■ Instead of motion detectors and cameras, use the valet parking idea as the front end to the process above. The valet gets the person's name and radios this information ahead to us. We now have time to get ready to greet the client.

Of course, there are many things that could go wrong in these ideas. Don't worry, we will evaluate them later. For now, remember to think positively (wear the yellow hat) during idea generation. Cautious, critical, negative thinking (the purple hat) has its place later in the directed-creativity cycle.

The alternatives-from-fixed-points tool is a powerful creative technique that naturally appeals to process-minded quality management practitioners. If captured diagrammatically, as in Figure 6.3, the result resembles a flowchart.

As we have seen, this branch of tools for directed creative imagination (see Figure 6.2) provides a rich kit of techniques. The key points to keep in mind from this section are summarized in a box.

When using tools that provoke the imagination directly, remember:

- These tools can be a fun, easy way to get people started in directed creativity.

- Key words, synonyms, manipulative verbs, prepositions, conjunctions, and nouns provide mental starting points for imagination (see resources in the appendix).

- There is no way to know beforehand which words will stimulate the best ideas; select several at random and go with them.

- Photographs, videotapes, physical objects, doodles, and drawings also provide mental starting points for imagination.

- Whenever you notice that you typically think of something as going in one direction, try reversing the direction and see where mental movement takes you.

- Consider reversing performance indicators, relationships, assumptions, and processes.

- When looking for creative alternatives, it is useful to back up and explicitly identify the fixed concepts.

- In a creative challenge we are not seeking an argument or logical explanation, we are searching for fixed concepts from which we can generate alternatives.

- Refrain from premature negative judgment; be positive, keep moving.

- Laughter and initial puzzlement may be signs that you are exploring mental connections that are rarely explored; there may be significant creative possibilities.

Leaping

The tools for imaginative leaping are closely related to the tools in the previous section. Both sets are directly based on a modern understanding of the mechanics of mind, but the tools in this section will involve a large mental step—we will simply jump over time, space, reason, and rules to find a new valley from which to commence our mental movement. The term *leaping* is meant to convey this sense of distance between our topic valley and the provoking valley.

We have already seen some leaping with scenarios and the stepping-stones tool. Scenarios stimulate imagination by allowing us to leap over time and details, while the stepping-stone method leaps over all sense of reason with an outrageous suggestion.

de Bono (1972) has coined the word *po* to signal a provocation statement for creative leaping. Po is a shorthand way of saying

> *I know that what I am about to say makes no sense. I have no reason for saying it other than the possibility that it might stimulate a creative thought. I do not know where it might lead, it might lead nowhere, but we will never know until after I say it and we think about it. While it will sound silly, I want us to take it seriously—as if it was very wise of me to say it. So here goes . . .*

de Bono points out that po is a syllable in words like *suppose, hypothesis, poetry,* and *possible.* He goes on to suggest that po is the "laxative of language" because it totally frees us to say whatever we want to say.

We can generate stepping-stones and illogical statements using the word *po* simply by asking people to say outrageous things pertaining to our topic of interest. There does not have to be a reason behind the statement.

Po, let's murder all of our clients.

Po, junior accountants have six ears.

Po, let's advise all of our clients to just stop paying taxes.

Totally outrageous! But if we treat them as mystical wisdom statements and let our minds move, we may get a good idea. For example,

- Murder clients. Do our clients have wills? Have they done adequate estate planning? Do they have succession plans for the leadership of their businesses?

- Clients stop paying taxes. There are ways to shield assets from taxes legally by placing them in trusts and offshore accounts. Perhaps we could invite someone to conduct a seminar on this topic. If our clients seem interested, we could develop a service to make it easy for them to do this.

We can also leap purposefully over any rule, law, or paradigm. Rather than trying to dismantle rules directly, creative thinkers often find that it is easier to simply leap over them temporarily to investigate what might be on the other side. Sometimes, we are so compelled by what we see on the other side of a rule, that we decide that it really is time to dismantle it. In other cases, we find that while the excursion was nice, we want to go back and live with the rule the way it is. This is okay. The more times we can get people to explore the world beyond a rule, however, the higher the likelihood that someday we will take it down.

Rules, laws, and paradigms that govern an accounting firm like SJ&D might include

Senior partners handle big accounts, juniors do delegated work.

We have an office; that is, a building, a physical structure to work in.

We must abide by the laws of our country and state.

Leaping over these rules, we could let junior accountants take on a few big accounts on their own to free up time for the senior partners to be more involved in the development of the innovative new services that are coming out of this exercise. We could experiment with letting people work from home offices. We could set up small satellite offices in office parks in order to be closer to our customers. We could develop a mobile office in a van, complete with computers, cellular phone modems, and so on. We could take this service on the road at tax season, set up in shopping malls and neighborhoods, and do individual tax returns. All of these ideas are worth exploring, even if we do not decide to use them all.

It may not be clear what creative ideas we can come up with by leaping over the legislated laws of the land (the final item on the previous list of rules). It does make me wonder if there is an accounting firm anywhere that specializes in overseeing the financial matters of convicted white-collar criminals while they are, shall we say, otherwise engaged. I do not know if SJ&D wants to take on this dubious distinction, but you must admit it is a novel idea. SJ&D could become like a celebrated defense attorney who takes on even the most disgusting criminals as clients. There may be something useful in this idea. We will keep it for now.

Creative leaping can be great fun. Most people find that they really enjoy it, once they get the hang of it. For most people, this means learning to take the scenarios, stepping-stones, po statements, and rule-breaking suggestions seriously for a moment. We are so conditioned to think of laughter and pretending as not businesslike, that we often find ourselves immediately rejecting these tools. It helps me to think of approaching creative leap provocations initially as wisdom statements—like the statements that teachers of Eastern philosophy make. If I force myself to assume that there is wisdom there, my analytical mind is challenged to find the wisdom in the seemingly

When using creative leaps, remember:

- There does not need to be a reason for why you have said something; the only point is to stimulate imagination.

- We can leap over time, space, reason, and rules to explore the worlds on the other side.

- *Po* is a useful shorthand way of signaling to others that you are about to suggest a creative leap.

- You do not have to dismantle every rule or past pattern in order to be creative; it is enough to simply be open to exploring the world beyond the rule.

- The biggest challenge in creative leaping is getting people to take it seriously.

- It may help to approach creative provocations as though they were wisdom statements from Eastern philosophy; challenge your mind to uncover the hidden wisdom.

nonsensical words. Again, I do not know how generalizable this is. Find what works for you. Be prepared to deal with this directly, or you will find few creative ideas from the tools of leaping.

Combining Concepts Systematically

As we have noted before, all creative ideas involve associations among existing concepts. The distinction in this branch of tools in Figure 6.2 is that, rather than relying solely on mental processes, we are now going to make those associations systematically and mechanically. Because these tools are systematic, I find that they appeal to even the strongest analytical thinkers. These might be the first tools of directed creativity that I would introduce if I were working with a really tough, initially unimaginative group. If you can get such groups to use these systematic tools, they may then be willing to go further with you into the other tools of directed creativity.

Systematic tools for generating creative ideas date back to the 1930s and the work of Professor Robert P. Crawford at the University of Nebraska. Crawford (1954, 1964) taught that one could generate creative ideas by listing and combining attributes in a situation. Zwicky (1966) and Koberg and Bagnall (1981) built on Crawford's concept by suggesting various tabular formats for the information.

To illustrate the basic idea behind all these tools, let us apply Koberg and Bagnall's method of "morphological forced connections" to the situation of quarterly financial statements produced by an accounting firm. Begin by identifying key elements in the situation. We will work with the elements of medium, content, audience, and format of quarterly financial statements. (In practice, we can work with any number of elements, but we will keep it simple here.) Now, under each element list several alternatives. A tabular listing of alternative attributes for these four elements would include

Medium	Content	Audience	Format
Paper	Summary only	Owner and key leaders only	Tables of numbers and text
Computer files	Include details	Employees	Include graphs
Broadcast fax	Include comments	Local newspaper	Include face plots
Conference call		Financial magazines	Include sounds

Now, force several connections by running through the table picking up items from each column. For example, we could have financial reports on paper, including comments, sent to financial magazines, with standard tables and text. Or we could release the quarterly report via a conference call to the local newspapers, including comments, and including background music that reflects the tone of the report. There are at least $4 \times 3 \times 4 \times 4 = 192$ possible combinations from this simple four-element table. A more complicated table would yield even more possibilities.

We can apply the general concept of systematically combining items to any list of ideas. For example, we used a morphological approach in generating ideas from the list of alternatives from fixed points in Figure 6.3. Our final ideas were combinations of specific alternatives. We could have systematically generated a large number of ideas by taking one, two, three, or more of these alternatives at a time.

When using tools to combine concepts systematically, remember:

- Make a multidimensional list of alternatives, and then systematically make combinations from the items on that list.

- These tools appeal to strongly analytical people; therefore, they can be a good entry point for teaching others the methods of directed creativity.

Organizing and Displaying Ideas

We have seen a rich variety of methods for stimulating the imagination to generate innovative ideas. It is now time to begin winding down the idea generation and looking forward to action.

One of the first things we need to do is organize the many ideas that we have generated. The purpose of this is twofold. First, organizing and displaying the ideas may trigger even more creative thoughts. We might be able to combine ideas, or we might see an opportunity to extend our creative thinking into underdeveloped areas. Second, organizing our ideas prepares us for the more analytical tasks of harvesting and developing.

As a basic organizing technique, I almost always use notebooks. A simple notebook would comprise a listing of ideas, in no particular order, with each idea expressed as one to four sentences. The ideas can be entered into the notebook following each idea generation session. Keeping the list on a computer allows us to bring a bit more order to the compilation by listing the ideas under category headers.

I have compiled such a categorized idea notebook to capture the work we have been doing for the accounting firm of SJ&D—an excerpt appears at the end of this chapter. (Ignore the harvesting notes in italics for the moment. I will explain these later.) We have already generated a total of 54 ideas under 10 headings! Not bad—especially when you consider that I was just trying to illustrate the various tools. Imagine how many ideas we could have gotten if we really tried. The number could well be several hundred. With so many ideas, organization is imperative.

A quick scan of the idea notebook and the number of items under each heading suggests that we might want to do some more focused thinking on several topics: retirement planning, teaching clients to do for themselves, and, of course, ideas to explore further. In addition, while bookkeeping, estate planning, and trusts are major areas of business for an accounting firm, we have not yet done much creative thinking in these areas.

While the concise idea descriptions in our notebook give us a crisp summary of our work thus far, you may have noticed that we have lost many of the explanatory comments that went along with the ideas when we initially generated them. Therefore, I often supplement my idea notebooks with more detailed idea capture worksheets, like the one shown in Figure 6.4. Note on this worksheet that I provide space to record positives, negatives, and data needs associated with the idea (de Bono's green-, yellow-, purple-, and white-thinking hats). You might also want to record feelings about the idea (red hat) or other information such as impact, potential cost, and so forth.

Recording the ideas on individual sheets opens the possibility of using various slip methods to organize and display the ideas. For example, Fiero (1992) and Krone (1990) describe the Crawford Slip method, in which participants' ideas are written on individual note cards and later organized by a facilitator into categories. This, and other methods described by Tatsuno (1990) and Michalko (1991), are variations of what quality management practitioners would call a storyboard, or affinity diagram. (See Brassard 1989 or Higgins 1994.)

While storyboards and affinity diagrams tend to organize items into a tabular format, mind maps are more free-form and visual in nature. (Buzan 1989; Wyckoff 1991) Figure 6.2 in this chapter and Figure 5.2 in the previ-

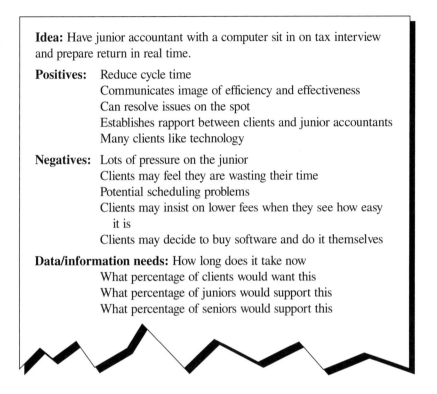

Idea: Have junior accountant with a computer sit in on tax interview and prepare return in real time.

Positives: Reduce cycle time
Communicates image of efficiency and effectiveness
Can resolve issues on the spot
Establishes rapport between clients and junior accountants
Many clients like technology

Negatives: Lots of pressure on the junior
Clients may feel they are wasting their time
Potential scheduling problems
Clients may insist on lower fees when they see how easy
it is
Clients may decide to buy software and do it themselves

Data/information needs: How long does it take now
What percentage of clients would want this
What percentage of juniors would support this
What percentage of seniors would support this

Figure 6.4. Example of an idea capture worksheet.

ous chapter are simple mind maps. Mind maps in thinking are like fishbone diagrams in problem solving. Each is a diagrammatic layout of information. There is no particular significance to the shape of a mind map. The key feature of a mind map is that it displays the whole of something on a single page. This makes it somewhat easier for the mind to make connections.

Another visual layout technique, one that I strongly favor, is de Bono's (1992) concept fan. A concept fan is an extension of the picture we drew in Figure 6.3 when we discussed alternatives from a fixed point. Figure 6.5 is a partial concept fan for processes in an accounting firm. Note that it includes the previous Figure 6.3, but goes on to explore concepts and alternatives associated with other steps in the process. You could construct a process-oriented concept fan deliberately by assembling a group, starting at the beginning of the process,

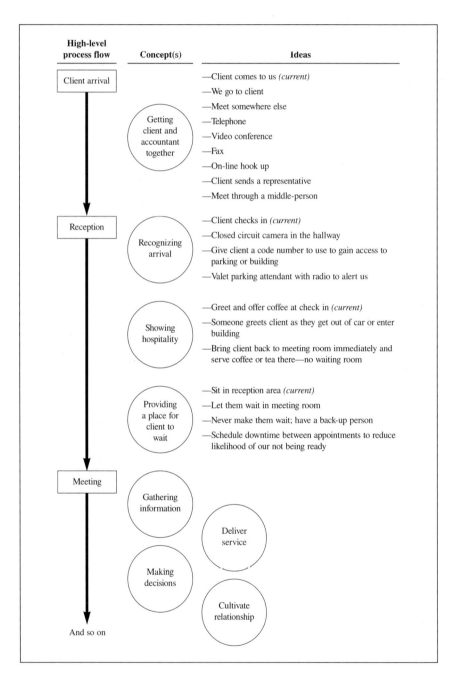

Figure 6.5. Portion of a concept fan for an accounting firm business process.

and working your way through to the end. Or you could assemble a concept fan from the pieces and ideas generated by multiple groups over time. In any event, you will probably want to use a systematic (morphological) technique for extracting complete designs from among the many alternatives on the fan.

When organizing and displaying ideas, remember:

- Organizing and displaying the ideas may trigger more creative ideas.

- Organizing the ideas is essential for transitioning into the next steps of analysis, evaluation, and action planning.

- Notebooks and idea capture worksheets are simple, straightforward means for organizing and displaying ideas.

- Slip methods, storyboards, affinity diagrams, and mind maps are alternative means for organizing and displaying; choose the methods that you like best or that your organization is familiar with.

- A concept fan is a powerful tool for displaying ideas along with the fixed points from which they emanate; it is a systematic way to both organize the ideas and stimulate more.

Harvesting ideas

Having organized our ideas, we are now ready to begin our initial evaluation by conducting a harvest. Just as a farmer harvesting grain brings in the entire crop for subsequent sorting and processes, so we will want to look at each idea that has been generated. In this initial harvesting, our objectives will be to do a rough sorting based on feasibility and then see if we want to make any final efforts at idea generation prior to moving on toward action. We will conduct a second, final harvest as we begin the development phase of the directed-creativity cycle.

Osborn (1953), Clark (1958), and de Bono (1992) suggest various approaches to harvesting. These approaches involve sorting the ideas into from three to 10 categories, depending upon how immediately useful we judge them to be. These, and other authors, offer further advice as to who should do the harvesting and when. Some authors suggest that harvesting should be done by the group that generated the ideas, as the final activity in the session. Other authors (notably Osborn and Clark) emphatically insist that the harvesting be done by a separate group several days after the ideas were generated. The rationale behind this was Clark and Osborn's belief that premature judgment had such a negative effect that it was best to put maximum distance between generation and evaluation.

Personally, I favor fewer categories, rather than many. I also favor doing this initial harvesting in the imagination phase with a small group of three to five people, separate from the idea generation sessions. I favor these approaches because I also favor multiple idea generation sessions, involving many people, over time, around a broad topic. As a consequence, I routinely expect to have from 50 to 300 ideas to work with at this point. Complex, large-group harvesting schemes are simply too tedious for this first, rough cut. We will involve a larger group in the final harvesting that begins the development phase. (I do not wish to be dogmatic about this. There is certainly nothing wrong with allowing groups to do a little on-the-spot harvesting immediately following idea generation. This does provide a useful feeling of closure.)

The small harvesting group should be made up of people who have a generally positive outlook and a good intuitive sense about what is doable in the organization. I recommend sorting the ideas into four categories (adapted from de Bono 1992).

Ready to use (RTU)	Ideas that we could act on very quickly. Need only a minimum of further study in order to get started on detailed implementation planning.
Seedlings (SEED)	Beginnings of a useful idea. Usable concept, but may not be able to do it exactly as stated. The basic idea itself needs more study and development before it is ready.
Useful directions (UD)	A useful broad concept or general idea, but not really fleshed out well enough at this point to evaluate. Could be sent back for more specific idea generation.
Not ready (NR)	An idea that is simply unusable at this point in time. Maybe someday, but not any time soon. Use this category sparingly.

It is important to note that, with the exception of the not-ready category, we are rating the creative content of the ideas themselves, not our readiness or capability to implement them. A creative idea can be ready to use in the sense that we do not need more large doses of creative thought, but it may still take us six months and lots of detailed work to implement.

The harvesting category abbreviations for the ideas that we have generated thus far for Steven Ross and his colleagues at SJ&D are shown in the Harvesting Notes column in the idea notebook excerpt at the end of this chapter. In total, we have 20 ready-to-use ideas, 17 seedlings, 17 useful directions, and 3 not-readies (some ideas are counted in multiple categories). Further, notice that the notes that go along with the ratings give additional information about the idea itself or what is needed to take it further. These notes are a combination of gut reactions (see, for example, ideas number 8 and 36); information requests (see numbers 7 and 28); and honest admissions of lack of knowledge (see numbers 17 and 35).

A final thing to notice are the gaps in our efforts. As we pointed out earlier when we talked about organizing and displaying the ideas, we have not

When harvesting ideas, remember:

- Our objectives are to do a rough sort based on feasibility and to identify any areas for a final round of idea generation; we are not making major decisions or commitments at this point.

- Keep your sorting categories simple, in line with the objectives.

- Harvesting can be done by the idea generation groups themselves or by a separate group convened specifically for harvesting; if you have hundreds of ideas generated by several groups over time, the separate harvesting group is probably the best approach.

- We are rating the creative clarity and content of the ideas themselves, not our ability to implement them (with the exception of the not-ready category, which can be a value judgment on our willingness to implement an idea).

- Also identify underdeveloped areas—subsets of the topic where we have few ideas at the moment.

yet touched on our current service areas of bookkeeping, estate planning, and trusts. We could simply add these three words to our idea notebook and mark them UD so we don't lose track of them. We should probably also note that while we have several ideas in the category of internal operations and logistics, we are a rather complex organization and should do some more thinking in this area. Perhaps it would be helpful to generate ideas systematically against a backdrop of a list of key business processes.

This simple sorting and evaluation has accomplished the purposes of our initial harvesting. We have not made any final decisions yet; we are not committed to anything. That will come later. We now know where we can focus our development and action efforts if we want some immediate hits (the RTU items). We also are now in a position to commission some specific feasibility studies (the SEED items). We can also now set up our final round of idea generation sessions (the UD items). Soon, we will be ready for full-scale critical evaluation, decision making, development and action—on our way to visible innovations in the marketplace.

Summary of the Imagination Phase, on to Development and Action

Like the last chapter, we have covered a great deal of ground here. This is to be expected. Preparation and imagination are the heart of directed creativity. Deliberateness and thoroughness are the keys to success. I hope that I have forever driven from your mind the notion that great, creative ideas can be had by casually assembling a group of people for an hour or two of brainstorming.

The key messages of this chapter are the following:

- Like anything else of value, innovative ideas are the product of much hard work, over an extended time, by dedicated people.

- Imagination uses the concepts and observations of the preparation phase as raw material for creative mental associations.

- Imagination utilizes primarily the principles of escape and movement.

- Imagination is boundless. There is always another novel mental association to be made, there is always an idea, there is always a place to go in thought. Never let yourself say, "I can't think of anything." You can always think of something.

- Premature judgment is a barrier to imagination. Set up environments for yourself and others that set it aside.

- Imagination depends on the personality trait of flexibility. Cultivate this trait in your life.

- Imagination can be deliberately provoked.

- You do not have to commit to any idea that your imagination dreams up. It is enough to simply imagine.

There are many tools for stimulating the imagination in this chapter. Use them as described, mix and match them, or invent your own. Use the mind map in Figure 6.2 and the various boxed summaries scattered throughout the chapter as reminders of the various approaches you might take. Give it some thought, select or design methods that you believe will work in your situation, and then give it a try. If you use multiple groups, even an occasional flop is tolerable. In keeping with the theme of randomness that runs through many of these tools, I have occasionally simply taken the mind map of Figure 6.2, closed my eyes, and selected a method to try. You can count on the imagination to take care of itself; for most of us, the imagination just needs a little help getting started.

So now Steven Ross and his colleagues at the accounting firm of SJ&D have a sorted and annotated collection of imaginative ideas. We have achieved creativity, per the definition we developed in chapter 2. Now we need innovation, concrete implementation of our ideas in a way that gets us noticed. This is the challenge of the development and action phases of the directed-creativity cycle.

Excerpt from Idea Notebook for the Accounting Firm of Smith, Jones, and Duzkiwitz

Original topic statement: Develop innovative pilot services that would please the customers of an accounting firm.

Idea	Harvesting Notes
Tax Returns and Tax Planning (4 ideas)	
1. To save the entrepreneur's valuable time, we could conduct the tax interview and collect the input information over the telephone, via fax, via computer linkage, or a combination of the above.	*RTU or SEED? Need to decide on appropriate medium for this*
Retirement Plans (2 ideas)	
5. Make it easy for small businesses to set up Keogh and 401(k) retirement plans by developing a "kit" of plans and forms (perhaps on computer disks).	*RTU*
6. Develop a relationship with a discount brokerage firm who could seamlessly handle the investment side of retirement plan work. Could offer this on a national basis.	*SEED*
Teaching Clients to Do for Themselves (1 idea)	
7. We could set up training programs to teach practical accounting to designated employees of the client's company. We would then provide a service of supervising these people.	*UD—Lots of study needed re: curriculum, licensing, ethics, and so on*
Communications and Image (9 ideas)	
8. Instead of always wearing tailored suits, we dress casually when we meet our clients.	*RTU—Let's just do it!*
9. Offer a finance seminar at a nice resort exclusively for owners of small start-up businesses and guests.	*SEED—Can we do within budget?*
16. Start a series of lunchtime seminars exclusively for our clients on current workplace trends that we know they are already engaged in. For example, we could get a well-known speaker to come and talk about the trend toward casual dress in the workplace (or sports teams at work, or community service at work, and so on).	*RTU.*
Helping Clients Better Understand Their Finances (4 ideas)	
17. Using Internet search technology, we could develop a software worm that could search in the background through files on the client's computer system that are potentially relevant to constructing a comprehensive financial picture of the organization.	*UD or NR? Is this technically feasible?*
20. Some clients might appreciate a regular conference call with us to review their financial situation.	*RTU—Let's just do it!*

Partnerships and Cooperatives (6 ideas)

21. Partner with accounting schools at universities via the Internet. Customers could designate a school; usually their alma mater. We would then contact that school to form teams of students who would work under our supervision.   *SEED—Neat idea, but lots of work needed*

• • •

26. Offer services in partnership with quick-copy centers, banks and their ATM network, cable TV companies.   *UD*

Totally New Directions for Us (8 ideas)

27. Offer consulting service to help clients improve their evolving financial systems to reduce their exposure to potential embezzlement.   *RTU—We know how to do this*

28. Develop a mobile office in a van, complete with computers, cellular phone modems, and so on. We could take this service on the road at tax season and set up in shopping malls and neighborhoods to do individual tax returns.   *SEED—Cost vs. benefit?*

• • •

Internal Operations and Logistics (9 ideas)

35. We could experiment with letting people work out of home offices.   *SEED—Are we ready for this?*

36. Experiment with 24-hour accounting services. Many of our entrepreneurial small business owners work odd hours; they might appreciate being able to conduct business with us on their schedule.   *NR—We just don't like this; we have plenty of other good ideas to work with*

• • •

Financial Reporting (3 ideas)

44. Find ways to communicate a better feel for the numbers in financial reports.   *UD*

• • •

Ideas to Explore Further (8 ideas)

47. Need to explore the various restatements of the topic in our purpose hierarchy.   *UD*

• • •

54. What services can we bring directly to the client's home or business? What services can we offer over the telephone? Via the Internet? In a shopping mall? In partnership with a quick-copy center? In partnership with a bank via its ATM network? Over a cable TV channel?   *UD*

CHAPTER 7

Development and Action: The Bridge Between Mere Creativity and the Rewards of Innovation

〽 ✓ ♪ ⸮

> *To put your ideas into action is the most difficult thing in the world.*
>
> Goethe

> *To dare is to lose one's footing momentarily. To not dare is to lose oneself.*
>
> Soren Kierkegaard

> *Make it so.*
>
> Jean-Luc Picard, Captain, *Starship Enterprise*

Let me say it again: *Creative ideas have no value until they are put into action.* While the preparation and imagination phases of the directed-creativity cycle are the heart and mind of innovation, the development and action phases are the hands and feet.

Practitioners of quality management have a great deal of experience implementing change in organizations. We know how to develop and execute plans. We are also familiar with the challenges on the social side of change—resistance to change, importance of involvement, power struggles, what's-in-it-for-me thinking, and so on. Consequently, I do not intend to provide an exhaustive look at the implementation of change in this chapter. There are many good books on this subject, and you have your own experiences to guide you.* There are, however, some special considerations that we should be aware of as we develop and implement truly novel ideas. Let's look at them.

Activities and Heuristics That Support Development and Action

In the imagination phase of the directed-creativity cycle we stressed escape and mental movement. We also emphasized the importance of suspending judgment. Here, in the development and action phases, we will focus on attention and a slightly different type of movement—we will want to pay attention to details and move on to action. Further, while we do not want to rush to judgment, it is now time to begin progressively applying critical thinking. Imaginative ideas sometimes turn out to be novel, but not very practical. We need to focus attention on the weaknesses of our ideas and either revise or reject them.

The activities of the development and action phases of the directed-creative cycle are depicted in Figure 7.1. These activities are a concrete application of directed creativity heuristic 8: Make a deliberate effort to harvest, develop, and implement at least a few of the ideas you generate. Think of them as a restatement, in innovation terms, of the familiar Shewhart-Deming PDSA cycle.

Let me walk you through the activities in detail. We begin development with a continuation of an activity that we started in the imagination phase of the cycle—harvesting. The implement-a-few-ideas heuristic allows us the freedom to not try to do everything. After the exhilaration of imagination, there is a great temptation to take on too much. If we do, we will only end up frustrated by ideas that fail because we do not have the time to think them through thoroughly.

The final harvesting that begins the development phase will be a bit more selective than what we described in the last chapter. Recall that our initial harvesting at the end of the imagination phase comprised a rough sorting of our ideas based on feasibility, so that we could determine the subjects for

---

*Good books on the management of change in organizations include (in alphabetical order by author), Atkinson 1990; Beckhard and Harris 1987; Dalziel and Schoonover 1988; Hutton 1995; Kanter 1983; Kanter, Stein, and Jick 1992; and O'Toole 1995.

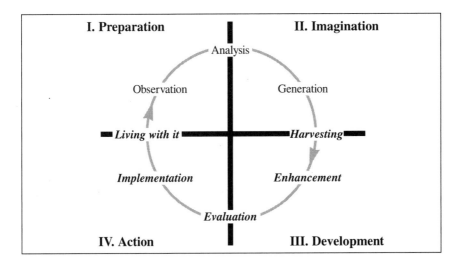

Figure 7.1. Activities in the development and action phases of the directed-creativity cycle.

any final idea generation sessions. We now need to make some initial choices from among all these ideas and initiate focused efforts to further develop them.

"Further develop" typically means the appointment of people to champion a specific idea, work out the details (what we will call enhancement), and shepherd the idea through to either final rejection or implementation. These champions might be groups, individuals, or a combination. A champion might be focused on a single idea, or several together. As before, you will need to mix and match approaches to suit your situation; there is no one, right way.

The selection of people to champion ideas is just as critical as the selection of people to serve on traditional quality management teams. (See Scholtes 1988 or Juran 1989.) We need people with what LeBoeuf (1980) calls "intelligent persistence." Similarly, Sternberg and Lubart's (1995) review of the research literature on creativity shows that successful innovators share several personality traits. They (1) persevere over obstacles, (2) are willing to take risks, (3) are willing to grow personally, (4) tolerate ambiguity, (5) are open to experiences, and (6) believe in themselves. von Oech

(1983, 1986) sums it up with his metaphor of the innovator as a warrior—devoted to the cause.

These character qualities are needed because people are better critics than creators (Perkins 1981). Typically, the implementation of an innovative idea faces many challenges; some valid and others simply veiled resistance to change. Therefore, in the development phase, we will need a healthy dose of both positive thinking and critical thinking. The heuristic of focus, care deeply, and work purposefully is just as important here as it was in the preparation phase. Further, the people selected to develop the ideas must also be comfortable with the heuristic, judgment is based on past patterns, no inherent right or wrong. We need passionate, action-oriented people with flexible, but critical, judgment skills. It is a tall order, but in many ways it is not dissimilar to the challenge we have always faced in engaging the people in our organization to lead quality management efforts.

The team or individual idea champions are charged to enhance the ideas. Enhancement is the process of critically evaluating an idea with an eye toward making it even more attractive. We will strive to further strengthen the strong features of the idea and shore up its weak ones. Later in this chapter we will look at a checklist to guide our efforts in doing this. For now, let me simply say that every idea can use some enhancement. Ideas rarely hatch in the imagination fully developed. Indeed, trying to hatch a fully developed idea will activate judgment, which we will probably defeat the imagination. It is important, therefore, to stress during idea generation sessions that enhancement is in the plan for later. Knowing that there will be a time later to focus on the idea and work out all its details relieves performance pressure during the imagination phase.

Our efforts to enhance our ideas might require another dose of imagination. We may need some creative thoughts about how to overcome barriers and weak points. We might find further uses for analogies and assumption challenging. We might end up laughing at an enhancement suggestion, and then pausing on it to extract a new idea (heuristic 6). We may decide to combine pieces of other ideas to strengthen the one we are working on. (This is why every idea should be recorded in an idea notebook. Even if it is infeasible on its own, it might help later.) Compared to our use of these tools in the imagination phase, our imaginative thinking here in the development phase will be more focused and smaller in scale.

Eventually, all creative ideas must face the test of cold, hard evaluation—the final step in the development phase of the directed-creativity cycle. We will strive for objective judgment based on quantifiable criteria, but there are important limitations and inherent dangers in this. Recall from chapter 1 how Seagate Technologies rejected the innovation of 3.5-inch disk drives because the numbers failed to meet the required thresholds. In 1943, Thomas Watson, the chairman of IBM, analyzed the creative notion of a machine that could think and declared, "There is a world market for computers of about five." Decca Recording rejected the Beatles in 1962 because the numbers showed that "Groups of guitars are on the way out." And the August 2, 1968, *Business Week* magazine looked at automotive industry figures and boldly declared that "The Japanese automotive industry isn't likely to carve out a big slice of the U.S. market for itself."*

Deming (1986) reminds us that the most important numbers are unknown and unknowable. If an idea is truly an innovation, there is no way to evaluate it with total objectivity. In the end, our evaluations must rely to some extent on intuition as well as numbers.† Hoping for certainty in evaluation is a deep pitfall that we must avoid; the best we can hope for is to minimize risk. 3M's Dennis Nowlin (1994, 40) sums it up best: "Productive mistakes are not merely tolerable in a culture of innovation, they are essential to creating it." Living with this principle may be one of the biggest challenges in directed creativity for practitioners of quality management.

This difficulty in judging innovative ideas can be mitigated through the use of prototypes. A prototype is a mock-up of a new product, service, or process that is realistic enough to allow people to experience it. The physical experience of an idea enables us to judge it better. You may have experienced this phenomenon yourself in your past quality improvement efforts. Have you ever implemented a change over some resistance, only to find that the objections went away once people actually experienced the change? "Oh, this isn't as bad as I thought it would be," is a common anticlimax in change efforts. At the same time, you may have also experienced the opposite effect: a

---

*These and other examples of how wrong the numbers and the experts can be are in a delightful book by Cerf and Navasky (1984), *The Experts Speak*.

†For more on the role of intuition in decision making, see Agor 1989; Rowan 1986; Ray and Myers 1986, 162–174; and Perkins 1981, 104–109, 253–256.

change that everyone agreed sounded great, but was a bomb when implemented. The lesson here is that it is hard to accurately imagine something that has never been done before. The physical experience of a prototype activates sensory perception, which carves the mental valleys that judgment needs in order to be more rational.

The formality of our efforts in the development phase will obviously depend on the nature of the idea. If it is a simple change like initiating a regular conference call with clients about their financial situation (idea 20 in Steven Ross' idea notebook at the end of the last chapter), our efforts to further develop might be a simple 10-minute meeting with one of the senior accountants who is willing to give it a try. On the other hand, putting together a retirement and 401(k) plan kit on computer disks for our clients' use (idea 5) will be a more complex effort requiring a multidisciplinary team, several months of effort, a budget, and a business plan. At the far extreme, developing a software worm to glean financial information from a client's internal information system (idea 17) may call for some serious R&D beyond our current capabilities. You will need to use your judgment and your organization's internal policies and infrastructure in deciding how exactly to proceed in a given situation.

The product of the development phase is either a firm commitment for implementation or a firm decision to reject the idea. Even if the idea is rejected, that should not be the end of it; we never throw away a creative idea. Its time may come later. We may be able to use pieces of the idea elsewhere, or the germ of it may serve as an analogy, creative scenario, or challenge-provocation for a future idea-generation session.

If it is on to implementation, then we still have significant work to do. Depending on the complexity of the idea, we will need implementation plans, communication, education, measurements, control and improvement systems, human resources plans, and contingency plans. Your experience in implementing change via quality management efforts will again be your best guide.

As noted in our discussion of the implement-a-few-ideas heuristic in chapter 3, it is important to hold ourselves to a commitment to implement in a timely manner. Fritz (1991, 300) advocates the use of deadlines to "organize your actions . . . build energy and momentum . . . and position yourself for your next creations." Most of us are so busy that we do not have time to work on things that do not have deadlines.

Make sure that your deadlines do not rush things unproductively. The people who will be impacted by our new idea must have a chance to be involved in it and feel that they have contributed to it. This will take some time. As with your quality teams, you should involve key stakeholders directly on your idea development and implementation planning teams. They may not have come up with the idea in the original idea generation sessions, but there is still plenty of room for them to contribute here in the development and action phases.

Be patient with people. The implementation of a truly innovative idea challenges deeply held beliefs and assumptions and can radically impact the social and political system in an organization. New ideas are inherently uncomfortable. Use prototypes to reduce the anxiety and help establish a mental valley for the idea to rest comfortably in, but be firm in your resolve to implement. It would be a shame to have come all this way only to end up with nothing.

Finally, it is critically important to integrate our quality management and innovation work. Rarely will a creative idea be so well thought through that it is perfect in its initial implementation. Often, better ideas only emerge after we have tried the first idea. We should be practicing continuous improvement from day one. A commitment to continuous improvement also guards against the mental judgment pitfalls we noted in chapter 2—believing that what we have is the best it can be already (belief preservation) or is at least as good as it has to be for us to reap the rewards (satisficing). Further, there is no reason to quickly give up our edge to me-too competitors who take our ideas and better them. We have already put in a great deal of work and thoughtful effort into the idea, we should be in the best position to improve upon it.

Living with our creation, the final step in the directed-creativity cycle, is also the first step in the next cycle. Though we have a right to celebrate our creative achievements, we should be back to the purposeful observation and analysis of the preparation phase on the morning after the big party. Creeping complacency is the enemy of creativity. If we expect to be an innovative organization we must apply continuous creative thinking to everything we do. The best time to dream up and implement new ideas is just after you have had a success with your last idea. Even if your last idea didn't work so well, your best hope is to generate another idea and quickly erase the impression of failure. In the spirit of continuous learning, we should also reflect on our experiences in the past round of the directed-creativity cycle prior to embarking on the next round.

The development and action phases of the directed-creativity cycle will not be easy. In the end, your unique experience at implementing change through your quality management efforts in your organization is more meaningful than anything that I or the innovation literature can say. The key points to keep in mind during the development and action phases are summarized in a box. I urge you to be reflective and purposeful as you enter these final phases of the directed-creativity cycle.

Key Features of Models for Organizational Change

There are many models for the process of organizational change. Understanding their key points can help us be more effective in implementing innovative ideas. My favorite model comes from Harvard's John Kotter (1995) and is depicted in Figure 7.2. I will use Kotter's model as a framework for this section and tie in the work of other authors to support points as needed.

The first four steps of Kotter's model present the greatest challenge when it comes to implementing creative ideas. In contrast, the final four steps present roughly the same challenge as they do in implementing incremental change. Therefore, I will devote this section primarily to a discussion about establishing urgency, forming a coalition, creating a vision, and communicating that vision in the case of truly innovative change.

Kotter asserts that effective change is born of a felt sense of urgency. He also notes that more than 50 percent of the more than 100 companies he has watched ended up failing in this first step. Change leaders in these companies routinely overestimated the shared sense of urgency in their organizations and, therefore, proceeded too quickly into the details of the change. Argyris (1990) also makes this point in noting that many top-down management communications tell the troops how to, but never tell them how come? In a similar vein, Beckhard and Harris (1987) have as the first step of their change model the question: Why change?

This is a critical point for innovators because, while it is an obvious point, it is often overlooked. Creativity is exciting. Idea champions can be enthusiastic about ideas simply because they are new ideas, but they soon

Key Points in the Development and Action Phases of the Directed-Creativity Cycle

- Now is the time to pay attention to details, move on to action, and begin progressively applying critical judgment.

- You do not have to implement all of your creative ideas. Select a few that you think will be successful innovations and save the rest for later. It is better to successfully implement a few ideas than to attempt many changes and fail.

- Each idea selected needs an idea champion. This can be either a group, individual, or combination of both.

- Select idea champions with care; you need warriors.

- Each idea selected needs purposeful enhancement. Enhancement further strengthens the strong points of the idea and shores up its weak points.

- Each idea selected must be evaluated to get a definite rejection (at least for now) or definite commitment to implement.

- Evaluation of innovative ideas is inherently an intuitive process. While we will strive for objectivity, the numbers can be misleading. We must implement the idea in order to truly know what will happen.

- Prototyping contributes significantly to the evaluation of innovative ideas by giving decision-makers a concrete experience upon which to base judgment.

- Do not expect to be right all the time in your evaluation. Remember the experience of highly innovative companies: "Productive mistakes are not merely tolerable in a culture of innovation, they are essential to creating it" (Nowlin 1994).

- Use your judgment and your organization's internal policies and infrastructure in deciding how exactly to proceed in developing, evaluating, and implementing ideas. Whatever has worked for you in chartering and supporting quality teams will probably work for innovation.

- Deadlines can contribute positively to the goal of innovation by giving you healthy pressure to push on to implementation. But, do not use deadlines as a way to run over people. Change is hard and scary, especially when the change is a true innovation with no past history of success. Involvement is helpful, but be persistent about the need to reach implementation.

- Begin continuous improvement now. Also start immediately preparing for the next cycle of directed creativity. There is no need to let the advantage of the innovator slip away to others.

- Never throw away an idea. The mental valley it has formed may be useful in the future.

Eight Steps to Transforming Your Organization

1. Establishing a Sense of Urgency
Examining market and competitive realities
Identifying and discussing crises, potential crises, or major opportunities

2. Forming a Powerful Guiding Coalition
Assembling a group with enough power to lead the change effort
Encouraging the group to work together as a team

3. Creating a Vision
Creating a vision to help direct the change effort
Developing strategies for achieving that vision

4. Communicating the Vision
Using every vehicle possible to communicate the new vision and strategies
Teaching new behaviors by the example of the guiding coalition

5. Empowering Others to Act on the Vision
Getting rid of obstacles to change
Changing systems or structures that seriously undermine the vision
Encouraging risk taking and nontraditional ideas, activities, and actions

6. Planning for and Creating Short-Term Wins
Planning for visible performance improvements
Creating those improvements
Recognizing and rewarding employees involved in those improvements

7. Consolidating Improvements, Producing Still More Change
Using credibility to change systems, structures, and policies that don't fit vision
Hiring, promoting, and developing employees who can implement the vision
Reinvigorating the process with new projects, themes, and change agents

8. Institutionalizing New Approaches
Articulating connections between the new behaviors and corporate success
Developing the means to ensure leadership development and succession

---

Reprinted by permission of *Harvard Business Review.* An exhibit from "Leading Change: Why Transformation Efforts Fail" by John P. Kotter, March–April, 1995. Copyright ©1995 by the President and Fellows of Harvard College; all rights reserved.)

Figure 7.2. John P. Kotter's model for organizational change.

become frustrated with their organization because others do not share their enthusiasm. In contrast, successful innovators know that it is not enough to have a good idea if you cannot sell it. Change theory suggests that the first step in selling it is to tie it directly to an urgently felt need. This is why innovation is such a challenge in "successful" organizations—they have few urgently felt needs.

Quality management systems can help provide some sense of urgency through customer needs analysis, satisfaction surveys, competitive benchmarking results, cost-of-poor-quality accounting, and internal performance measurements. Therefore, we have an important role to play in stimulating and supporting innovations.

Likewise, idea champions (both individuals and teams) have an obligation to answer the how-come question as they harvest, develop, and present their innovative ideas for how to. Innovation leaders, like 3M, make it easy by making innovation itself a deeply held corporate value (Nowlin 1994). If you are not so fortunate to work for an organization that values innovation for its own sake, you will need to work on establishing some sense of urgency around the innovative idea you are proposing.

To return to Steven Ross and his colleagues at SJ&D, a key initial question that change models raise is, "To what extent do people here feel the need to innovate?" The firm's partners certainly see the loss of business to other firms, but has that information been shared with all staff? Here's a creative idea. Estimate the falling revenues and staffing needs of SJ&D over the next five years if current trends continue. Then have an all-employee meeting in a large auditorium. Pass out cards with numbers on them as people enter. During the presentation, pause several times and ask people within certain number blocks to get up and stand in the back of the room. The number of people standing in the back is in proportion to the projected loss of jobs at SJ&D as time goes by. While you might feel that this is a bit dramatic, urgency is a dramatic feeling. Drama is exactly what we are after.

Kotter's next step for successful change (see Figure 7.2) is to establish a powerful guiding coalition. Kotter notes that most change efforts start as a germ of an idea in one or two people's heads, but it is rare that these few individuals have the complete power to pull off the change. The guiding coalition is a larger group that is powerful enough to lead the change. This typically means that the guiding coalition must be made up of people who have the power to allocate resources and to ask for constructive participation by others in the change effort. Kiechel (1988), Kanter (1983), and others draw similar conclusions about involvement from the top and the allocation of resources from their studies of innovative organizations. Of course, this point is no surprise to quality managers. I know of no serious book on the topic of quality management that does not advocate strong senior-level involvement in the effort.

I emphasize the point here to dispel the myth of the innovator who works outside the corporate structure. It is true that creative thinking is often found outside the bounds of the organization's structure. Challenging sacred cows and deeply held beliefs in an organization is the essence of creative escape. But you cannot be an innovator outside the bounds of the organization's structure. You cannot implement your ideas unless the organization at least permits it. The skillful innovator (whether individual or team) must learn to work the organizational structure to secure resources and support. Stated another way, while the preparation and imagination phases of the directed-creativity cycle can occur without a powerful guiding coalition, the development and action phases cannot. (Of course, the potential innovator does have another choice: Leave the company and form his or her own organization. Anecdotes about people who have chosen this route are no doubt the source of the innovator-outside-the-corporate-structure myth. In fact, such innovators are not outside the corporate structure. They have simply created a new corporate structure in which they are the guiding coalition.)

The next two steps in Kotter's change model involve creating and communicating a new vision. In the language that we have been using in this book, simply substitute the word *idea* for *vision*. Whether the idea is small or grand, we need to explain it to others in a way that they can understand. Kiechel (1988, 132) makes a similar point in saying that "it helps to hold up a cause that everyone can rally around."

An obvious, but again often overlooked, point is the necessity for clarity. Kotter provides a concrete rule of thumb that we can apply to the issue of clarity in communicating innovative change ideas. If you cannot communicate the idea to someone in five minutes or less and get a reaction of both understanding and interest, you are not ready to proceed to implementation. This five-minute test requires that we focus on the key aspects of the idea and avoid loading it down with extraneous detail.

The importance of broad communication is another key point that cannot be overemphasized. Kotter asserts that most organizations undercommunicate their new ideas by a factor of 10. Hammer and Stanton (1995, 147) suggest the rule of seven times seven: "The same thing must be communicated seven times in seven different ways before anyone will believe it." Failed organizational innovators are often heard to lament, "I don't get it, we held a meeting (or sent out a memo, or distributed a procedure, or whatever) about this; how could people not know about it?" If you hope to be successful, overcommunicate. My rule of thumb is: You are ready to implement the change only when you reach the point that people interrupt you in the middle of your explanation of the idea and say with some exasperation, "Okay already, we've heard this . . . when are we going to do it?!"

Kotter points out communication also occurs through the behavior and example of leaders. In many ways, what leaders do is much more important than what they say. Leaders who ask members of their organization to place themselves in the uncomfortable position of accepting a radically new way of doing something, without being willing to put themselves in the same uncomfortable position, are naive to expect enthusiastic cooperation.

The implication of this is that early on we should purposefully select one or two innovative ideas that let the leaders of the organization be seen as embracing radical new ways. If the guiding coalition is unwilling to pursue this for its symbolic value, it is a bad omen for the rest of the innovation effort. If the guiding coalition will not take on a significant change or a significant visible role in a change, either set your sights low or be prepared to undertake a very thorough communications effort to sell your new ideas to the rest of the organization. (Do not give up too easily. To the extent practical, be prepared to live out the warrior metaphor. Paradoxically, in order to succeed, you may need to put everything on the line. This, unfortunately, is the lesson from the study of creative lives.)

The final four steps in Kotter's model of change in Figure 7.2 should be second nature to practitioners of quality management. Empowering others to act, getting rid of obstacles, encouraging risk taking, making improvements, recognizing and rewarding those who participate, modifying organizational infrastructure, selecting new themes, and institutionalizing the new ways are basic concepts in the quality literature. Given adequate resources, committed and active leaders, and intelligent people who are crying to "just get on with it," I am confident to leave actual implementation as an exercise for the reader.

Key Points from the Study of Change Management

- Even with a great idea, the implementation of change is hard, emotional work.

- Effective change is born of a felt sense of urgency. You must create urgency.

- Amid the excitement you feel for your creative ideas, do not forget to answer the how-come question for those who must participate in implementing the change.

- While creative thinking often requires that we escape the organization's structure and rules, implementing innovation requires that we engage the organization's structure and rules, at least enough to gain permission to do something radically new.

- Every idea needs a guiding coalition whose members are wide ranging and powerful enough to allocate the necessary resources and ask for constructive participation by others.

- Be prepared for defensive routines and fancy footwork in response to innovative ideas. Be patient with others, but insist on getting on with implementation. (Prototypes may help.)

- If you cannot state the innovative idea clearly and compellingly in five minutes or less, you are not ready to proceed into implementation.

- Overcommunicate. You are ready to implement only when people start saying to you, "Enough already, when are we going to do it?!"

- Implementation of innovative ideas is scary. Leaders have the responsibility for leading the way by their own actions to put themselves on the line with a bold, untried innovation.

Tools That Support the Development and Action Phases

Let us now turn our attention to some specific tools that help us carry out the activities of the development and action phases of the directed-creativity cycle. Again, I do not intend to be comprehensive here. I will instead assume that you are familiar with many general management tools that support planning and action taking. Do not hesitate to use tools beyond those that I mention here if they have worked for you and your organization.

Final harvesting. We may well have more than 100 ideas coming out of the Imagination phase of the directed-creativity cycle. Typically, more than two-thirds of these ideas are now in the RTU and SEED categories, meaning that with a bit of work they could be implemented. Of course, implementing this many ideas would quickly overwhelm the organization. It is important, therefore, to do a final harvesting to develop a manageable list of ideas that have an above-average chance of being successfully implemented.

I recommend harvesting about twice as many ideas as you think you can reasonably expect to implement over the next 12 months. I suggest this liberal harvesting policy because several of the ideas initially selected in the harvest will not make the grade on the final evaluation. Other ideas will end up being combined or streamlined. Most important, going into the development phase knowing that you will want to eliminate several ideas helps avoid satisficing and belief preservation.

Returning to our SJ&D accounting firm, let us say that 10 high-impact ideas is all the innovative change that this relatively conservative firm can expect to digest over the next year. Therefore, we will be searching for only about 20 ideas, from among the hundreds generated, as the output from this final harvesting. While this number is somewhat pulled from the air, it does give us a starting point. You might develop a similar number for your organization's efforts by asking several people what they think. "Could we implement five ideas in the next year? 10? 15? 20? 25?" and so on until you identify a consensus comfort level. In subsequent years, you might challenge the organization to continually stretch its capacity to implement innovative change.

Final harvesting is a good time to get more people involved in the process. The final harvesting might be done by a relatively large group of 12 to 20+ people. This group should include many of the leaders from your powerful guiding coalition, several people that might end up being idea champions, several people who were involved in the preparation and imagination phases, and several people whose opinions are representative of key stakeholder groups that will be impacted by the implementation of the innovations. You might also consider rounding out the group with several people who are known for their critical (purple-hat) thinking. We have plenty of ideas in our notebook; we should weed out the marginal ideas at this session.

Majaro (1988) has developed a nine-cell screening matrix that can be helpful at a final harvesting meeting. As shown in Figure 7.3, ideas are placed on the grid based on subjective ratings for attractiveness and compatibility. *Attractiveness* refers to the idea's impact on the external and internal customers, or the public at large. Think of this much like Kano's (1984) notion of "attractive quality." Will it get us noticed? Will people like it? *Compatibility* refers to our assessment of the ease with which we could implement the idea. In other words, can we do it? Ideas that fall in the shaded cells are the best ideas to move forward to the next stage of development.

The leader of the harvesting session could use any comfortable group process to get consensus on which ideas fall into the desirable cells. Just make sure to allow plenty of time for discussion of minority opinions. Remember, you have invited people to the session because you believe that they will play some key role in implementing the ideas. If anyone feels

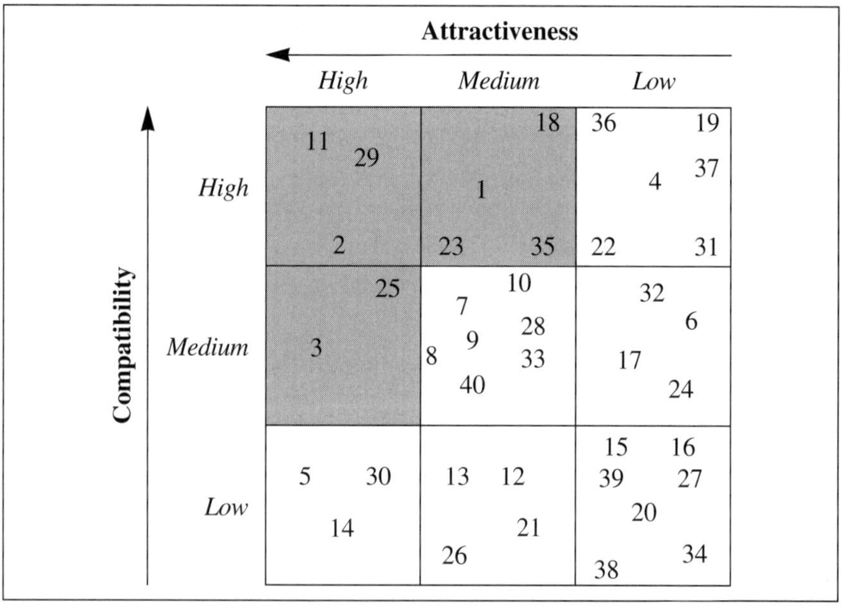

Adapted, with permission, from S. Majaro, *The Creative Gap: Managing Ideas for Profit.* New York: McGraw-Hill. Copyright 1988.

Figure 7.3. A screening matrix for final harvesting of ideas.

strongly that an idea does not belong in the desirable cell, you must think carefully before proceeding with it.

Enhancement. As previously mentioned, every idea selected in the final harvesting needs an idea champion to further develop it. This can be an individual or a team who might be assigned a single idea or multiple ideas. Use the same care in selection and the same formality in structure that you would in forming quality teams.

The idea champion's main task is to further develop the idea and get it ready for implementation. Figure 7.4 presents a list of questions, adapted from de Bono (1992), to guide this work. Notice how the questions guide thoughtful analysis aimed at increasing the chances of success. They guide us to consider emotional and people-related issues, the strengths and weaknesses of the idea, systems effects and consequences, and the need for trials and prototypes. Though the list appears in one-question-at-a-time order, the questions are really meant to be taken together. Start anywhere on the list, consider multiple questions at the same time, and be prepared to reevaluate your work on earlier questions as you go along. When you think you are done, go through the list one final time to make sure you have not missed anything.

The Six Thinking Hats is a useful tool in conjunction with the list in Figure 7.4. Whether working alone or with a group of people, remind yourself to work from good data (white hat), be attentive to intuition and feelings (red), emphasize positives (yellow), consider negatives and be critical (purple), and take creative approaches (green) with each of the enhancement questions.

You should expect to spend some time in enhancement. Unless the idea is very straightforward, enhancement is not a one-hour meeting. Shortcutting enhancement is a common pitfall, leading to half-baked ideas that fail. Your experience with designing solutions in the context of quality improvement projects is a guide to estimating the amount of time that you should allocate here. Typically, enhancement involves two to 20 hours of thoughtful work, perhaps spread out over several weeks. Of course, allow even more time if the idea requires some fundamental R&D (like SJ&D's idea 17 about developing a software worm to analyze files on a client's information system).

While shortcutting enhancement is a common pitfall, overdoing enhancement is equally problematic. We will have difficulty in implementation

---

Shaping. How can we modify the idea to address objections that would otherwise cause rejection?

Tailoring. Can we modify the idea to even better fit our needs?

Strengthening. How can we increase the power or value of the idea?

Reinforcing. What can we do about weak points?

Looking toward implementation. What can we do to the idea to enhance the probability of implementation? Who must be involved?

Comparison to current. How does the idea compare to what it is replacing? Should we do further enhancement, expand, or scale back the idea?

Potential faults or defects. What could possibly go wrong with this idea? What can we do?

Consequences. What are the immediate and long-term consequences of putting the idea into action?

Testability and prototyping. How can we try the idea on a small scale?

Preevaluation. How can we further modify the idea to meet the needs of those who will evaluate it next?

Figure 7.4. An idea enhancement checklist.

if we load down the idea with too many clever features. The comparison-to-current question in the enhancement checklist in Figure 7.4 suggests that we consider scaling back the idea. It might be helpful to plan a version 1, version 2, and so on to enable us to get the basic idea in place now, and then systematically add features over time.

Quality management tools can play an important role in addressing the enhancement questions in Figure 7.4. The concept of multiple customers and the methods of customer needs analysis can help identify potential objections and strong points from others' points of view. Surveys and focus groups might be helpful. We can develop flowcharts of new processes, and requirements documents for new products and services, as a way to focus our thoughts. Benchmarking visits may enhance our thinking further. Statistical analysis tools and designed experiments (DOE) can help us choose among alternatives and demonstrate improvements over current practices. We can use failure mode and effects analysis (FMEA) to explore potential faults and defects. We can also use systems diagrams to identify potential unintended consequences. In summary, our traditional strengths in analysis can be very helpful.

Enhancement is the meat of the development phase of the directed-creativity cycle. The product of our work here is a more well-thought-out idea. While the enhancement questions guide us to critical thinking (purple hat), we should maintain an overall positive attitude (yellow hat) throughout this activity. We want to do everything we can to see the idea accepted by all stakeholders and successfully implemented.

Documenting the idea. We now need to document and communicate our enhanced ideas. Various authors in the creativity and innovation literature have proposed formats for doing this. These range from relatively informal, one-page summaries to full-scale business plans. Again, you will need to apply some judgment in choosing what is right for you.

In chapter 6, I introduced a simple idea capture worksheet (see Figure 6.4). Expanding on this notion, we might document the output of our enhancement work using a simple framework like the one described in Figure 7.5. Note that it presents, in sequence, green-, yellow-, purple-, white-, and red-hat thinking. I have used this format with clients to get one- to three-page write-ups of ideas to circulate to the guiding coalition for evaluation.

In the end, keep in mind the immediate next step in the directed-creativity cycle: evaluation. While we want to be clear and comprehensive in communicating our ideas, avoid burdensome documentation requirements. You need enough documentation to enable the guiding coalition to decide whether the idea should proceed to action. It is okay if there are still many implementation details left to be worked out. The guiding coalition may not need to know every technical detail in order to be convinced of the value of the idea. You can also supplement your documentation with discussion, role plays, simulations, models, and prototypes.

Evaluation. The activities of the development phase of the directed-creativity cycle culminate in evaluation. We have been using judgment throughout these activities, but we have been purposefully avoiding final judgment. The time has now come.

Evaluation is an activity conducted by the guiding coalition—the group of leaders who collectively possess the power to allocate resources and ask

The Idea. Explain the idea in two to three clear, informative, compelling paragraphs. (If you cannot do this, you must question whether your idea is ready to move on to action.) Use complete sentences and paragraph structure, not bullet lists. It is too easy to cop out, oversummarize, and overassume in preparing a bullet list. If appropriate, you could present the idea as a scenario; describing how a person would experience the idea. Attach flowcharts and other supporting details, but write the description here in such a way that the reader can understand it fully without referring to the supporting details.

Benefits and Positive Aspects. Describe three to 10 key benefits of the idea. Here, it is okay to use a bullet list. Consider benefits to multiple customers both internal and external. Remember, everyone that is impacted by the idea will be asking, "What's in it for me?" All key stakeholders need to find something that appeals to them listed in this section.

Remaining Negatives and Potential Downsides. If you have done a good job of enhancement, there should be few things to report here, but no idea is perfect and there are always things that cannot be fully known until we implement. Demonstrate your objectivity by identifying potential objections, negative points, and consequences here. While you may be reluctant to do this, these points will surface eventually and could completely undermine all your hard work. Better to be upfront and show that you are thinking about them proactively, than to be put in a reactive or defensive position later.

Supporting Information. Use this section to report facts and the numbers. How much will it cost in staff time and money? How many tangible benefits can we expect to get in terms of increased customer satisfaction, revenues, cost savings, reduced cycle time, and so on? What data exist to further support the notion that this is a good idea? Just summarize here; use attachments to provide the details of any analysis. Be conservative. Do not be afraid to point out that the most important numbers are unknown and unknowable, but also do not use this as an excuse for being lazy.

Intuitive Conclusion. You have expended a great deal of effort on this idea. In one or two sentences or phrases, tell us how you really feel about it. Use emotive, descriptive, metaphorical language. Communicate how excited or unexcited your are. Use the following examples as guides for communicating various shades of feelings that you might have. "This idea is a home run!" "Wow! What are we waiting for?" "We really think customers will like it." "A solid idea, we should do it; but we won't win any prizes for it." "It's better than doing nothing." "Perhaps this idea's day will come later." "All things considered, not worth the effort."

Figure 7.5. A format and set of instructions for documenting an idea after enhancement.

for constructive participation by others. Many of these people will have been involved in the earlier final harvesting activity that led to the identification of idea champions and the initiation of enhancement. This group's role now is to

- Select the final set of ideas that will be implemented (recall that we purposefully harvested about twice as many ideas as we thought we could implement).
- Allocate the resources needed to carry them out.
- Empower people to carry them out.
- Visibly communicate support for the changes.

The evaluative work of the guiding coalition might take the form of a special meeting, an off-site retreat, a Delphi method (where opinions are expressed, tallied, and fed back via mail or computer compilation without a face-to-face meeting), or a combination of these three. Regardless of the logistics, the evaluation activity needs inputs, evaluation criteria, a decision process, and an output. The inputs are the documented ideas as described in the previous section. The outputs will be formal decisions, authorities, and budgets, or clear explanations for decisions to not pursue a given idea at this time.

The creativity literature provides many suggestions relative to evaluation criteria and processes. Majaro's (1988) criteria of attractiveness and compatibility, and his nine-cell screening matrix is one approach that we have already examined (see Figure 7.3). If you used this approach for final harvesting, you can simply repeat it here with a more critical eye on the enhanced ideas. LeBoeuf (1980), Michalko (1991), Parnes (1992), and others suggest additional, multidimensional evaluation criteria such as the following:

Effectiveness in achieving objective	Customer reaction
Cost to implement	Revenue or cost avoidance potential
Uniqueness of the idea	Potential for enabling other innovations
Moral or legal implications	Degree of positive feeling evoked by idea
Likelihood of success	Freedom from adverse consequence/risk
Ease of implementation	Timeliness of the idea

Availability of technology   Match with organizational strengths

Simplicity of the idea   Degree of internal support

Sense of urgency of need

Ask guiding coalition members to select three to seven criteria from this list (or develop additional criteria) that seem to be a good fit for your specific situation. It is best to do this prior to seeing the ideas to avoid biasing the process, but do not be dogmatic about it. Guiding coalition members could either rank order the ideas with the selected criteria implicitly in mind, or score each idea on each criteria using a high-medium-low, or 1–10, scale.

LeBoeuf (1980), Koberg and Bagnall (1981), Michalko (1991) and others recommend the use of various relative weighting schemes, multi-column matrices, and ranked comparisons for processing this information. Practitioners of quality management will be familiar with such methods as part of group process and the seven management and planning tools. (See Brassard 1989, Brightman 1988, Plsek 1993b, and Scholtes 1988 for more information.)

The most interesting idea evaluation technique that I have come across, from Ray and Myers (1986), is designed to tap into your intuitive judgment. If you have a choice between two alternatives where there is no clear winner based on analysis, flip a coin. When informed of the result, immediately sense your feelings. Are you happy and relieved, or uncomfortable and disappointed at the outcome? Do you find yourself wanting to go two out of three on it? Go with your intuitive feelings and either accept the coin's outcome or reverse it. As goofy as this may sound, I have used this method to break ties after voting or scoring and have found it surprisingly appealing. Try it. (I should warn you that this method often does not work in large groups. When you tally the intuitions, you often end up with at least a few people on both sides of the issue, which simply brings you back to where you started. Extended dialogue or compromise are the only ways to resolve this. Even in large groups, it only takes a second to flip the coin. So it's worth a try.)

Planning for implementation. As I have noted previously, the implementation of creative ideas is not substantially different from the challenges encountered in implementing any type of change in an organization. Creativity authors describe various tools that we would recognize as variations on flowcharts, matrices, action plans, quality function deployment, Gantt charts, timelines, simulations, and model building.

I advise clients that they need, at a minimum, an action plan, communications plan, training plan, measurement plan, contingency plan, and improvement plan. Depending on the complexity of the innovation, the action plan might be broken down into subsections covering procurement, final design, information systems, human resources, and other issues. All these plans should be keyed to an integrated timeline of events.

While such plans cover the technical and logistical aspects of implementation, anyone who has ever participated in the implementation of change will know that the psychological aspects give rise to the greatest problems. Hammer and Stanton (1995) advise us to expect resistance to change when implementing innovative ideas. They further suggest that the key mechanisms for overcoming such resistance are the Five *I*s: incentives, information, intervention, indoctrination, and involvement. You probably have your own favorite tools and frameworks to support planning for the psychological aspects of change in the context of your quality management efforts.

While we normally focus on overcoming resistance to change in others, we should not overlook the importance of overcoming our own internal fears as idea champions and change leaders. This is easy to overlook because it is hard and uncomfortable to reflect on one's own attitudes and beliefs. Because satisficing and belief preservation are such strong properties of the mechanics of our minds, I strongly urge you to face up to this challenge proactively.

In addressing this issue of confronting our own fears, Basadur (1995, 121–124) suggests a number of good techniques for prompting oneself to act. Among these are

- Write down the worst thing that could happen. (Often you find that it is not so bad.)

- Ask yourself, "If I wait, how much better will things be?"

- Break big tasks down into smaller pieces and start tackling them.

- Reverse-prioritize to say no to less important tasks that you might use as an excuse to avoid pushing ahead with your innovation.

- Set deadlines for yourself and share these commitments with others.

- Use the broccoli-first principle: Do the part you hate most first to get it out of the way.

Whatever you chose to do, be proactive and open. Admitting your own fear of the unknown will help others to deal with theirs. Acting frustrated and superior is a common mistake that many change leaders make in implementation.

When using tools for development and action, remember:

- Use your past experience with the implementation of change as a guide to what will work and not work in your organization.

- Use some structured decision-making method to do a final harvest of about twice as many ideas as you think your organization can effectively implement over the next 12 months.

- Assemble a relatively large and representative group for the final harvesting; beware of proceeding with any ideas that someone strongly opposes.

- The idea enhancement questions in Figure 7.4 and the Six Thinking Hats can be used together to do a thorough job of enhancement.

- Remember to be clear, concise, compelling, and continuous in communicating your ideas; communicate through documentation, discussion, role plays, models, and prototypes.

- Do not be afraid to use some intuitive and subjective judgments; no amount of analysis can predict precisely the outcome of a truly innovative idea.

- There are many structured decision-making processes for evaluating creative ideas; select a method that you believe will fit your situation.

- If you have done a good job of enhancement, implementation will go smoother; but it is never easy.

- Expect resistance to change; plan proactively for it.

- Deal openly and proactively with your own natural fears of the unknown.

Summary of the Development and Action Phases

Let me end where I began in this chapter. Creative ideas have no value until they are put into action. Therefore, be deliberate and thorough in enhancing your ideas. Be tough and intuitive in evaluating your ideas. Be committed and courageous in implementing your ideas.

The key messages of this chapter are

- The development and action phases are hard work, but without them the preparation and imagination phases are meaningless.

- You do not have to implement all of your creative ideas. Be selective. It is better to successfully implement a few ideas than to attempt many changes and fail.

- Do not scrimp in the enhancement activity, but keep your ideas free from excess baggage and clever features that only distract from the main concept.

- While it is possible to be creative outside the organization's structure, you must work effectively within an organization's structure in order to implement your ideas and be innovative.

- A sense of urgency and active leadership are necessary conditions for the implementation of innovations and change.

- Do not forget to answer the how-come question for those who must participate in the implementation of the innovation.

- Overcommunicate. Be clear, concise, compelling, and continuous.

- The traditional tools of quality management and general project management are very useful in the development and action phases of the directed-creativity cycle.

- In the excitement of completing a trip through the directed-creativity cycle, do not forget to prepare for the next cycle. Customers are increasingly demanding innovation. Competitors are increasingly supplying innovation. Today and in the future, it is the rate of innovation that is decisive.

This concludes part III on methods and tools for directed creativity. I hope that you now see that directed creativity is a possibility for anyone. Throughout these tools chapters, I have purposefully been careful to present the tools as examples of what one can do. I honestly do not care if you ever use any of the tools in this book exactly as they are described. I invite you to invent your own methods, or mix and match the tools described here as you see fit. There are a limitless number of ways to accomplish directed creativity.

PART IV

Applying Directed Creativity to the Challenges of Quality Management

CHAPTER 8

Process Design, Reengineering, and Creativity

☺ ♪ 〰 ♫

Any valuable new process design will at first appear to be whacko. If someone approaches you with a proposal for a new process design that strikes you as interesting and plausible, our advice is: Throw it away.

Michael Hammer

It's easy to come up with new ideas; the hard part is letting go of what worked for you two years ago, but will soon be out of date.

Roger von Oech

Even if you're on the right track, you'll get run over if you just sit there.

Will Rogers

This chapter begins the final part of the book, in which we will sharpen our focus on the practical application of directed creativity to the specific challenges of quality management. In this chapter, we will examine the use of directed-creativity methods for designing and reengineering processes.

I chose to start with this topic because I feel that it is the most natural, straightforward, and urgent application. Many practitioners of quality management are currently serving on or leading process design and reengineering

185

teams. While the goal of such efforts is a radical restructuring of the way work is done, the experience is that many of these projects fail to meet their objectives. (See, for example, the research of Hall et al. 1993.) Hammer and Stanton (1995) attribute at least some of this failure to a lack of creative thinking. While decrying the lack of creative thinking, the reengineering literature contains more exhortation than method. The key question that readers of the process design and reengineering literature should be asking back to authors is, "How exactly do I go about getting a radically new, innovative idea for restructuring the process?" That is precisely the question I intend to answer in this chapter.

Reengineering: Controversies Leading to Creative Provocations

The term *reengineering* has been the source of much controversy. The basic issue is this: Is reengineering just another name for quality management, or is reengineering a fundamentally new approach to things?

Hammer (1990) defines reengineering as "using the power of modern information technology to radically redesign our business processes to achieve dramatic improvements in their performance." Currid (1994), Petrozzo and Stepper (1994), and others offer similar definitions revolving around the themes of radical redesign, use of information technology, organizational role restructuring, and dramatic performance improvement. Based on these definitions, many proponents of reengineering claim that reengineering is completely different from quality management, which they see as being about incremental improvement. The misunderstanding comes from the assumption that incremental improvement is the whole of quality management.

At the same time, I feel that practitioners of quality management are misguided in asserting that reengineering is nothing more than quality management. It is true that reengineering and quality management share a common base of principles; for example, about customers, process focus, and the role of leadership. It is also true that the original reengineering project reported by Hammer (1990)—Ford's reengineering of its accounts payable system in the factory—was not a reengineering project until Hammer so named it. The people doing the project thought that they were a quality improvement team. Despite the common base, the no-inherent-right-or-wrong heuristic reminds us that there is something to be gained creatively by focusing for a moment on the differences between quality management and reengineering.

For instance, reengineering adds a key focus on the use of modern information technology as an enabler of change (Hammer and Champy 1993; Petrozzo and Stepper 1993; Davenport 1993). While quality management has never precluded the use of information technology as a means for bringing about improvement, the literature of the field has also not explicitly pointed our thinking in that direction. For example, quality expert Joseph Juran's (1992) text on process design, *Juran on Quality by Design,* does not even contain an index entry for *information technology.* Petrozzo and Stepper (1993) further point out that none of the classic quality management texts explicitly mention information technology.

This heuristic also frees us from the tyranny of the need to decide which side is correct on this issue. It does not matter whether reengineering is the same as or different from quality management. We should simply celebrate the fact that we have extracted a new attention provocation: "Po, blow up the current process and rethink it using the capabilities of modern information technology as a starting point." This is helpful. Arguing about who is right and wrong is not.

Another difference in emphasis between reengineering and quality management has to do with the scale of change. Quality management embraces both incremental improvement *and* redesign. Reengineering insists on radical redesign. Again, both approaches are useful. If we take a creative pause, however, we might notice that often people shy away from large-scale change because they believe that it will be much harder to do than small-scale change. Maybe change is inherently hard no matter what the scale. If that is true, then why not go for the greatest impact? This is a thought-provoking question worth exploring. The reengineering approach of insisting on large-scale change can also be thought of as a creative escape provocation: "Po, they have passed a law making it illegal to do small-scale change—it is either leave it as is or blow it up and radically restructure—now what are we going to do?"

A third key difference to focus on, and the final one I will mention, is the notion in reengineering of concurrent redesign of processes, organizational structures and roles, and information systems. (See, for example, Petrozzo and Stepper 1994.) The diagram in Figure 8.1 illustrates this expansive scope. I believe that the failure to work simultaneously in all three circles is one of the reasons why so many reengineering projects fail to bring about dramatic performance improvements.

As practitioners of quality management, we must admit that as part of our tradition we have focused on process redesign and have deemphasized organizational role restructuring and information technology. For example, many local implementations of quality management have ground rules that explicitly preclude teams from addressing role-definition issues. Many practitioners of quality management also emphatically insist that information technology should be applied only after process redesign has occurred. (See, for example, Harrington 1991.)

We can now use these observations to generate two more creative attention and escape provocations. "Po, leap over control and improvement of the current process—redesign the processes and install information

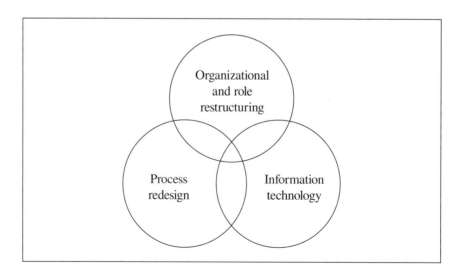

Figure 8.1. The scope of true reengineering: A true reengineering project simultaneously addresses all three circles in the diagram.

technology at the same time." "Po, simultaneous change of processes, organizational structure and roles, and information technology."

The point, creatively speaking, is that we do not need to defend or discredit either side in the reengineering-versus-quality-management debate. There doesn't have to be a right or wrong on these specific issues. While it is okay to feel quite strongly about one side or the other, simply recognize this as your belief, to which you are entitled. Do not let belief preservation overwhelm imagination. Have the flexibility to explore the world on the other side of your beliefs and you might make a creative mental association that changes the world that you will eventually return to.

Using Directed Creativity to Redesign Processes in a Medical Clinic

With our minds appropriately flexed, let's apply the heuristics, principles, models, and tools of directed creativity to a process design project. A health maintenance organization (HMO) plans to set up physician clinics in a new building that is being constructed in a suburban location. Construction has just begun on the building, so its location, overall physical size, and interior load-bearing walls are fixed. (You might say we should have applied creative thinking before we even designed the building. It is too late for that now. In any creative-thinking application, there are always some things that are givens.) The HMO is engaged in fierce competition and sees innovation, quality, customer service, and cost control as its four keys to success. The new clinic is not scheduled to open for another eight months, and the senior leadership team sees this as a golden opportunity to design a showcase for innovative services. They have commissioned a four-person team to oversee an effort to produce an innovative design for the clinic. The team consists of the organization's quality manager, information systems director, medical director (a physician), and a nurse manager. These four people plan to work about 25 percent time on this project, while they maintain their normal responsibilities. The group is also empowered to pull others into the effort as needed. How might this group proceed?

Preparation phase. Beginning at the beginning of the directed-creativity cycle, the group's first thoughts ought to be about preparation. It might be helpful to think about four types of preparation.

- Preparation for teamwork
- Preparation for leadership and project management
- Preparation in general skills for directed creativity
- Preparation for the imagination phase of this specific project

I mention these four types of preparation because the need for the first three is frequently overlooked. Again, it is the brainstorming syndrome that suggests that we can simply assemble a group of people, have them knock out a few ideas, and then just do it. It will not be that simple.

For the sake of focus here, let's say that the group has, or gets, preparation on the first three items (that is, they read books, attend courses, teach each other, bring in others to facilitate, and so forth). What tools and methods of directed creativity might they use to get prepared for imaginative idea generation for the new clinic?

The mind map of methods for preparation in Figure 5.2 is a good place to start. It would also be helpful to review the key points in the various boxes scattered throughout chapter 5. Finally, recall that during this preparation phase we want to work on attention and escape, and create a storehouse of mental valleys.

Most of the tools depicted on the mind map in Figure 5.2 can be used to support preparation in a process design or reengineering project. Since a process is a concrete thing and we typically have some existing way to do it, the looking-closer-and-analyzing branch of the mind map is a logical place to start. It will also be helpful to spend some time refocusing the topic—playing with words and various statements of purpose. As an input to this refocusing, we might want to do some creative customer needs analysis in conjunction with the new design effort. (We will explore creative customer needs analysis in chapter 9.) Searching for analogies and seeing other points of view will help us do a little escape-oriented preparation. The possibilities for analogies and points of view are limitless, so we will want to set a time limit on the use of these tools. Of course, pausing and noticing is obviously a background part of any preparation experience. Creating new worlds, the only branch of the preparation tools mind map that I have not mentioned, is more applicable to product, service, and strategic planning applications. In many ways, creating a new world is the output we are trying to achieve in an innovative process design effort, rather than an input. Let's apply these thoughts now to our medical clinic design project.

We will begin by paying attention to our current mental valleys on the topic of medical clinics. Under the looking-closer-and-analyzing branch of the preparation tools mind map, we could try surfacing assumptions, seeing the obvious, and answering questions. We might begin this at a two-hour meeting of the group at one of our existing clinics. In the first 45 minutes, we can do some analyzing based on what is already in our heads. We'll make a list of assumptions and rules about what has to happen or has to be true in a medical clinic. We could also start a list of obvious things in a medical clinic. (There could be some redundancies between these two lists, but that is okay.) Finally, we will list some expansive questions in response to who, what, when, where, why, and how.

When the 45 minutes are up, we will leave the meeting room for a pause-and-notice excursion. With the lists that we have just prepared fresh in our minds, we will take a leisurely walk through the clinic with notebooks in hand to record observations. We might even use cameras to take pictures of scenes. The previous discussion will have carved fresh mental valleys, so it should be pretty easy to notice additional items to add to our lists or additional concepts to store up. After 30 minutes of strolling, we can return to the meeting room to compile our new observations onto the lists previously generated.

In the final 30 minutes of the meeting, we could make a list of potential analogies (or randomly select a few from the other worlds list in the appendix). Potential analogies for a medical clinic might include: a department store or shopping mall, an airport, a job interview at a large corporation, or doing research on a topic in a library. (Pause and reflect for a moment; in what ways are each of these situations like a medical clinic? With mental movement, what creative insights do you get? Can you add to the list of analogies?) Each person could take one to three analogies to research prior to the next meeting of the group. Through reading, conversation with others, or visits to places, each member of the group will prepare a list of facts and insights from the analogous world that might serve as raw material for the imagination.

At the next meeting of the group, we could begin by compiling the input from the analogy search into several one-page summaries suitable for handing to future brainstorming groups. We will also add to our previous lists any things we have noticed recently. (Every member of the group should have a notebook or other insight recording technique.) If we haven't already discussed it, now probably would be a good time to agree on the format that we will use to document imaginative ideas. Even though we are technically still in the preparation phase of the cycle, it will be difficult (and unnecessary) to hold back the imagination once we start discussing analogies and actively pausing and noticing. We should have a system for capturing these ideas. Besides, this will give us a chance to fine-tune this documentation format within the small group before we start receiving ideas from others.

The bulk of this second preparation meeting might be spent refocusing the topic. Recall that we want broad topics that leave plenty of room for the imagination to move (heuristic 3). Our basic, initial topic statement is this: Develop innovative process designs to use in our new suburban medical clinic. By asking why and how come, and exploring larger and smaller statements of purpose, we can generate a purpose hierarchy.

Beat the competition.

Surprise and attract customers.

Get a reputation for being innovative.

Be a showcase for innovation in healthcare delivery.

Be a test site or model for innovation that could be spread to other clinics.

Innovative process designs for new suburban medical clinic.

Improve a few key processes in our new suburban medical clinic.

Create a sense of excitement among staff that might rub off in better service.

Be creative and innovative.

Later, in the imagination phase, we can give these statements—collectively or individually—to various groups and ask them to generate alternative ideas based on the statements.

We can continue refocusing the topic through word play. Since we already have the multiple statements in the purpose hierarchy, let's circle key words in each of these statements. Then we will close our eyes and point to the page to generate 20 word pairs. Alternatively, we could arrange the words in a matrix and generate all possible pairings or go around the group purposefully selecting pairings that group members think might be interesting. It doesn't much matter how we do it; we are going to parcel these out to imagination groups later. We could go on to explore synonyms and antonyms as time permits. There are so many possibilities, we should probably just stop when the time is up. We can always add additional items later if noticing suggests a particular insight.

At our third preparation meeting, we can add any new observations to our lists. At this point, we might be feeling pretty anxious to get going. Checking the directed-creativity cycle model and noticing the word *analyze* as the final step of the preparation phase will turn us back to the looking-closer-and-analyzing branch of the tools mind map in Figure 5.2. It might be helpful to do a quick pass through the Six Thinking Hats to make sure we are balanced in our thinking. We have used the green (creative) hat in developing analogies and refocusing the topic. The yellow (positive) hat suggests that we might compile a list of positive attributes that we want the new clinic to possess. We could use such a list later in evaluating ideas. We might also use it to form creative reversal provocation for the imagination phase. (For example, "Po, let's make the patients wait a very long time before they see the doctor." Mental movement leads me to think about setting up a system where patients could receive information and reassurance to treat themselves at home in situations that lend themselves to a wait-and-see approach.) The purple (negatives) hat suggests that we compile a similar list of negatives. The red (feelings) hat suggests several expansive questions, such as: How should the new clinic feel to patients? What is known about the use of colors, smells, sounds, plants, and so forth to create positive feelings? We can research this and bring the findings into future idea generation sessions. Finally, the white (data) hat could lead to a long list of information inputs that we could compile. For instance, it would be nice to have high-level flowcharts of existing clinic processes, information from focus groups of patients, data about our competitors, and data on current performance on key indicators. We can use this information to help us identify fixed points from which to generate alternatives.

An additional, interesting, white-hat thinking activity that I always try to do in a process redesign effort is what I call the circa exercise. *Circa* is a Latin word meaning *about*. It is used in archeology and history to indicate approximate dates of things. Similarly, in the circa exercise we date our existing process concepts. For example, a doctor's waiting room is probably circa 1950. That is about the time that doctors stopped routinely making house calls and started seeing patients almost exclusively in their offices. Except for cosmetic differences, the basic process of handling patients in a doctor's waiting room has not changed much since the 1950s. Since that time, patients have been walking up to a counter, stating their names, being told to take a seat in the common area with other patients, and waiting until their name is called.

The purpose of the circa exercise is to overcome the mental process of satisficing. When we realize that a process has remained conceptually the same since the 1950s, we are likely to react by thinking, "It really is time for a change, isn't it?" Be prepared to introduce the results of your circa analysis whenever you sense that a group is favoring the status quo. Ask, "How long have we been doing this process basically this same way?" It may be helpful to ask, "What did we used to do before we did it this way?" and then ask, "When did it change?" Try it yourself on processes in your organization and notice how it makes you feel.

We have now prepared quite a collection of resources to bring into the imagination phase. Recapping, we have the following items (text in parenthesis indicates a possible use in the imagination phase).

- List of assumptions and rules in medical clinics (po these)
- Obvious things in a clinic (how can we use these creatively?)
- Expansive questions (explore with escape and mental movement)
- Things we have noticed (use these as starting points for movement)
- Analogy summaries (stimulate connections and adaptations)
- Purpose hierarchy (generate alternatives)
- Word pairs, synonyms, and antonyms (stimulate mental associations)
- List of positives and negatives (use for reversal provocations)
- Fixed points extracted from information on processes, customers, and competitors (alternatives from fixed points)
- Circa dates for major processes (use to overcome satisficing)

A nice collection! In addition, we still have random words and other such on-the-spot provocations that we can use. We clearly have enough raw material to feed dozens of idea generation sessions. This is exactly what we need if we expect to generate breakthrough innovations.

Transition to the imagination phase. The planning group might spend another meeting or two, with homework between meetings, polishing up these preparation materials and planning specific idea generation sessions. The planning group may decide to use some of the material in its own idea generation sessions, or each of the four members of the group could convene and facilitate separate idea generation sessions. We might decide to involve dozens of people in the effort or only a few. Some preparation materials might be used multiple times to see what ideas various groups come up with. Provocations could be put out on bulletin boards or distributed in the cafeteria or break rooms with a request that people jot down their ideas . . .

There is no end to the approaches we could use. Therefore, it is important to have a plan. Lay out a timeline on the wall and use note cards to represent the various idea generation activities. Do not forget to schedule training for directed creativity. Participants need to know enough about mental mechanics to understand what their minds are supposed to be doing during the idea generation session. (Just-in-time training in the context of a specific session is usually adequate.) In addition to these logistical matters, the planning group should keep in mind the various heuristics and advice that we covered in the chapter on imagination.

Our clinic design group might spend four to six weeks in the preparation phase and then plan to spend another four to six weeks in imagination. With an eight-month total project window, this still leaves five to six months for development and action. This distribution of time is typical for the directed-creativity cycle in a process design or reengineering project: 20 percent preparation, 20 percent imagination, 20 percent development, and 40 percent action. (As we will see in subsequent chapters, the amount of time we spend in each phase of the cycle will depend somewhat on the application.)

Imagination. The mind map of imagination tools in Figure 6.2 again serves as the starting point for our thinking about how to proceed in a process design or reengineering project. Of course, our preparation-phase materials have already led us to several types of imagination-phase tools. If you have prepared analogies (a branch on the mind map in Figure 6.2), use them. Also remember that we can use analogies on-the-spot, through random forced analogies. You should also plan to work with the be-someone-else tool (that is, role-play) in most process design projects. People hired from other industries often bring with them seemingly innovative ideas about ways to do things when they come into our companies. We can simulate this effect by imagination.

The leaping and provoking-the-imagination-directly branches of the imagination mind map provide natural tools to use in any process design and reengineering project. In addition to the methods that follow naturally from the materials developed in the preparation phase, do not overlook the potential use of random words, visualization techniques (for example, make a videotape of the current clinic intake process, play it slowly or backwards, and practice attention and movement), stepping-stones (for example, "let's just kill patients the first time they get sick so we never have to deal with them again"), and illogical statements (for example, "doctors have huge noses"). If you plan to use some of these tools, you should spend some time preparing.

The tools in the combining-concepts-systematically and organizing-and-displaying-ideas branches of the mind map in Figure 6.2 are essential in process design and reengineering efforts. In addition to idea notebooks (or slip methods or mind maps) to capture most ideas, nearly every creative process design project will want to construct a concept fan. Further, it is important to note that in the context of process design and reengineering, there must be some sort of systematic approach to combine ideas and harvest them as a package. We are not so much interested in harvesting individual ideas as we are sets of ideas that will flow together as a process.

Let's continue now with our example of process design in a medical clinic. Space does not permit a full development of ideas here, but I will try to provide enough to give you the flavor of it.

Let's look in on a idea generation group using the be-someone-else tool (imaginative role play). The nurse manager on the planning team is facilitating this group of a dozen people. She spends the first 15 minutes of the session orienting the group and explaining basic mental mechanics: that creative ideas are the combination of mental valleys and that different people have different mental valleys. She then tells the group that she is going to read off a list of types of people and occupations. Each person has a pad of paper. When they hear the person or occupation, they are to try to imagine what that person would say or think if asked to help design processes in the new clinic and then jot these thoughts down on a sheet of paper. Outrageous or laughable thoughts are welcomed. After two minutes of thinking, each person is to pass his or her ideas into the box in the middle of the table. The nurse manager will then read off another person or occupation and repeat the process with two more minutes of silent idea generation. After eight rounds of this (about 16 minutes), group members will randomly select sheets from the pile and read off the ideas. Participants will have the opportunity to contribute new ideas as they think of them. We have chosen to use this silent brainstorming methods because of our past experience with dominating members in such mixed groups.

Examples of provocations and potential ideas include the following:

- The manager of a fast food restaurant (A drive-through clinic.)

- A horse (Something to munch on, space to exercise; would patient satisfaction improve if we provided these?)

- A rent-a-car company employee (They know you're coming and your car is waiting with the engine running, so have the patient walk right into an exam room that has her name flashing over the door.)

- A mail-order catalogue manager (What clinic services can we provide over the phone?)

- An Indy 500 racing car pit crew (Instead of a single doctor, a group of doctors and nurses, each with a narrowly defined task to perform, descends on the patient, and the entire visit is completed in a matter of seconds.)

With 12 participants, imagining eight different people and occupations, we will have close to 100 ideas. Allowing for duplicates, we should still have at least several dozen ideas from this one session alone.

The information systems director on the planning team was intrigued by our earlier discussion about the debate between advocates of reengineering and quality management. She has formed two teams to examine the provocations we generated. One team is charged with developing three innovative designs from the provocation, "Po, blow up the current process and rethink it using the capabilities of modern information technology as a starting point." This team will complete its work in four, two-hour meetings over the next month. The second team is charged with suggesting organizational and role restructuring based on the provocation, "Po, we live in an alien world where everyone is socialized to value equality. No one stands on hierarchy, everyone is paid the same and respected the same, regardless of title, profession, training, and skills. How would we organize and assign roles in the medical clinic in such world?" Its output is expected to be a two-page write-up that directly answers the provocation question in the context of the alien world, followed by a list of creative but plausible suggestions for adapting what has been learned into the real world. Given the strong traditions and hierarchical roles in the medical profession, we may not be able to implement very many of the ideas that are generated. But recall that in the imagination phase, it is enough to simply explore the world on the other side. If we can implement even a few ideas from this effort, we will be moving in the right direction.

The planning group itself will meet for an idea generation session using the provocation tool of visualization. The physician in the group sent his daughter, an aspiring photographer, into a clinic with a camera and asked her to photograph typical scenes. A slide carousel is now loaded with the pictures. As each scene is projected onto the wall, group members note the obvious elements in the scene and other elements that can be presumed, even though they are not pictured (creative attention). The first photograph shows an appointment-scheduling secretary taking a call. What are the elements of this scene? There is a patient (not pictured), the secretary, doctors' schedule books, a telephone, the secretary's desk, and so forth. Now let's systematically change these elements to see what creative possibilities emerge . . .

- Instead of a phone, substitute a fax machine. Patients could fax in their requests for appointments (like faxing in a pizza order). Secretaries could then utilize slow times in the day to respond to these requests.

- Instead of a paper-based doctor calendar, put the calendar on the computer. With the calendar on the computer, patients could use a modem (instead of a telephone) to schedule their own appointments (thereby substituting for the human secretary). Or they could send in their requests via modem, let the computer (or a human) do some screening and matching, and then have the computer generate an e-mail message back to the patient with the scheduled date and time. Another way would be to allow patients to use a bank's ATM network to schedule appointments.

- Instead of the secretaries sitting at desks, let them work from home. This would be a great way to employ people with disabilities or who have other needs to work from home. It would also save valuable clinic space for more examination rooms.

- Why not just eliminate schedules all together and go to a no-appointment-necessary system?

As another imagination-phase activity, the organization's information systems director (a member of the four-person planning team) selects a random noun every morning and e-mails it to 32 people who recently attended a training session on directed creativity. The e-mail is a one-line message: "What creative ideas for the new clinic come to mind when you think of this word?" (Notice that, consistent with the broad-focus heuristic, we are keeping our topic broad—anything about the clinic.) Today's word is *umbrella*. Here are two of the ideas submitted.

- An umbrella can be opened quickly when you need it. We can design the clinic such that we can quickly open new exam rooms and staff them instantly to meet the needs of fluctuating demand. If nurses were cross-trained to do other clinic jobs such that every employee was a nurse, we could quickly shift them to nursing roles when needed. We could also design movable partitions to quickly convert all the space in the clinic into temporary exam rooms when needed (for example, a sliding partition covers the filing cabinets, and a pad is fitted onto the table to quickly convert the file room to an exam room.)

- An umbrella has spokes that come out from a central post. This makes me think about the possibility of a distributed laboratory system. Drop a blood sample into a device in the exam room, the lab is alerted, the device in the exam room sends information to the lab, and the results quickly appear on a screen in the exam room. No physical movement of the specimen! One could begin to develop such a device by analyzing current lab equipment and separating the parts of the machine that handle the physical specimen (locate these parts in all the exam rooms) from the parts of the machine that process information about the specimen (locate one of these in the lab). Perhaps a manufacturer of laboratory equipment would be willing to work with us on this.

Again, this process can generate a lot of ideas with relatively little effort. Thirty-two people working with just one random word per day for two weeks could easily generate 200+ ideas.

As mentioned earlier, a concept fan can be a very useful tool for designing and reengineering processes. To develop a concept fan, we begin with a high-level flowchart of the traditional or current process. If your organization already has key business process maps, these are great. The left side of Figure 8.2 depicts the beginning of one key business process in our clinic: patient intake. To construct the concept fan, we have assembled a cross-disciplinary group for a half-day retreat session. The quality manager on the planning team is facilitating the retreat and providing the necessary background training in directed creativity.

Now let's step back from the current high-level process flowchart and identify the underlying concepts behind the various steps. As indicated in the second column in Figure 8.2, one underlying concept in the clinic process is that the patient and the provider (for example, doctor, nurse, psychologist, or therapist) must come together. Creative possibilities emerge when we note that the current way (patient comes to clinic) is only one way of achieving this underlying concept. Are there other ways? Instead of the patient coming to visit the provider,

- The provider could travel in a van that comes to the patient.

- The patient could interact with the provider via telemetry equipment and a video phone at home.

And so on.

These ideas, and others, are captured in the third column of the concept fan in Figure 8.2. Over the course of the half-day retreat, the team could proceed similarly with the other steps and concepts in the process. We might want to establish a time limit for each step to assure that we get all the way through in the allotted time.

We can also add to the concept fan additional ideas that have been previously recorded in our idea notebook from other idea generation sessions. In this way, the concept fan becomes a major documentation mechanism for the process design project. (Of course, some ideas in our notebook might not lend themselves to such a process-oriented documentation method. For example, some ideas might completely replace entire steps of our existing key business processes. These ideas could remain in a shortened version of the idea notebook or be shown on the concept fan as spanning or replacing sections of the flowchart.)

With the complete concept fan in hand, our next step would be to run through it picking up ideas from each concept to generate a potential creative design scenario for the clinic's key business process. (In chapter 5, we

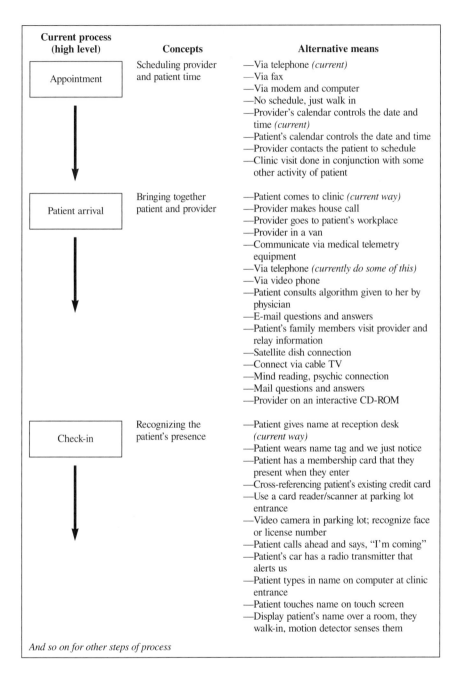

Current process (high level)	Concepts	Alternative means
Appointment	Scheduling provider and patient time	—Via telephone *(current)* —Via fax —Via modem and computer —No schedule, just walk in —Provider's calendar controls the date and time *(current)* —Patient's calendar controls the date and time —Provider contacts the patient to schedule —Clinic visit done in conjunction with some other activity of patient
Patient arrival	Bringing together patient and provider	—Patient comes to clinic *(current way)* —Provider makes house call —Provider goes to patient's workplace —Provider in a van —Communicate via medical telemetry equipment —Via telephone *(currently do some of this)* —Via video phone —Patient consults algorithm given to her by physician —E-mail questions and answers —Patient's family members visit provider and relay information —Satellite dish connection —Connect via cable TV —Mind reading, psychic connection —Mail questions and answers —Provider on an interactive CD-ROM
Check-in	Recognizing the patient's presence	—Patient gives name at reception desk *(current way)* —Patient wears name tag and we just notice —Patient has a membership card that they present when they enter —Cross-referencing patient's existing credit card —Use a card reader/scanner at parking lot entrance —Video camera in parking lot; recognize face or license number —Patient calls ahead and says, "I'm coming" —Patient's car has a radio transmitter that alerts us —Patient types in name on computer at clinic entrance —Patient touches name on touch screen —Display patient's name over a room, they walk-in, motion detector senses them

And so on for other steps of process

Figure 8.2. Beginnings of a concept fan for the key business process of patient intake.

discussed this morphological procedure under the mind map header, combining concepts systematically.) This could be done by the team that generated the concept fan or by a separate group.

One such creative clinic design scenario would be that heart patients are furnished telemetry equipment at home that measures vital signs and blood pressure. At appropriate intervals, the equipment signals the patient that it is time for a check-in. The patient connects herself to the equipment and pushes a button to upload new vital sign information to the clinic's medical record database. The clinic computer checks to see if the vital signs are within normal limits for that patient, as established by the physician. If so, the equipment tells the patient that all is well and automatically processes established billing information for the consultation. If the vital signs are outside limits, the computer is programmed to signal the patient to increase the dosage on her blood pressure medicine and then send an e-mail message for the physician to read the following morning. If the values are far outside limits, the computer could check the physician's schedule and give the patient a menu of available appointment times.

Another creative scenario would involve issuing magnetic-strip smart cards to all patients. When the patient arrives at the clinic, a valet swipes the smart card through a reader indicating arrival and then parks the patient's car. The patient enters the clinic lobby and finds his name on the TV screen indicating his exam room number. Motion detectors signal the physician when the patient enters the exam room.

When the physician enters the exam room, she swipes the patient's smart card through a reader, which instantly displays the patient's medical record on a screen. The physician conducts the exam. If new medications are indicated, the order is electronically transmitted to the clinic's pharmacy, which fills the order and delivers it to the car parking valets. When the visit is over, the physician again swipes the patient's smart card through the reader, initiating the billing process and signaling to the valet that the patient is on the way to pick up his car. The valet puts the medication bag in the car and pulls the car up. The patient exits through the lobby, presents the smart card to the valet to validate his identity, gets in the car, and drives away.

All of the technology described above is either currently available or well within reach in the next few years. Imagine how such a clinic would revolutionize our concept of what it means to go to the doctor's office.

We could go on to generate as many design scenarios as we wish. Notice how these purposeful runs through the concept fan accomplish a type of harvesting. When we run through the concept fan trying to construct creative yet plausible scenarios, we implicitly disregard ideas that do not fit together or are not feasible. These morphological runs have the desirable by-product of dramatically reducing the number of ideas that we have to consider in harvesting, enhancement, and evaluation.

Harvesting, enhancement, and evaluation. Harvesting in a process design project is done on the creative scenarios gleaned from the concept fan and the remaining ideas in the idea notebook. Again, the initial harvest should come about two-thirds of the way through the time allotted to the imagination phase so as to allow time for any additional idea generation sessions that may be needed. Majaro's screening matrix, with its criteria of attractiveness and compatibility, is a good tool to use here (see Figure 7.3).

It is now important to establish a powerful guiding coalition to spearhead the drive that will take our imaginative ideas on to action. To avoid a time lag and attendant loss of momentum, the four-member planning team should probably begin assembling the guiding coalition at about the time of the initial harvesting. Indeed, it would be good to have had this group actively involved from the beginning of the effort. The guiding coalition might participate in the initial harvesting as a way of getting familiar with process and the tone of the ideas being generated.

In addition to dealing with the questions on the enhancement checklist in Figure 7.4, the development groups also need to produce flowcharts and detailed plans for the new processes. This is standard process design or quality planning work. Again, as practitioners of quality management, we should be well equipped to contribute significantly to this work. (See, for example, the tools and methods outlined in Juran 1992.) Give the development groups access to the full concept fan and idea notebook. They may be able to enhance their process design scenarios by simply adapting previously generated ideas.

The guiding coalition and original planning team need to agree on a schedule that will allow adequate time for implementation. We will have a better feel for how much time will be needed after we see the magnitude and scope of the ideas coming out of the final harvesting.

An issue to watch for in the development phase in a process design project is the problem of process design gaps. All of our energies thus far have been focused on new, creative process ideas, but we need to recognize that we may very well be dealing only in pieces of a system. For example, while we may have wonderful ideas for innovations in patient intake in our new clinic, we did not generate any new ideas for the process of ordering supplies and stocking the patient exam rooms. These uncreative processes need to be designed as well, and they need to mesh seamlessly with the more innovative pieces of the system. This is not hard to deal with, once we recognize the process gaps, but it is easy to forget in all the excitement that comes with our focus on innovation.

The planning team might take responsibility for developing the less innovative processes in the system. Or they might commission specific teams to do this. Remembering to do this is the big challenge; how you do it doesn't much matter.

The guiding coalition's final evaluation will involve some decisions among options presented and approval of a final design plan. This approval should include funding for implementation and commitment to an implementation timeline.

Communications and implementation. Since the implementation of process innovations is, by nature, a disruption of internal operations, expect resistance. The change management and reengineering literature offers plenty of advice on these matters. I cited several references in chapter 7. I will not repeat all of that here. Besides, all of the advice in the world does not make it easy. The implementation of change is hard work.

One point that I do want to make with regard to communicating about innovations is that the challenges of implementing innovations in a product or service are different than those involved in implementing innovations in a process. Innovating in the realm of products and services most often involves selling the idea to senior managers and securing the resources to pull it off. The ability to present ideas and the ability to prepare a good business case are key skills. Innovating in the process realm most often requires convincing middle managers and frontline staff to accept changes in their work. The abilities to listen, communicate a vision, plan details, and reassure others are the key skills here.

Awareness of this distinction is crucial for success. Many talented idea champions become frustrated when they run into difficulties implementing process innovations that, after all, have been approved by senior leaders. Because they have not paid attention to the appropriate groups at lower levels in the organization, they find their creative ideas subverted and compromised. Similarly, product and service innovators can waste a great deal of effort building internal coalitions to support their creative ideas when the important decisions will be made based on the strength of the business case and the intuitions of the senior decision-makers involved.

Summary of the Application of Directed Creativity to Process Design and Reengineering Efforts

Process design and reengineering efforts are a natural application for the principles and methods of directed creativity. The tools of the preparation and imagination phases of the directed-creativity cycle help us get beyond mere exhortation to creativity. With these tools, it is relatively easy to generate many creative ideas for new ways of doing things.

While there are challenges inherent in creative process design, practitioners of quality management have key skills to offer. We have relevant experience in the management of change. We have the generic tools of process planning and project management. We also have a vested interest in seeing to it that processes are well designed and well implemented. Use the quick reference section at the end of this chapter to help add to your current skills some newly developed skills at directed creativity.

Quick Reference:
The Application of Directed Creativity to
Process Design and Reengineering

Key Principles to Keep in Mind

- Avoid the brainstorming assumption; if you expect creative ideas, provide specific tools to help generate them.

- True reengineering involves simultaneous redesign of processes, organizational structure and roles, and information systems.

- Be open to using the differences between reengineering and traditional quality management as creative provocations.

Preparation Phase

- Consider specific preparations for teamwork, leadership and project management, and skills in directed creativity.

- Reread the material in the various boxes scattered throughout chapter 5 and refer to the preparation tools mind map in Figure 5.2 for ideas about methods you might employ.

- Especially consider preparing the following items.

    Lists of assumptions, rules, and obvious things
    Expansive questions
    Analogies
    A purpose hierarchy for the process
    Word plays from the purpose hierarchy
    Lists of positive and negative attributes of the current process
    Fixed-point concepts for the process
    Circa dates for major process concepts

- Plan to spend roughly 20 percent of your total project time in the preparation phase.

Imagination Phase

- With so many potentials directions to go in, you will need a plan for idea generation sessions in the imagination phase.

- Provide training in directed-creativity theory and methods for all those involved.

- Involve lots of people, go for quantity of ideas, create in short bursts, develop team environments free from judgment, set a deadline on idea generation, and have an idea-capture system ready to go from the start.

- Consult the mind map in Figure 6.2 for tools to use in the imagination phase. Many of your choices will be natural follow-ups from materials developed in the preparation phase.

- Especially consider the following tools.
  Analogies
  Role playing
  Reversals, challenges, provocations, breaking the rules, and word plays
     based on preparation-phase materials
  Random nouns
  Videos, photographs, and other visualizations from the current process
  Concept fans
  Morphological combinations

- A concept fan is an essential creative tool in process design; think of it as a creative flowchart and consider using it as one of your main documentation tools.

- Plan an initial harvest about two-thirds of the way through the time allocated to the imagination phase.

- Plan to spend roughly 20 percent of your total project time in the imagination phase.

Development Phase

- Reread the material in the various boxes scattered throughout chapter 7.

- If you have not already done so, now is the time to assemble the guiding coalition that will see the creative ideas through to implementation.

- Use the enhancement checklist, the concept fan, idea notebooks, and the quality management tools of process design to work out the details of the harvested ideas.

- Watch out for process design gaps; the lack of integration among the pieces of the innovative design.

- Plan to spend roughly 20 percent of your total project time in the development phase.

Action Phase

- Reread the material in the various boxes scattered throughout chapter 7.

- Expect resistance to change; plan for it and deal with it directly.

- Communicate, communicate, communicate.

- Do not expect that implementation will go forward as planned simply because the guiding coalition has approved the new design. You must sell the ideas to the middle managers and frontline staff whose work lives are impacted by the change.

- Plan to spend roughly 40 percent of your total project time in the action phase. Even the best conceived implementation plan can run into unexpected snags.

CHAPTER 9

Creativity and
Customer Needs Analysis

It will not suffice to have customers that are merely satisfied. A satisfied customer may switch . . . It is necessary to innovate, to predict needs of the customer, give him more."

W. Edwards Deming

The concept of understanding and exceeding customers' needs is central to quality management. Quality is judged by the customer, using the criteria the customer chooses. Likewise, recalling that our definition of creativity included the phrase "that others judge to be useful," the customer is the ultimate judge of our creative ideas.

Companies spend millions of dollars each year to gather data about customers through market research, surveys, and focus groups. All of this marketplace research is aimed at answering two basic questions: How do you like what you get from us? and What more would you like from us?

Our understanding of the mechanics of mind tells us that the first question is answerable with reasonable accuracy. When a customer experiences our product, service, or process, he or she creates a mental valley that records the experience. The mind has the ability to encode both the facts and the feelings associated with that experience. When we ask customers, "How do you like what you get from us?" we are asking them to retrieve and play back a previously stored mental valley. This is a relatively straightforward request.

The second basic question of market research, "What more would you like from us?" requires a different set of mental gymnastics on the part of the customer. In essence, we are asking the customer to look at a familiar situation in a new way, notice something that is not there, and make mental associations that result in ideas about what could be added. We are asking the customer to be creative on our behalf! Further, we are once again falling into the brainstorming assumption. We assume that the customer has potentially innovative ideas for new products, services, and processes, we just need to call them forth. To be sure, sometimes this does work; sometimes customers do have creative ideas and are waiting to be asked. But should we rely on this to work all the time? Of course not.

The bottom line is this: Customers can rarely tell us exactly the new product, service, or process they need. Customer research does not, itself, reliably generate innovation (Ackoff 1995). On the other hand, if we pay attention . . . escape . . . and move . . . we can use customer input to feed the engine of innovation. That is the point of this chapter.

The discussion of tools here will not be organized around the phases of the directed-creativity cycle. In contrast to problem solving and the design of products, services, and processes, customer needs analysis is most often an integral part of some other effort, not a stand-alone effort itself. For example, we might conduct customer needs analysis as a part of the preparation phase of a project to generate innovative service ideas. Or we might perform customer needs analysis to help us in the evaluation step of a creative problem-solving project. Therefore, my emphasis here will be more on individual tools that you can plug in as needed in your creative endeavors.

The Evolution of the Understanding of Customer Needs in Quality Management

Successful businesspeople have always understood the importance of pleasing the customer. In the days of quality control by inspection, where quality was defined as conformance to specifications, the author of the specification had an implicit sense of the needs of the ultimate customer. The main feedback loop from the customers was sales figures in a competitive marketplace. Unfortunately, the implicitness and long, noisy feedback loops of this system destined it to drift further away from a real understanding of customer needs. "Tell them they can have it in any color they want, as long as it is black" is the classic joke about the arrogance of companies toward their customers that this system bred.

In the mid-1940s, quality expert Joseph Juran (1964) defined quality as "fitness for use" as judged by the customer. It seems trivial to us now, but Juran's notion of fitness for use was a radical, foreign concept to the legions of quality control inspectors who just wanted to know if the part they had selected off the assembly line measured 1.63 mm ± 0.20 mm. In the 1970s, quality expert Philip Crosby (1979) combined Juran's idea of explicitly including customer needs in the definition of quality with the more traditional view when he defined quality as "conformance to customer requirements." Crosby disseminated this thinking widely through his popular writing and his "Quality College." Crosby can be credited with reaching masses of managers and leaders in business with the notion that, in understanding quality, it is important to know explicitly what the customer wants.

David Garvin (1988) made what I think was the next major evolutionary step toward improving customer needs analysis in quality management with his "dimensions of quality." Garvin researched competitive success and customer judgments of quality in several industries and noted that quality was a multidimensional concept. Products and services could be understood as excelling in certain dimensions of quality—for example, performance, features, reliability, or aesthetics.

The key insight Garvin contributed was that it is possible to compete successfully in the marketplace by focusing on only some dimensions of quality: those that are most important to your customers. Garvin illustrated this marketplace dynamic by reflecting on the revolutionary changes in the automobile industry brought about by the Japanese in the 1970s. At that time, American automobiles excelled in performance (in terms of things like acceleration), features, and durability. The new Japanese imports, however, excelled in another aspect of performance (fuel economy), conformance (great paint jobs and fit-and-finish), and reliability. Both countries produced high-quality cars, but for a variety of reasons customers of that time were more attracted to the dimensions of quality in the Japanese vehicles.

Astute readers will immediately see the creative power inherent in Garvin's concept of the multidimensional nature of quality. The dimensions of quality provide mental attention valleys for us to work with. We can use the dimensions to help us better pause and notice customer behaviors and needs. We can also use the dimensions as fixed points from which to generate creative alternatives.

The final relevant development in our understanding of customers' needs is Noriaki Kano's (1984) model of customer perceptions. Kano points out that the characteristics of a product or service can fall into one of three categories, based on customer judgments about quality.

- *Must Be.* These are characteristics that customers take for granted; they expect them to be there and only notice them when they are missing. For example, when you buy a new computer, you expect it to come with a power cord and to work when you turn it on for the first time. It is unlikely that you would mention these things as requirements to the computer salesperson, but you would certainly be back in the store quickly if you did not get them. Kano sometimes refers to this as "take-it-for-granted quality."

- *More Is Better.* These are characteristics that bring increased customer satisfaction as we provide more. In a computer, processor clock speed, RAM size, hard disk size, and friendliness of service are examples of more-is-better characteristics.

- *Surprising Quality.* These are characteristics that customers do not expect, but that delight the customers when they experience them. Kano and others also refer to these as "attractive quality" and "delighters." For example, customers were delighted when, a few years ago, computer manufacturers began bundling useful software with their machines. The customers did not expect the computer to come with software; that was something that they expected to buy separately. (Of course, yesterday's surprising quality can become today's take-it-for-granted quality; witness bundled software.)

Implicit in Kano's model is the insight that in order to satisfy our customers, we need continuous quality control (of must-be quality), continuous quality improvement (of more-is-better quality), and continuous innovation (for surprising quality).

Like Garvin's dimensions of quality, Kano's model also gives us some direction for creativity. We can challenge the assumptions around must-be quality. We can look for innovative ways to give more-is-better, and we can purposefully set out to find surprising quality.

The understanding of customers' needs is a broad topic in quality management. I have left out and glossed over large expanses of the subject. I have also not mentioned parallel developments in the field of market research. Comprehensiveness was not my intention, rather, I want to set up the minds of quality practitioners to take a fresh, creative look at the concept of understanding customers' needs. We can do this without abandoning our past and current methods. We just need to take a creative pause and then make some novel connections among what we already know.

Some Directed Creativity Tools for Customer Needs Analysis

The coming together of directed creativity and the quality management notions of customer needs analysis is a natural. Models from the field of quality management give us creative attention points. Directed creativity adds the notion of escape and movement from these points.

The eight tools that follow in the next subsections are, again, not intended as an all-encompassing catalogue. My goal will be to demonstrate how we might think about the topic. I invite you to invent your own methods.

Let me briefly set up two concrete situations that I will use as running examples throughout this chapter. Sharon Bower is a quality manager for Apex Cameras. Apex is small manufacturer of amateur photography equipment: camera bodies, lenses, and related accessories. The company does okay in the competitive marketplace, but would really like to break away from the pack with an innovative product concept that will attract customers. The company's vice president of marketing has asked Sharon to work with her in doing some up-front customer needs analysis to feed to the research and development department.

Tim Johnson is a quality management specialist in the corporate catering division of BSB Foods. The corporate catering division of this large food vendor provides contract food service and cafeteria management in large office buildings. The recent trend in outsourcing has been a big boon for this division of BSB Foods, but it has also brought forth a host of competitors. Tim's boss asked him to compile customer intelligence that might help the organization pinpoint problems and redesign services as needed.

Sharon and Tim's challenges are typical entry points for practitioners of quality management. Because we are seen as customer advocates and have access to relevant data, quality managers are often asked to contribute their views on the needs of the customers. Often implicit in these requests is the notion that better analysis will yield better insight. But I am suggesting that in addition to the analytical skills that we traditionally bring to this challenge, we can also apply what we now know about directed creativity. While those who initially requested our involvement might have done so for our analytical skills, in the end, what they want is innovative new ideas and solutions to problems.

Who is the customer? Let us start simply. Ever since Ishikawa (1985) expanded our notion of what is meant by the term *customer,* we have been escaping the traditional notion that the customer is only the person who ultimately uses our product and service, or who pays for it. A natural first step, therefore, is to pay attention to who we are defining as a customer.

For example, Sharon Bower could use the looking-closer-and-analyzing tools from the preparation phase mind map to make an expansive list of customers for amateur photography equipment. In other words, she might purposefully escape the obvious and think beyond the person who purchased the camera or who is taking the pictures. Here is a partial list of other customers that I compiled quickly.

- Friends of photographers
- Children and grandchildren of people who take pictures
- People who think they can't take good pictures
- Film developers

We now have a few new, creative attention points to work with. We can select a few of these nontraditional customers and ask, "What are their needs and desires?" For example, consider children and grandchildren of amateur photographers. For one thing, children would like to be involved in their parents' or grandparents' vacation or trip. (We could learn more from a focus group or other research method.) Having focused some attention on this need, let's now take it and practice creative escape and movement. Here are some potential new product ideas . . .

- I have noticed that my children love stickers. How about a disposable camera that comes with a set of stickers indicating the types of pictures that the children want to see. Stickers might include animals, flowers, people you meet, fire engines, and so forth. The kids can peel off the stickers and place them on spaces on the camera before their parents or grandparents leave. The parent or grandparent is thereby sensitized to the wants of the child and will probably go well out of their way to collect the appropriate pictures to bring back.

- Building on this idea, how about a sophisticated electronic camera that could store a list of requests from the children and automatically print the category on the photograph using the same technology that is currently used to print the date on pictures. Imagine the children's delight at being able to sort the photographs into the categories that they asked for. In the enhancement step of the directed-creativity cycle, we might want to explore a partnership with a video game maker to develop an electronic interface to the camera that enables the children to enter the category requests into the camera themselves.

- That last bit of mental movement put me in the electronic interface mental valley. How about a new digital camera that has a self-contained modem? Dad or grandmother takes pictures all day during their trip. The camera stores the images digitally (cameras that do this already exist). At night, hook the camera to a telephone line and press a button. The camera automatically logs you onto the Internet and transmits the pictures to the children's e-mail account. When they get up the next morning, the kids rush to the computer to see the latest photographs.

- Looking back at the customers list, I now notice film developers. Expanding on the camera-with-modem idea, we could set up the camera to automatically also transmits the digital images to a local film developer who prints the photos in the traditional way. This would be nice for people who do not have computers to download the pictures. This service could be modeled on the highly successful network that allows you to order flowers from anywhere in the world to be delivered by a local florist.

I spent some time on this example to illustrate what directed creativity adds beyond the traditional practice of customer-needs analysis in quality management. We already know how to make lists of customers beyond the obvious customer. We already know how to imagine or get data on these customers' needs. Directed creativity adds the notion of going just a little further out in casting our nets for customers and their needs. Further, if we have been practicing active pausing and noticing, we will have many things stored away in our minds to connect with these needs. Finally, directed creativity screams *mental movement* in response to customer needs. These ideas are the products of continuing free association. If we can avoid bringing our old mental valleys with us when we look at customers' needs, we can use information about those needs as creative attention points to develop a limitless number of surprising quality ideas.

How could we use it? Juran's (1964) fitness for use definition of quality provides us with another creative attention point. Typically, we consider *use* to be a fixed point. Our quality improvement efforts usually involve trying to move our product or service closer to the customers' use-need. A creative customer-needs analysis approach would be to consider the product or service already fit for a use (a creative reversal); we just have not yet clearly identified that use. We will take our product or service, or a piece of it, and go exploring in our customers' world for uses.

For example, consider the company cafeterias that Tim Johnson's organization, BSB Foods, operates. Tim takes out a pad of paper and walks through the cafeteria noticing what is there. Let's see . . . tables, chairs, long counters and rails that people can slide their food trays on, a computer-terminal cash register, dishwasher, and so forth. With these things in mind, Tim now goes on a search for uses in the customers' world. A walk-through of the offices of the corporation that owns the building shows groups of people meeting in cramped offices. Idea: They could meet in the cafeteria! Of course, some people already do this, so this is not so novel an idea. Why don't more people use the cafeteria space? Suppose we wired the cafeteria tables for computer network hook-ups and offered computers on rolling carts that people could reserve for meetings. We could also rent out portable electronic white boards and easel pads.

Walking on further, Tim notices a group of clerks putting together packets of materials to be mailed out. They have several stacks on various desks and filing cabinets. The clerks are walking around (and bumping into each other) to get a sheet from each stack to stuff in the envelopes. They could use the cafeteria's counter space for this. We could even lease our cafeteria employees to do this task at off-hours. Now that we think about it, our computer-terminal cash registers go unused most of the day. We could reconfigure these and tie into the company's information system so that we could lease out our cashiers' time to do typing and accounting tasks during slow periods.

With a little exploration, we could find lots of uses. Even if we do not generate new revenues from these ideas, we could use them to build customer loyalty. Our new marketing slogan could be: "We go beyond the call of duty to serve you!" or "When was the last time your food services vendor offered to roll up its sleeves and help you out?"

Tim could do this exploring alone or with a group. He could make it a special project or a routine creative-noticing exercise. Another way would be to reverse the situation and invite customers to come and explore the cafeteria looking for things that they could use to help them in their work.

Search for underlying concepts and customer needs drivers. A basic principle in market research and customer needs analysis involves looking underneath what customers say to identify their real needs. In directed-creativity terms, this involves searching for fixed concepts that can be used to generate alternatives.

For example, one of the top 10 complaints in BSB Foods' cafeterias is, "It takes too long to make it through the line." A traditional approach would be to try to speed up the line by identifying and removing bottlenecks in the system. In this context, we are treating speed of getting through the line as what Kano would call a more-is-better characteristic. Let's look underneath the complaint by asking, "Why do customers care about this?" Resist the urge for premature judgment; in other words, resist the urge to give the obvious answer or to dismiss the question. "No, really, why do they want to get through the line faster?" We could generate several answers from the customers' point of view and use these as fixed points for creative alternatives. For example,

Underlying Need	*Creative Alternatives*
"I'm busy and need to get back to work quickly."	■ Room service like a hotel. For a service charge, we deliver your order, off a limited menu, directly to your office.
"I have errands to run."	■ A concierge service; we do errands for you.
	■ Install telephones at cafeteria tables so people can make local calls while they eat.
"I want to get seated so I can talk with my friend."	■ Install a special line for parties of two that want to talk. The ground rule here is that people want to be next to their friend in line. So it is socially acceptable to cut in this line.

This notion of looking underneath applies to traditional customer-needs analysis focus groups as well as to complaint analysis. For example, let's join Sharon Bower in a focus group of people who use photographic equipment. At the surface level of the conversation in the focus group, we hear the customers offering improvement ideas about cameras. The results of such traditional customer needs analysis provides us with incrementally better cameras, but probably not a lot of innovation.

On the other hand, if we listen to the conversation with the goal of underlying concept extraction in mind, we can hear something different. What underlying concepts are these customers talking about when they talk about a camera? One such concept might be: record a memory. When you pay attention to what they are saying, this is what they really want to do.

Extracting this concept as part of customer needs analysis is good preparation in a directed-creativity cycle for new product development. So let's escape the current paradigm and move in our thinking to develop innovative alternatives. What is a memory? In the context of a focus group of photographers, a memory is a picture. Escaping this notion momentarily, we might note that sounds, smells, and feelings can also be memories. What if we developed a camera that took a picture and also recorded a 10-second sound bite from the situation onto the picture? (I have noticed that the technology for this exists. I recently bought a greeting card with a prerecorded message stored on a tiny chip embedded in the card.) A small, instant-developing camera that records a memory in this way might be a surprising innovation to a camera buff!

Dimensions of quality analysis. Garvin's (1988) notion that quality is multidimensional has powerful creative possibilities. We might choose to think in a dimension that has historically been ignored, or we might use the dimensions as fixed concepts for the generation of alternatives.

As a starting point, this table lists various dimensions of quality. (See, for example, Garvin 1988; Plsek 1987; Zeithaml et al. 1990; and Usrey and Dooley 1996.)

accessibility	aesthetics	appropriateness
assurance	conformance	continuity
durability	effectiveness	efficacy
efficiency	empathy	features
freshness	performance	personal perspectives
reliability	reputation	responsiveness
safety	serviceability	timeliness

In creative customer needs analysis, we can separate the dimensions into those that are well-developed in our context and those that are less-developed. For example, in Sharon Bower's camera industry, the concepts of features, reliability, and aesthetics are relatively well-developed. We are comfortable using these terms in the context of talking about cameras.

On the other hand, what do words like *responsiveness, empathy,* and *continuity* mean in relationship to a camera? What would a camera have to be for a customer to say that the camera was empathetic? Here is an idea: Combine a camera with the old mood rings that changed colors according to the mood of the person wearing the ring. Sensors on the camera body detect the mood of the person taking the picture and transmit this information in some way to the photograph; maybe in the form of an icon, printed word on the photograph, or a color tint. This is just the seed of an idea, but it could be further developed into something that might delight customers. We could generate similar novel, customer-oriented ideas by exploring other dimensions on the list.

If applying a specific dimension in this way to your product, service, process, or problem feels a bit goofy, you should get excited. As we noted in heuristic 6, laughter is probably a signal of a novel mental connection. It is likely that no one in your industry has ever given that particular dimension serious thought before. Pepsi's recent introduction of freshness dating on soft drink cans is an example of innovation through application of an previously unexplored dimension of quality.

Even the dimensions that are fairly well-developed in a particular context have creative potential as fixed points. For example, efficiency is a well-developed concept in Tim Johnson's corporate cafeterias. When customers talk about an efficient cafeteria, they mean one where they can find things easily and get through quickly. There are many things we might do to provide a more-is-better type of efficiency.

On the other hand, suppose we convened a focus group of customers to explore the topic of efficiency. We could say, "Tell me about an experience you have had recently with any type of business where you feel that the word *efficiency* was a good description of what you liked about it." The response to this question would give us customer-suggested analogies that we could explore later. Or we could ask, "What are some synonyms for efficiency?" Alternatively, we could take synonyms for efficiency from a thesaurus, introduce these in a customer focus group, and ask for ideas for new services that we could offer.

By exploring several such dimensions in this way, we could develop a customer-oriented concept fan in which the various dimensions of quality are fixed points with creative alternatives fanning out from them. As with the process-oriented concept fan that we discussed in the last chapter, we could then make several morphological runs through the fan to develop innovative scenarios.

Escape from must-be quality. The discussion so far primarily has involved looking for surprising quality ideas or creative approaches to more-is-better quality from Kano's model. If you are developing the creative characteristic of mental flexibility, you should have had an immediate reaction to Kano's term *must be*. In directed creativity, we realize that where the imagination is concerned, there is nothing in the business world that must be. We should experiment, therefore, with various provocations around these so-called must-be, or take-it-for-granted, characteristics of quality.

It is easy to identify these must-be items through traditional customer research. We can ask customers directly, "What are some things that you expect from us that you would assume are taken for granted?" A focus group or survey of corporate food services user might compile the following list: do not make me sick, give me clean dishes, I shouldn't be overcharged, and so forth. These could then be used as input to an idea generation session aimed at elevating these must-be characteristics to more-is-better or surprising quality status.

To illustrate, the provocation, "Po, make me sick" might lead to the creative idea of offering meals-on-wheels food service to employees who are at home sick . . . or to employees' children who are at home sick . . . or to employees' elderly loved ones who are shut in. We could charge for this service as it is used . . . approach the corporation's benefits manager about making it a fringe benefit . . . or offer it on a fee-for-service basis exclusively to members of our frequent lunchers club (people who are loyal to the company cafeteria instead of going out for lunch). In this way, we are elevating a take-it-for-granted quality characteristic (safety and basic performance) and using it for surprising quality.

Teach customers to search for surprising quality. We have noted that the traditional approach of asking customers directly for new product ideas suffers from the brainstorming assumption. It is exhortation unless we accompany the request with something that answers the question, "How do I go about getting a creative idea?" So if your company sponsors ongoing customer panels or user groups, teach directed creativity to these groups. They will then be better equipped to suggest new ideas, and you will be better able to tap into their unique mental valleys and judgment processes. A related idea would be to do some just-in-time training in directed creativity in a focus group meeting of customers. As we have seen throughout this book, directed creativity is not hard, people just need to be shown how to do it.

Multimodal thinking in customer needs analysis. As we have seen in other applications, de Bono's Six Thinking Hats provide general guidance in any thinking task. We might structure a customer needs analysis focus group or telephone survey around the different modes of thinking represented by the hats. For example, we might ask participants to list every positive thing they can think of when they think of our product, service, or process (or those of our competitors or the topic in general). We could do a similar exercise with the hypothetical purple hat calling for negatives and the red hat calling for feelings. As before, these lists can serve as input for challenge and reversal provocations in a subsequent idea generation session. The twist is that we have had the customers generate these preparation phase materials directly.

Another way to involve customers using the six hats in the directed-creativity cycle would be to convene a focus group of customers to help with the harvesting and evaluation activities of the development phase. Take ideas generated in idea generation sessions directly to a group of customers and ask for positives, negatives, feelings, and enhancements. This is certainly better than our use of implicit knowledge of customer needs in evaluating the ideas.

Bring prototypes and scenarios into customer needs analysis. A final approach that I want to present in this chapter picks up on the notion that it is difficult for a customer to imagine what he or she might do or feel in experiencing a creative idea. Because of the mental mechanics of valleys in memory and the subsystems of judgment, it is much easier to answer the question, "What do you think about what you have experienced?" than the question, "What new things would you like?"

So in addition to asking customers in focus groups the open-ended question, "What more would you like from us?" also bring in some prototypes and detailed scenarios and ask the more closed question, "What do you think about this?" Alternatively, bring in a prototype and simply watch what the customers do with it. This is a popular concept in Japan, where many companies have consumer testing laboratories in which average customers get to play with and evaluate models of new products from the research and development arm of the company.

A pitfall to avoid in using this approach is taking the customers' feedback too literally. Even if the customer rejects the proposed innovation, it may still represent a promising concept. They may be simply rejecting the alternative you have chosen from the fixed point. The multimode thinking of the six hats again provides a helpful framework. Ask customers to detail positive, negative, and feeling points after their experience of a prototype or detailed scenario (yellow-, purple-, and red-hat thinking, respectively). Then explicitly identify the underlying, fixed-point concept behind the idea and repeat the feedback. Do this both for accepted innovations and rejected innovations. Always present multiple ideas to aid the comparison and leave open the possibility that the final implemented innovation may be a collage of the best features from previously independent ideas.

Summary of Creativity in Customer Needs Analysis

These are but eight ways to be more creative in customer needs analysis. I hope that I have piqued your interest and encouraged you to experiment a bit in your next customer needs analysis assignment. The basic idea behind all of these methods involves casting a wide net when thinking of customers, finding something to pay attention to, escaping the usual way of thinking, and continual mental movement. The quick reference section at the end of this chapter captures the key points to keep in mind the next time you conduct a customer needs analysis as part of a design or problem-solving quality effort.

Before leaving this topic, I think that it is important to address a crucial question: Can the techniques of creative customer needs analysis presented in this chapter overcome the attackers advantage, and the trap of listening too well to your customers, as cited in the innovation literature (Foster 1986; Bower and Christensen 1995)? Recall from chapter 1 that there are many documented cases of successful organizations losing their competitive positions to upstart innovators precisely because they paid too much attention to the results of traditional financial and customer needs analyses. Would the outcomes have been different had they used some of the methods described in this chapter? I think so, but there is no guarantee.

I think so because I know the intent of the various tools I have developed for inclusion in this chapter. For example, the who-is-the-customer tool and dimensions of quality analysis directly provoke us to think broadly, listen to customers that we do not normally think of as customers, and explore under-emphasized aspects of generic customer needs. If Seagate Technologies had spoken seriously with nontraditional customers like Compaq Computers and had participated actively in showing customers prototype systems built around small disk drives, it may have increased it revenue projections for 3.5-inch drives significantly and avoided losing its marketplace position.

These methods cannot offer guarantees against the attackers advantage and other pitfalls because, by nature, creative thinking offers no definitive answers. We cannot hope to explore all of the creative possibilities that might exist, and so, we will always be open to the possibility of having missed something. Paradoxically, this reality of endless possibilities is both the joy and pitfall of innovation. Further, the concept that it is enough simply to explore the world beyond a provocation contains in it the possibility that, having explored the possibilities, we will incorrectly decide to return to the status quo.

In the end, it is down to the mental judgment processes of intuition, risk-aversion, and courage. No matter what tools we use or how hard we try, we could always be wrong. The tools of creative customer needs analysis that I have presented in this chapter greatly improve our odds of successful innovation, but no methods can guarantee it.

Quick Reference:
The Application of Directed Creativity
in Customer Needs Analysis

Key Principles to Keep in Mind

- Asking customers to tell us what innovative products and services they want from us is probably asking too much. It is the brainstorming assumption again.

- Creative customer needs analysis is often an adjunct to other design or problem-solving efforts.

- Evolution in quality management has led us to the concepts that customers are the ultimate judges of quality; there are multiple customers; quality is a multi-dimensional concept; and customer judgments about quality can fall into the three categories of must-be, more-is-better, and surprising quality.

- When customer needs analysis provides a new attention focus, our creative instincts must be to escape and move.

Some Useful Approaches

- *Who Is the Customer?* Make a list of nonobvious customers or people who could be beneficiaries of the product, service, or process in question. Then ask, What are the desires of these people? Use the extracted concepts as fixed points for alternatives.

- *How Could We Use It?* Take parts of existing products, services, and process and go on a deliberate hunt for a customer need that they might fulfill. The goal is to surprise the customer with a new use for a familiar item.

- *Search for Underlying Concepts and Customer Needs Drivers.* Take a complaint, customer comment, or customer behavior and ask, "Why do customers care about this?" Resist the urge to give the obvious answer or to dismiss the question. The goal is to identify purpose concepts that can be used as fixed points for alternatives.

- *Dimensions of Quality Analysis.* Separate the dimensions of quality into those that are well-developed in your context and those that are not. Explore with customers ways to deliver on the poorly developed dimensions and different ways from the current approach to deliver on the well-developed dimensions. Construct a customer-oriented concept fan using the dimensions as fixed points.

- *Escape from Must-Be Quality.* Identify must-be or take-it-for-granted quality characteristics through traditional customer research methods. Use these to create escape and reversal provocations. Look to turn must-be quality characteristics into more-is-better and surprising quality ideas.

- *Teach Customers to Search for Surprising Quality.* Teach directed creativity to customers and let them use their unique mental valleys to generate creative ideas for you.

- *Multimodal Thinking.* Use de Bono's Six Thinking Hats as a framework to ask customers to generate lists of positives, negatives, feelings, and creative ideas. Use these to create provocations for future idea generation sessions.

- *Bring Prototypes and Scenarios into Customer Needs Analysis.* Remember that it is difficult for a customer to imagine what he or she will do or feel in experiencing a creative idea. Make the idea more concrete with a prototype or detailed scenario and analyze customers' reactions. Debrief the customers' experiences of both the specific idea and the concept behind it using the six thinking hats framework.

- Experiment with your own methods for creative customer needs analysis.

CHAPTER 10

Innovative Product and Service Design

We're never going to out-discipline the Japanese on quality. To win, we need to find ways to capture the creative spirit of the American worker. That's the real organizational challenge.

Paul Allaire, CEO, Xerox

Everything that can be invented has been invented.

Charles Duell, Director U.S. Patent Office, 1899

The most common application of the tools of directed creativity is in the design of new products and services for the competitive marketplace. In the end, this is where the money is. A good, innovative new product or service can generate millions of dollars of revenue for the company that creates it.

We have already seen many examples of new product and service designs. The SJ&D accounting firm is planning to offer an innovative service that involves partnerships with universities around the country. Sharon Bower's company, Apex Cameras, has several innovative camera designs that allow children to share the experience of their parents' and grandparents' travels. BSB Foods is poised to revolutionize the outsourced food services industry by offering to roll up its sleeves and pitch in to help its customers with various clerical tasks during slow hours for cafeteria workers. These are just a few of the many ideas that we have generated.

We also know that product and service design will involve a complete trip around the directed-creativity cycle. While there are certainly anecdotal reports of on-the-spot generation of great new product and service concepts, the vast majority of such ideas come from hard work over an extended period of time (Sternberg and Lubart 1995). To be successful, we must be purposeful in our preparation, imagination, development, and action.

A New Role for Quality Management in Design

The role of quality management practitioners in design efforts varies greatly from organization to organization. Sadly, many organizations today still see quality management as primarily an operational challenge. After the design is done, we must find a way to manage the quality of the production or implementation of that design. In these organizations, design is seen as the purview of the R&D, design, or marketing departments.

In other organizations, design is still seen as mainly the job of these special departments, but quality management is integrated into the fabric of the design process. In these organizations, quality managers are involved in design efforts, but not focused necessarily on the content of the design. For example, quality managers will remind design teams about the need to develop customer-based design requirements, to involve manufacturing and operational people on design teams and in design reviews, to interact early and in a partnering spirit with suppliers, and so on. QFD and various quality planning and statistical methods are specific tools to support these efforts. (See, for example, Juran and Gryna 1980; Juran 1992; Eureka and Ryan 1988; King 1987; and Plsek 1993b.)

I believe it is safe to say that in most organizations practitioners of quality management are not routinely looked upon to contribute to the creative aspect of design. I am boldly suggesting here that we now take on this new role, in addition to the role we may already be playing on the analytical side. We have a vested interest in facilitating innovations because our customers want them and our competitors are poised to provide them. We also have good skills in teaching and facilitating others. We may lack the depth of specific subject matter knowledge that others in the R&D, design, or marketing departments possess, but creativity is more about connecting mental valleys than digging them deeper. While deep subject matter knowledge is essential in the development phase of the directed-creativity cycle, modest levels of knowledge are all that we need in the preparation and imagination phases. The tools of directed creativity give us something new to contribute.

Using Directed Creativity in the Design of New Products and Services

As noted earlier, innovative design involves purposeful activities in all four phases of the directed-creativity cycle. Building on the concepts and examples that we have already explored in previous chapters, the following subsections describe tools and methods that we can employ at each phase of the cycle. In contrast to previous chapters, I will simply leave it to you to generate your own examples of creative design in areas of interest to you and your organization.

Preparation phase. The tools of the preparation phase are outlined on the mind map in Figure 5.2. Recall that during the preparation phase, our goals are to pay attention, pause, notice, extract meaning, and store up mental valleys for later use. Anything you do that engages these mental activities will help you prepare for making a positive contribution in design efforts. We can perform these mental activities in general or with specific product and service design tasks in mind.

One of the most productive things that you can do to prepare for creative design is to maintain a notebook (or computer file or voice recording) of things that you have noticed and briefly analyzed. The process of recording thoughts in a notebook not only preserves the thoughts in tangible form, but also deepens the mental valleys associated with the thoughts. This makes it easier to recall the past observation even without the notebook. Many people report that they have experienced this phenomenon in the mundane context of making a grocery list. Have you ever noticed that it is easier to remember what you need from the grocery store if you take the time to make a list? Even if you leave the list at home, the items come back to you; often in the exact order that you wrote them down. The explanation for this phenomenon is that writing down the list engages more senses than simply repeating the list to yourself in your mind. The additional sensory input coming through the perception subprocesses in our mind enriches the mental valley established by the memory subprocesses and thereby makes the items easier to recall.

A review of the preparation mind map in Figure 5.2 reveals several types of observations that we could include in a design-aid noticings notebook. To remind yourself to engage in pausing and noticing richly, consider designating separate sections of your notebook for

- Things I have noticed
- Concepts extracted from conversations
- Concepts extracted from reading
- Obvious things about our current products and services
- Assumptions underlying our current products and services
- Analogies that have occurred to me

Keep in mind that these headings are more for the purpose of reminding you where to look, than for strictly categorizing your observations. If you notice something, write it down; it does not matter which category you place it in.

Set a goal of recording an observation or two every day. After a while, pausing and noticing will become second nature to you and you will find yourself recording ideas frequently. With time, you will find that you no longer need the headers to remind you where to look; if so, simply drop them.

While most people prefer to keep their own individual notebook of observations, there are some benefits to maintaining a collective notebook to which many people contribute. Reading someone else's observations can be very stimulating to your own powers of both observation and imagination. The group effort might help some people develop the habit of doing it. The group effort also signals that in your organization, design is everyone's job; a team responsibility. This can go a long way in combating the counterproductive secrecy and competitiveness that often accompany design efforts. Of course, all of these benefits need to be weighed against the effort required to maintain such a database in a consistent format. I would suggest that you begin with individual notebooks to develop the habit and then evolve to a collective notebook over time if many people support it.

These activities comprise continuous preparation; we will notice anything and everything, we have no specific design needs in mind. In addition to this undirected preparation, we should also engage in some specific preparation for the design project at hand. Again, the preparation tools mind map of Figure 5.2 gives us several possibilities. Once we know the topic for our design effort, we can engage in purposeful noticing, conversation, and reading. Our new observations can be recorded in the notebook along with our undirected thoughts.

The pitfall to watch for here is that of overanalysis. As you notice, converse, and read in the specific topic area, remember that you are not searching for an answer or trying to figure out what is right or wrong. Instead, the goal is simply to enrich and store up mental valleys. If mental movement causes an idea to pop into your head at this point, certainly capture that idea. If you set out to generate an idea immediately from your noticing, you are more likely only to find a strong pull back into the mental valley of the status quo. It may become increasing difficult for you to participate constructively in imaginative design.

The preparation tools mind map in Figure 5.2 also suggests several other items that we can prepare with our specific design topic in mind. For instance, make a list of potential role plays. What would a computer look like if it were designed by a child? a horse? an auto mechanic? a stay-at-home parent? a person living in the frozen land of Antarctica? Remember, the goal here in the preparation phase is simply to write down expansive questions. You do not need to answer them or even wonder if you can answer them.

Similarly, you might make a list of assumptions inherent in the current product or service: obvious things; positive attributes; negative attributes; feelings; information sources; direct analogies; or responses to who, what, when, where, why, and how questions. An FCB grid, or other such pattern search tool, might also be helpful. (For a review of these methods, see chapter 5.) In all of this preparation phase work, remember that there is no right or wrong. The only goal is the identification and storing up of mental valleys for later use in the imagination phase.

In keeping with the focus-on-broad-topics heuristic, it is always a good idea to construct a purpose hierarchy for your design topic. Write down the original topic and just keep asking why or how come. For example, "Why the service of training?" Because people need to learn how to do their jobs better . . . because the organization needs improved performance . . . because people want advancement . . . and so on. Later, each of these statements can serve to trigger creative thoughts about innovative new training services.

If one of the underlying goals of the innovative design is to position the organization better for the future, consider developing scenarios and idealized situations. For example, we might develop a scenario describing the corporation of the future as a backdrop for an idea generation session about the innovative training services we might offer.

Finally, don't forget to commission an effort to do some creative customer needs analysis to support the design work. Review the previous chapter for specific techniques for doing this.

Spend at least a few weeks in focused preparation around the specific design topic that you are working on. Prepare as many lists, analogies, scenarios, and so forth as you can in that time. If necessary, extend the time to include some specific customer needs analysis activities or research associated with analogies. When you have all of your materials collected, or at least know what materials you will have eventually, review them all and plan how you will use them for idea generation.

As with process design and reengineering efforts, there are many possible ways to go as you make plans for next steps. You might have a single design team that is charged with doing all of the idea generation. The people in this group might generate ideas individually, collectively, or both. In addition to this single design team, or instead of it, you might convene multiple-idea generation groups. Ideas could be generated via bulletin boards, e-mail, table tents in the cafeteria—wherever and however you want. Remember, the more people you involve, the more mental valleys there are for creative connection. The only limit will be the organization's ability to capture and process all of the ideas.

Imagination phase. The imagination tools mind map in Figure 6.2 reminds us about the many different tools that we can bring to the task of idea generation. In the imagination phase, we want to escape current thinking and premature judgment, move flexibly, explore mental valleys, and make novel connections. Anything that helps you do these things will help you imagine innovative product and service design concepts.

All of the tools cited on the imagination tools mind map are potentially useful for product and service design. I realize that I am not giving you much direction by this statement, but the simple fact is that it is true. Since product and service design are such common contexts for creative thinking, nearly every tool in the creative-thinking literature was designed with this application in mind.

Because there are so many different way to proceed, and no way to know which is the best or right way, you should use as many approaches as you can. It should not be hard to generate literally hundreds of ideas.

Plan to spend four to six weeks in the imagination phase. About two-thirds of the way through (three to four weeks) conduct an initial harvesting.

There are two classifications of the ideas that you might want to make in this initial harvesting. First, every idea should be rated as ready to use (RTU), seedling (SEED), useful directions (UD), or not ready (NR). You will want to design specific idea generation sessions around the SEED and UD items. (This was described fully in chapter 6.)

Another classification cut that is useful to consider when working with product and service design issues involves the scope of the idea. Is the idea a radically different product or service concept when compared to what we have now? Or, is it a creative idea that modifies a part of the existing product or service, without changing the fundamental concept? For example, in the area of computers, a cheap, Internet-access-only computer is a radical new concept because it redefines the multifunctionality that we have come to expect from computers. A computer that responds to voice commands is a creative modification of a part, the input device, without changing the fundamental concept of what a computer is and does. I will use the labels WHOLE and PART to distinguish between the two categories.

The distinction between these two categories is not always sharp and clear. You will have to use some judgment. If after much effort you cannot decide, mark it as both categories. (I just love creative thinking's permission to escape the tyranny of I-am-right-you-are-wrong thinking.)

Both categories of ideas are valuable. We will want to have some of each to bring into the development phase. The WHOLE ideas may, by nature, be more long-term. We may need to do some basic research and development on them. The radical nature of the idea may make it difficult to market test. We may have to work hard to gain customer acceptance. In the end, these ideas may involve higher risk. The PART ideas, on the other hand, may be realizable on a shorter-term basis. The scope of the development, market testing, customer acceptance task, and risk will probably be smaller than that for the other set of ideas. Of course, I am being noncommittal because these are only general observations, not definitive rules. A PART idea may be very difficult to implement successfully, while a WHOLE idea may turn out to be an easy winner. Still, the general trend and my suggestion remains: It is useful to look at ideas this way and to make sure that you have some of both to take into the development phase.

A final thing to look for as you analyze the list of PART ideas is whether or not creative thinking has been applied to all of the parts of the existing product or service. For example, a block diagram of a traditional computer would include: input device, CPU, memory, mass storage (for example, hard disk drives, CD-ROM), operating system (for example, Windows, MacOS), output device, and communications device. Have we applied creative thinking to each of these subsystems? Similarly, we could construct a block diagram of our existing service portfolio and ask, "Have we applied creativity to all the parts here?"

The goal of this initial harvesting is to identify any topics that should be the subjects of a final round of idea generation. When these final sessions are complete, you should have a nice and varied collection of creative ideas for new products and services.

Because imagination is so expansive, you will need to set a time limit for the imagination phase and then move on in the directed-creativity cycle. Otherwise, it is easy to get caught up in endless idea generation. If you allow yourself and your organization to get caught up in this, you risk falling into the pitfall of creativity without innovation.

Be firm, but not dictatorial, in calling an end to the imagination phase when you reach the preset time limit (four to six weeks). If someone simply must try just one more session, let them do it, but ask them to get it organized quickly. I have used Ray and Myers' (1986) flip-a-coin method as a way of deciding whether to extend the imagination phase further when faced with multiple great ideas for one more session. Regardless of your decision, if a fabulous new idea turns up after you have already done the final harvesting, it will be okay to commission another development group to work on it.

As another ambiguity here, I must point out that it is not entirely clear who I am referring to by the use of the pronoun *you* in the preceding paragraphs. It would probably be more accurate to say *someone* in place of *you,* but I tried that and it does not communicate the call to action that I want to communicate. *You* provides emphasis; *someone* sounds wishy-washy. At the same time, I realize that you (the reader) may not be in a position to carry out all of these things. Someone else may be leading the design effort, there may be a powerful guiding coalition in place, you (the reader) may have only influence power and not position power. The structure surrounding product and service design efforts can be very complex and highly political.

Therefore, I must again unfortunately leave it to you to adapt what I am saying here to fit your circumstance. While I am clearly advocating a stronger role for practitioners of quality management in the creative aspects of product and service design, there is too much diversity in the current situation to suggest a well-defined new role.

Development phase. The final harvesting that begins the development phase should pass on several ideas for further development. The screening matrix based on the criteria of attractiveness and compatibility that we illustrated in Figure 7.3 might be a good tool to use here. Since the customer will be the ultimate judge of the quality and usefulness of the ideas, you should also consider conducting some type of customer-needs analysis. This might be as simple as passing the ideas by a focus group, user group, or standing customer panel.

Again, a general rule of thumb would be to select about twice as many ideas as you think you could reasonably be expected to implement within a year. In the case of product and service design, however, this is a bit harder to judge. For instance, we might be able to implement several PART-type innovations, but only a single WHOLE-type idea that radically changes our concepts about the product or service.

Because of this, apply the twice-as-many rule of thumb independently to both the WHOLE- and PART-type ideas. Ask, "How many radical new design concepts could we reasonably expect to implement next year?" and "How many modifications to parts of our existing products and services can we handle?" Another fine-tuning would be to select three or four times as many ideas as we think we can handle, but designate some of the ideas for long-term development on a different timeline from the others that we might expect to implement this year.

While it might seem logical to forego development on any of the PART ideas because we think we have a killer WHOLE idea that will negate the need for smaller-scale innovation, this approach is not wise. Remember, by nature, creative ideas that radically restructure the current product and service are risky. Fabulous-seeming ideas may not work out when we explore the details. A key technology may not live up to its promise, costs may be prohibitive, someone may hold an obscure patent that blocks us. Even if all goes well through the development phase, there is no way to know if the marketplace will accept or reject the innovation until we try. Keep in mind that all innovative organizations have a few past flops. Investing all your energy into radical innovations may leave you with nothing to show for all your work. If you can invest at least some of your resources into parallel development of PART-type ideas, you will have something to fall back on.

A second reason for selecting some PART-type ideas for development is that work on these may eventually serve to further enhance a WHOLE-type idea. The development group focused on the PART may come up with something that the WHOLE group would never have dreamed because of its broader focus.

Each idea selected in the final harvest needs an idea champion. The idea champions should use the enhancement checklist (Figure 7.4) to guide shaping, tailoring, strengthening, reinforcing, and so forth of the basic idea. Each idea champion should approach their idea with positive thinking (yellow hat); expecting to produce a winner and not giving up on the idea without a fight.

Practitioners of quality management have several tools to add to this development process. FMEA, QFD, the seven management and planning tools, robust design methodologies, quality system planning, and requirements analysis are just some of the many tools that we can pull from our traditional tool kit. If you have been involved on the creative side of design up to this point and your organization does not usually practice disciplined design for quality, now is your opportunity. If your organization already uses quality management principles and tools in design, now is the time to apply these in the directed-creativity cycle.

Prototypes and simulations are a must in creative product and service design. It is difficult to imagine how we can do an adequate evaluation of an innovative idea without a concrete mock-up to experience firsthand. Once the prototype is available, we can involve customers in the development process.

The development phase of creative product and service design can take several months. While we do want to get to action eventually, we should not rush it. There may be many technical hurdles to overcome, and we may need several rounds of customer-oriented prototype testing to be sure that we have made the proposed implementation of the idea the best it can be. While there are no hard data on this, I suspect that many good, innovative product and service ideas are discarded due to flawed development.

In contrast to process design and reengineering projects where the major selling job must be focused on the middle managers and frontline employees whose work is changed by the new process, the major selling job for innovative new products and services should be focused primarily on senior-level decision-makers. The ability to construct a good business case and present ideas convincingly are key skills here. Typically, organizations have well-defined rituals regarding such things.

The preevaluation question on the idea enhancement checklist in Figure 7.4 is critically important. How can we further modify the idea to meet the needs of those who will evaluate it next? If you do not know the needs of the senior-level decision-makers who will evaluate the developed idea, you owe it to yourself and the idea to find out.

Decision-makers can greatly aid this process by being very clear about how they will evaluate the ideas—both analytical criteria and intuitive criteria. An example of an intuitive decision criteria is, "I can see how this idea is similar to another situation where we were successful." If the truth were known, such intuitive decision criteria often carry more weight than more analytical criteria like sales projections. Importantly, when evaluating truly innovative ideas where the numbers can be way off, such intuitive decision-making criteria are really quite sensible. If decision-makers would make these intuitive criteria known up front, idea champions could develop information that addresses them. Unfortunately, acknowledging the use of intuition in decision making is not considered socially acceptable in many organizations. We instead engage in what Chris Argyris (1990) calls "face saving" and "fancy footwork."

The bottom line is that many great, innovative product and service ideas are rejected because they are not presented well at the time of final evaluation. They are not presented well because the decision-makers will not tell the presenters the real rules of the game. This would be comical if it were not so tragic.

If you find yourself in the role of idea champion, point out directly the necessary role of intuition in decision making about innovative product and service designs. It is nothing to be embarrassed about; it is the nature of the situation. Then ask for clear criteria for how your idea will be evaluated— both the analytical and intuitive criteria.

If you are in the role of decision-maker, set aside your ego and be comfortable with the logic that intuition is essential in evaluating truly innovative ideas. Reflect back on past decisions you have made and isolate clearly for yourself what intuitive factors you used. Do your best to express these to the idea champions with enough lead time to give them the opportunity to present their ideas in ways that address your intuitive needs. To do otherwise is dishonest and wasteful of the time and creative spirit already expended in the three phases of the directed-creativity cycle leading up to evaluation. As a senior-level decision-maker, you cannot afford to frustrate the creative energies of your organization in this way.*

As a final note on the development phase of innovative product and service concepts, do not overlook the possibility of combining or otherwise integrating the work of separate idea champions. A technique to facilitate this would be to schedule a rehearsal of the presentations of the developed ideas for all the idea champions to attend several days before the final evaluation. Discuss creative ways to integrate the strengths of several of the ideas. The idea champions should be prepared to present these integration ideas as part of the discussion that takes place at the final evaluation meeting.

Action phase. Once again, there is little new to say about the action phase of the directed-creativity cycle. Most organizations have fairly well-developed rituals around the launch of new products and services. If your organizational role involves quality management, you have your traditional

---

*For research on the role of intuition in decision making by senior managers, see Agor 1989. Michalko 1991, 213–220 offers exercises to help one develop and identify intuitive thinking abilities.

job to do in the action phase. The only real point I want to make about the action phase is: Do it!

Summary of Directed Creativity in Product and Service Design

The key points about the application of directed creativity in product and service design are summarized in the quick reference section at the end of this chapter. The tools of directed creativity make it possible for everyone to contribute to the process of innovation in an organization, and that is good. The more minds we have applied to the challenge, the higher our chances of success.

Because customers are increasingly demanding innovative new products and services, quality managers should be taking an active role in creative design. While in the past our role in design efforts has been largely analytical in nature, we now have the tools to make creative contributions as well.

Quick Reference:
The Application of Directed Creativity
in Product and Service Design

Key Principles to Keep in Mind

- A good, innovative product or service can generate millions of dollars of revenue for a company. It is worth some effort to purposefully search for creative ideas.

- Practitioners of quality management have reason to want to participate in innovative design work; customers want it and competitors are offering it.

Preparation Phase

- Reread the material in the various boxes scattered throughout chapter 5 and refer to the preparation tools mind map in Figure 5.2 for ideas about methods you might employ.

- Especially consider preparing the following items.

  A noticings notebook in which you record concepts extracted from observations, conversations, and readings; obvious things; and analogies

  A list of role plays

  Lists of assumptions, positive attributes, negative attributes, feelings, information sources, and direct analogies relevant to the topic of the design effort

  Expansive questions based on who, what, when, where, why, and how

  An FCB grid or other pattern search tool

  A purpose hierarchy

  Futuristic scenarios

  Insights and expansive questions from creative customer needs analysis

- Plan to spend at least a few weeks in the preparation phase.

Imagination Phase

- Reread the material in the various boxes scattered throughout chapter 6 and refer to the imagination tools mind map in Figure 6.2; use as many different tools as you can.

- Conduct an initial harvest about two-thirds of the way through the time allocated to the imagination phase and plan additional idea generation sessions to fill in any gaps.

- In addition to the four, standard harvesting categories, separate the ideas into those that represent a radically different product (WHOLE) and those that represent a modification of a part of the existing product or service (PART). Look to see that you have addressed all of the parts of the existing product or service.

- Plan to spend about four to six weeks in the imagination phase. Be firm, but not dictatorial, about bringing the imagination phase to an end.

Development Phase

- Your final harvesting should include both WHOLE- and PART-type ideas.

- Consider involving customers directly in harvesting, developing, testing prototypes, and evaluating innovative ideas.

- Use the enhancement checklist and quality design tools to further develop the ideas.

- Prototyping is a must.

- Develop a business case and present your ideas clearly. Also understand that the final decisions about whether to go forward with an innovation are, of necessity, largely intuitive in nature. Discuss this openly and seek clarity on intuitive decision criteria.

- Consider integrating the strong points of several ideas to develop a better idea.

- The development phase can take several months. Do not delay unnecessarily, but neither rush the effort. Good ideas can be ruined by flawed development.

Action Phase

- Just do it! Consider your organization's usual procedures for launching new products and services.

CHAPTER 11

Creative Problem Solving and Incremental Improvement

᛭ ☺ ☺ ᚕ

Discovery consists of looking at the same thing as everyone else and thinking something different.

Albert Szent-Gyorgyi, Nobel Prize winner

Keep on the lookout for novel and interesting ideas that others have used successfully. Your idea has to be original only in its adaptation to the problem you are currently working on.

Thomas Edison

I'm a victim of coi'cumstances!

Curly, *The Three Stooges*

It has been said that the definition of lunacy is to continue to do the same things, but expect a different result. When you think about it, many efforts at problem solving would qualify as lunacy.

In the medication errors case in the prologue, I was a bit kinder and called this lunacy stuck thinking. As we have seen, the mechanism of mind is optimized to retrieve and play back patterns stored up from the past. What should we do when the past patterns fail to solve the current problem? Escaping the current mental valley and moving to another one is the only antidote to stuck thinking. Analytical thinking put us in the current mental valley and is keeping us there; creative thinking provides a way out.

Let me again reiterate that I am a firm believer in the power of analytical methods in problem solving and incremental improvement, but the issue here is: Are analytical methods always the best way to go? There are enough failures of analytical problem solving to make it clear that the answer to this question must be, "Well, not always."

Creative Versus Analytical Methods: The Tyranny of Wanting to Know Which Is Right

Individual preferences for approaches to problem solving range along the spectrum that I have caricatured in Figure 11.1. You probably know people all across this spectrum, and you can probably isolate your own preferred style by reflecting on how annoying those other people are to you. My preferred style is just to the left of the "Analytical, with a little creative/intuitive" spot in Figure 11.1. This is not a surprise. I am an engineer. A statistician is trained to think on the left side of the diagram, while an organizational development practitioner is trained to think on the right side.

The classic question that the spectrum in Figure 11.1 raises is: Which problem-solving approach is correct? By now, you surely know that this is a silly question. All the approaches are correct at some time, and none of them is correct all of the time. A good problem solver will develop an understanding and degree of comfort with each. It is not even as simple as choosing the right approach to fit the specific problem you are facing. The optimal approach may be a little bit of all of them. Importantly, you can never know if the approach you do end up with was the right approach for that problem. To be sure, you can know if your approach failed. If you succeed, however, you can never know if a different approach would have yielded greater success. In the end, arguments about the pros and cons, successes and failures, rightness and wrongness of various approaches to problem solving are just not helpful.

Style	Strong statistical/ analytical	Analytical, with a little creative/ intuitive	Creative/ intuitive, with a little analysis	Strongly creative/ intuitive
Heard to say	"In God we trust. All others bring data."	"Show me how you arrive at that. Surely there is at least some data on that."	"We studied it some, but then what occurred to us was . . ."	"Are you sure that's the problem? The data will only confuse you."
Typical profession, background, or training	Statistics	Engineering	Management	Organizational development and psychology

Figure 11.1. The spectrum of approaches to problem solving.

At the same time, it is okay to have preferences. It is honest and helpful to openly acknowledge these preferences. It is okay to start with your preferred problem-solving style. You may be successful. If you are successful with your preferred style, then you are probably also being efficient because you know how to execute that particular style well. It does not matter if you could have arrived at a solution by another way; you got there by your way.

The pitfall inherent in preferred problem-solving styles is stuck thinking. If you fail, but remain wedded to your preference, you will end up being frustrated, rationalizing the situation, and (most importantly) being stuck with the status quo. You do not have to settle for this. You merely need to develop the mental flexibility to try other approaches when your preferred approach leaves you stuck.

In the remainder of this chapter I want to explore the creative-thinking approach. I am not advocating this as *the* approach. I am not even suggesting that you adopt it as a new, preferred approach. Personally, I remain an analytical kind of guy. ("A serious gear head," a colleague once called me.) The only thing that I am advocating here is openness and flexibility in trying new ways of thinking.

The Symptoms of Stuck Thinking

So it is okay to prefer the analytical problem-solving approaches of traditional quality improvement, and it is okay to start with these methods initially. So when should we consider another approach? When analytical thinking leaves us stuck.

We need to be able to check periodically for indications of stuck thinking in our problem-solving and quality improvement efforts. The symptoms are varied, but the checklist in Figure 11.2 will direct your attention. The more of these items you check off, the more likely it is that you and your team are stuck.

Good students of mental mechanics will recognize three judgment subsystems at work behind these outwardly visible symptoms: emotional reaction, belief preservation, and satisficing. These judgment subsystems are not all bad. They provide the delightful human diversity that makes life interesting. They also provide stability of personality and the permission that we all need to just relax from time to time. The issues with these subsystems in the

---

- Frustration at being unable to either isolate a cause, propose a solution, or achieve your goals after implementing a solution

- Data collection and analysis efforts that have been going on for a long time, but do not seem to be providing any clear direction

- Reexaminations of data or past thinking that keep coming back to the same conclusions

- Tinkering with failed solutions without a clear and compelling theory as to what real difference these minor changes will make

- Accusations that others are simply not being reasonable, logical, or cooperative

- Rationalization of the seemingly unreasonable, illogical, or uncooperative behavior of others

- Calls for reconsidering the original goals of the improvement effort because we now realize that these expectations were unreasonable

- Calls for celebrating the achievements of the effort and accepting the new, better—but not as good as we hoped for—status quo

---

Figure 11.2. Classic symptoms of stuck thinking in problem-solving and quality improvement efforts.

current context is that, by definition, in a problem-solving effort we have a problem. The reason that we are working on the situation is that it is far enough away from satisfactory that it was called to our attention. It cannot be acceptable to have put forth all of the effort leading up to this point, only to end up with little or nothing to show for it.

The symptoms of stuck thinking outlined in Figure 11.2 are an indication that it may be profitable to supplement our analytical efforts with some directed creativity. Of course, there are no guarantees that the methods of directed creativity will resolve the matter either. It is my experience that once you get stuck in analytical thinking, thinking harder rarely helps. Thinking differently is the only thing that helps. The methods of directed creativity provide a way to look at the problem and think differently about it.

There are many reported cases where teams get unstuck by asking someone else to analyze their data. As a consultant in quality management, I often play this role. But I would argue that the point is still valid: the mechanism of getting unstuck was not thinking harder, it was thinking differently. When someone else reanalyzes your data, he or she uses a different set of mental valleys than the ones that the team was using. I have nothing against one last shot at analysis; try it, it might help.

Finally, let me point out that it is also okay to use directed-creativity methods before you get stuck in your thinking with analytical methods. If you are open and flexible, why wait? If someone else had been given the problem to work on, they might have started with these methods—and they might have been successful. There is no way to ever know the optimal starting point, nor the optimal thinking path toward a solution for real-world problems of even modest complexity. How ever you start in your thinking, just remember to keep moving flexibly. You can get stuck in the creativity mental valley just as easily as the analysis one.

The Use of Directed-Creativity Tools in Problem-Solving and Incremental Quality Improvement Efforts

The intent of the first portion of this chapter was to give you the proper attitude, motivation, and direction signals to support adding the methods of directed creativity to the standard tool kit of quality improvement. These exhortations now raise the questions: "What should I do that is different from what I am already doing?" and "How do I go about getting creative ideas in problem-solving efforts?" These are our topics for the latter portion of the chapter, in which I will highlight seven potentially useful tools.

Quality management has a mental valley about the number seven. There are the seven QC tools (Ishikawa 1985) and the seven management and planning tools (Mizuno 1988). The number *seven* comes from the Japanese legend surrounding the twelfth century samurai warrior Benkei. Benkei's mastery of seven basic weapons equipped him to take on any challenge. Metaphorically, the seven QC and seven management and planning tools are the basic equipment for practitioners of quality management. If we master the use of these tools, we will be equipped to take on many of the challenges of quality management. Of course, no one takes this literally. There are various lists of the seven tools; and some lists have eight or nine items on them! While the metaphor of the seven indispensable tools of Benkei is useful for stressing both simplicity and mastery, no one would suggest that these two sets of seven tools comprise an exclusive and all-sufficient set of methods for quality management.

With these cautions noted, I will continue in this tradition and outline here the seven directed-creativity tools for quality improvement. These methods are depicted in Figure 11.3. I hope that these methods will take their place along side the other lists of seven in the basic training that many organizations give to quality improvement teams. (Note: I have not included the rules of brainstorming here because this tool is already well-known. The rules of brainstorming provide basic ground rules for any idea-generation session and are, therefore, implicitly assumed in Figure 11.3.) Obviously, these are not the only methods that can help, but they do provide a good place to start. Again, I encourage you to experiment with your own methods and with variations on these methods.

Purpose hierarchy. A basic creative-thinking maneuver to combat stuck thinking in problem solving is to question whether or not we are solving the right problem. Research indicates that creative problem solvers are often successful primarily because they are good problem finders. (Various references were cited in chapter 3.) The Creative Problem Solving (CPS) process of

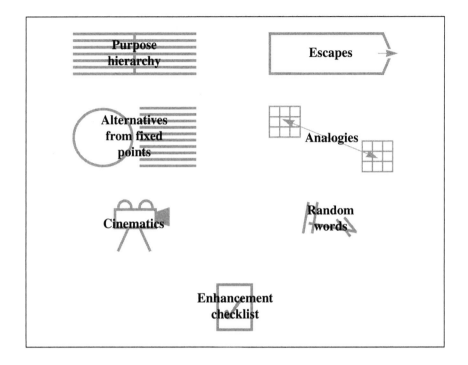

Figure 11.3. The seven directed-creativity tools for quality improvement.

Parnes (1992) and Isaksen and Trefflinger (1985) emphasizes this notion by including a specific step called "problem finding."

Problem redefinition is important in creative problem solving and incremental improvement because often the best way to solve a problem is to solve a different, but related, problem. Consider, for example, a quality improvement team chartered to reduce the waste associated with flaring in a chemical refinery. (When a chemical refinery produces off-spec product, it is diverted to a special pipeline where it is sent up a tall tower to be burned in a flare. When you drive by a chemical refinery and see a bright, roaring flame, you know that the plant is experiencing quality problems in production.) "Reducing the production of off-spec product" is one statement of the problem. This leads to a stream of analytical thinking involving investigations of raw materials quality, production processes, operator training, and so forth. "Finding new uses for off-spec product" is a creative restatement of the problem that leads us down an entirely different thinking path.

The purpose hierarchy is a tool proposed by Nadler and Hibino (1994) that directly supports the notion of problem redefinition. We have already cited the use of this tool in the case of the slippery packing crates in chapter 3. Recall that, on a consultant's recommendation, a national manufacturer of consumer goods was about to make a multimillion dollar investment in loading dock automation in order to solve the problem of damaged crates. A young staff engineer saved the company a great deal of money and effort by taking another look at the issue.

The consultant's solution had the implied purpose "to reduce damage by doing a better job of loading trucks" "But," asked the young engineer constructing the purpose hierarchy, "what is the purpose of loading trucks?" (Recall that we construct a purpose hierarchy by repeatedly asking why, how come, or what is the purpose?) The purpose of loading trucks is to consolidate shipments to dealers. Continuing with this line of questioning yields the purpose hierarchy (read from the bottom up, asking the question why between each line).

Improve the lives of customers
Satisfy the customers' demand for our product
Distribute the company's products to the marketplace
Ensure that dealers have adequate inventory on hand
Transport products to dealers effectively
Consolidate shipments to dealers
Load trucks

Each level of the purpose hierarchy associated with a problem provides us with a different mental attention and escape point. The loading dock automation solution proposed by the consultant solved the problem of damaged shipping crates at the load-trucks purpose level. At the consolidate-shipments-to-dealers level, we might consider developing a multiunit packing scheme that reduces the exposure to potential damage for individual product crates. This might cost a lot less than the loading dock automation solution, and there might be further benefits to our customer, the dealer.

The young engineer in Nadler and Hibino's story focused his problem-solving efforts at the distribute-products-to-the-marketplace level of the purpose hierarchy. He proposed a dramatic reduction in the company's warehousing network from 24 to four, with air shipments to these regional centers direct from the manufacturing plants. The problem of damaged crates was solved not by expensive loading dock automation, but by reducing the number of physical handling points in the company's vast warehousing network. The company saved hundreds of millions of dollars and improved its overall effectiveness in getting product to market.

The Seven Directed-Creativity Tools for Quality Improvement: Purpose Hierarchy

Synopsis: Multiple redefinitions of the problem or underlying purpose of the effort.

Primary creativity principles: Attention and escape.

When to use:
- The solution you have come up with to the original problem is unsatisfying in some way.
- You are just not getting anywhere with the problem as currently stated.
- Before you even begin your analysis of the problem.

Overview of method: Begin with the original statement of the problem, issue, opportunity, or purpose. Ask why, how come, what's the purpose of that?

Place in directed-creativity cycle: Preparation phase. Then use statements as fixed points for mental movement in the imagination phase.

Pitfalls to watch for: Trumping—suggestions that we work the problem at such a high level on the purpose hierarchy that we end up being unable to accomplish anything.

The major pitfall to watch for in using the purpose hierarchy is that of trumping. To avoid trumping, I suggest that you not share your purpose hierarchy too broadly until you have had a chance to decide the level at which you intend to address the issue. In keeping with the define-topic-broadly heuristic, you should select the highest level of the hierarchy that is practical.

Then, for public consumption, simply lop off any higher levels. The perception that you are already working at the highest level of the hierarchy reduces some of the psychological motivation on the part of others to trump you.

Escapes. The gestalt psychologist Carl Dunker illustrated the principle of escaping from constraints in creative problem solving with his famous nine-dots problem. The challenge is to connect the nine dots with four straight lines, without lifting your pencil once you begin. The answer is shown on the next page. Play with it for a minute or two before looking at the answer; there is learning in the experience. If you get it, repeat the challenge with three lines; again, without lifting the pencil. Then do it with one line.

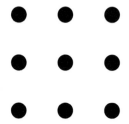

The learning point in the puzzle is that in order to solve it, one must escape the imaginary box formed by the dot pattern. This puzzle is the source of the expression "thinking outside the box." There is no solution if we confine our thinking (and our lines) to remain inside the box. The really key point is that the box that confines us is not even real. We assumed it. There was no law that mandated it, no instruction that required it.

Did you figure out how to connect the nine dots? In the four-line solution we escape the imaginary box restriction. In the three-line solution we escaped both the box restriction and the assumed restriction that the lines had to pass through the centers of the dots. In the one-line solution we escaped the assumed restriction of a skinny line. Another way would be to escape the assumed restriction of flatness and fold the paper until the dots are on top of each other. Adams (1974) provides many additional solutions.

The nine-dot problem dramatically illustrates the principle of escape—multiple escapes—in creative problem solving. Keep looking closely; you are probably assuming something. Escaping these assumptions opens the possibilities for previously unimagined solutions.

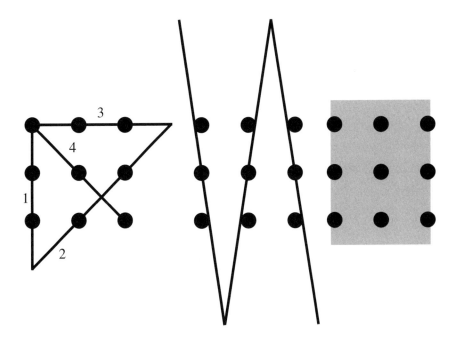

On our seven creative tools list, escape is not a single tool, but a family of tools. As we have seen in previous chapters, and now in the nine-dots problem, we should explore escapes from

- Rules
- The obvious things before us
- The paradigms in our industry
- The limits of current technology

- Assumptions
- The way we have always done it
- Logic and reasonableness
- Time and space

- The usual direction (for example, instead of increasing customer satisfaction, how could we decrease it?)

As noted in the summary box, one pitfall in using escape is that of too much escape. Because there are endless possibilities to explore through escape, consider setting a time limit and then moving on to harvest from among the ideas you have. Another approach is to keep up the loop of idea generation and initial harvesting until you reach a preset quota of promising ideas.

The Seven Directed-Creativity Tools for Quality Improvement: Escape

Synopsis: Escape rules, assumptions, paradigms, and so on that are blocking solution.

Primary creativity principles: Attention, escape, and movement.

When to use: ▪ The solution you have come up with to the original problem is unsatisfying in some way.

▪ You are just not getting anywhere with analysis.

▪ The problem system is steeped in strong traditions.

Overview of method: Identify rules, assumptions, current methods, paradigms, current logic, limits of technology, limits of time and space, the usual direction of thinking, or anything else you can think of that is connected with the problem. Announce that you are escaping these temporarily and explore the world without these restrictions. A po statement is a good way to announce this.

Place in directed-creativity cycle: The identification of the rules, assumptions, and so on is a preparation phase activity. The actual escape and movement is an imagination phase activity.

Pitfalls to watch for: Endless suggestions for escape. Unwillingness to explore the world envisioned by the escape provocation.

The second pitfall, nonengagement, is a bit harder to deal with, but there are several things you can do. Some people are such strong purple-hat (negative, critical) thinkers that they just cannot generate the mental flexibility to participate in this exercise. Be firm in enforcing the no-criticism ground rule of brainstorming. Consider adding the yellow hat to your idea generation session by stating a ground rule that the group must make at least one positive comment about every idea generated. Let purple-hatted people sit out the idea generation session. Or, bring extra people who are flexible thinkers into the group temporarily for the idea generation session.

Alternatives from fixed points. An important creative insight that aids problem solving is the realization that everything we now do is just the currently selected means of accomplishing some larger end. The end purpose or goal may be a fixed point, but the means we use to accomplish it are potentially variable. The alternatives from fixed points tool directly supports this notion.

The alternatives from fixed points tool is one of the many methods developed by de Bono (1992). We discussed it at length in chapter 6. The basic idea is to mentally back up from our current means of doing things and identify the fixed point(s). We do this by asking: What is the purpose here? What is really happening? Where is the value in this? The answers to these questions give us fixed points for mental attention. Next, we need to escape the thinking that the way we do it now is the only way and then move on to generate alternatives. We can show these alternatives on a diagram like the ones shown in Figures 6.3 and 8.2. Let's illustrate the use of this tool in the context of a problem-solving or quality improvement effort.

Consider the dilemma of a quality improvement team chartered to "improve the productivity of meetings in the organization." While this vague mission statement violates many of the guidelines for chartering quality improvement teams (see, for example, Scholtes 1988), many improvement efforts begin with not much more than this to go on. The analytical approach from quality management would send us down the thinking path of data collection, cause-effect analysis, stratification, Pareto analysis, and measurement of productivity. The engineer in me would encourage you to consider this approach and see where it leads you, but my experience with such vaguely chartered improvement efforts is that teams often end up displaying one or more of the symptoms of stuck thinking outlined in Figure 11.2.

One approach to combat this would be to do a better job of focusing the team's mission. "We want to reduce the overall amount of time spent in meetings" would be a more focused mission statement. Still, the team might only end up stuck with a smaller, but no less confusing, set of data to work with. In addition, there is the pesky issue that we really do want improved overall productivity in meetings. The amount of time spent in meetings (or the number of meetings, or the number of decisions made per hour of meeting time, or participant satisfaction, or whatever) are just imperfect surrogates for what we really want.

The creative approach would be to stay with the broader topic statement (per heuristic 3) and apply creative thinking in addition to analytical thinking. The creative insight would be to recognize that meetings are not preordained fixed points (although in some organizations they seem to be). Meetings are simply a mechanism for achieving some purpose or realizing some value. Meetings are a means to accomplish the ends of informing people, making group decisions, and encouraging teamwork. Rather than working to find ways to improve the productivity of meetings, what are alternatives to meetings that would still deliver these fixed point concepts? For instance, what are alternative ways of informing people? A newsletter, a memo, a broadcast voice-mail message, e-mail messages, one-on-one conversation, tell the notorious gossips in the organization and they will spread it, stamp the information "TOP SECRET" and everyone will know it by tomorrow, and so forth.

I bet you smiled at those last two suggestions, so let's pause on these for just a bit to explore (per heuristic 6). What I notice about the suggestion involving gossips is that some people really seem to enjoy telling other people about things. This, of course, implies that other people do not so much enjoy doing this. While most organizational communications systems utilize the management structure for information sharing—your boss tells you in a staff meeting—managers are not necessarily selected based on their reputations as people who really enjoy sharing information. So, the productivity of information sharing in staff meetings depends a great deal on the personality of your boss.

Stepping out of the scene for just a moment, I want to point out the critical importance of free-association and mental movement in using the alternatives from fixed points tool. Notice how we are ranging freely in our thoughts, but always remaining tied back to our fixed point.

Also notice that the insight produced by all this mental movement—that the productivity of information-sharing depends on the personality of the manager—is not an earth-shattering revelation. It is likely that it will be greeted with "Well, of course," "Everybody knows that," and similar dismissive comments. It is a logical conclusion—after you hear it expressed. While it is a logical conclusion, *it is highly unlikely that the analysis of data would have led us to it.* This is another important reason why we should balance the use of analytical and directed-creativity methods in all our quality improvement work. Some useful conclusions might be reachable only by one method or the other.

Continuing on the gossip line of thinking, we might propose that one alternative means of accomplishing the end of informing people would be to establish an information-sharing structure independent of the management structure. We could identify people who really enjoy sharing information with others and assign these people to lead an information-sharing cell of 10 to 12 people. An enhancement of this idea would be to construct these cells with people from different departments. This gets at the other fixed point of encouraging teamwork. We could go on to generate more alternatives by continuing in mental movement.

The Seven Directed-Creativity Tools for Quality Improvement: Alternatives from Fixed Points

Synopsis: Everything we currently do is but a means to some end. If we are experiencing a problem, maybe we should try an alternative means to accomplish the same ends.

Primary creativity principles: Attention, escape, and movement.

When to use: ▪ The objective as originally posed is vague, but it really is what you want to do.

▪ You are just not getting anywhere with analysis; you feel overwhelmed by all the data and possibilities.

Overview of method: Focus on the current way things are done, but acknowledge that this is just one means to a larger end. Identify the ends by asking, what is the purpose here? What is really happening? Where is the value in this? Consider these ends as fixed points and ask for alternatives. Construct a diagram to capture this creative input.

Place in directed-creativity cycle: The identification of the fixed points is a preparation phase activity. The generation of alternatives is an imagination phase activity.

Pitfalls to watch for: Unwillingness to explore the possibilities of alternatives to the current way.

The quality improvement team can now used its analytical skills to gather data and test out some of these ideas (white-hat thinking). For example, we could set up some experimental information-sharing cells and conduct a controlled experiment. (We would want to study this for a long enough period of time to avoid being fooled by a Hawthorne effect—the observed improvement is simply an artifact of the newness of the idea. If it is just a Hawthorne effect, after the novelty wears off information sharing will be just as poor as ever. Beware of the Hawthorne effect when studying creative solutions to problems.)

Analogies. Some creativity authors assert that analogy lies at the heart of all creative thinking (Koestler 1964). When we use analogies in problem solving and incremental improvement, we are seeking to identify some principle or concept from one situation that we can adapt to our own. For example, benchmarking teams use analogy when they take insights gathered while visiting another company and adapt them to solve a problem.

We can consider four types of analogies: direct analogies, random-forced analogies, excursions, and being someone else.

To apply a direct analogy to our problem, we ask, "What is the fundamental essence of our problem and who else (or what else or where else) deals with a similar situation?" Consider a quality improvement team at an airline looking into the problem of lost baggage. The fundamental essence of this problem might be stated as: "failure to keep track of things and move them about appropriately." Who, what, or where else deals with this problem? An overnight package delivery service . . . a school teacher with children on a field trip . . .

- Overnight package delivery services use bar code tracking systems. We already do this. They also place a great deal of the responsibility on the customer for getting the correct destination information. In contrast, our ticket agents take all of the responsibility for properly labeling bags. What if we asked passengers to verify the bag tag one last time before we sent it down the conveyor? What if travel agents were responsible for giving barcoded baggage tags to passengers when they picked up their tickets? Passengers would naturally examine the labels and alert us to any errors.

- A school teacher with children on a field trip often puts the children in groups and makes them hold hands to stay together. Can we group bags going to the same destination earlier in the baggage handling process? If we labeled bags both individually and as a group we might reduce the chances of misdirecting them.

To apply random-forced analogies to a problem, we select a parallel world from the resource list in the appendix and see what linkages we can come up with. For example, consider the problem of finish defects on automobiles discovered on final inspection at the factory. The parallel world I just selected from the list is "TV news." Your first reaction is probably, "What could television news possibly have to do with eliminating finish defects on cars?" Don't give up; the creative challenge is to find as many linkages as you can.

- Television news obviously uses video cameras. We could temporarily install video cameras every few feet on the assembly line to see if we can pinpoint the sources of the finish defects.

- Television news uses a combination of live and prerecorded reports. Which is more prone to defects: finishes we apply on the assembly line ourselves or prefinished parts?

It is sometimes helpful to take a problem-solving group on an excursion in search of analogies. For example, the automobile finish defects team could spend a profitable hour in a shopping mall searching for things that might help in its problem-solving efforts. Getting away from the world of the problem—in this case the factory—stimulates our perception processes and recasts our emotional judgment processes. During the visit to the mall, the team might notice and mentally move . . .

- The wax on the mall's floor protects that surface. What wax technology might we apply to our problem?

- Expensive evening dresses are covered in plastic to protect them while they hang on the rack. What types of coverings can we use to protect the automobile's surfaces during assembly?

Finally, we can use analogies to solve problems by thinking like someone else. How would a six-year-old child solve the problem of lost baggage for the airline? Perhaps by tying a colored ribbon on her bag so she could spot it easily. We could experiment with color coding or some other type of redundant baggage identification process in addition to the bar codes we already use. With redundant coding, we would be covered if one type of identification should become separated from the bag. We could also use different sensor technologies and cross-verify the destination of each bag to avoid misreads of the bar code label.

Of course, with all of these ideas, we still have plenty of research, development, and enhancement to do. We may need to spend some time learning more about the analogous situation before we can come up with any really good ideas. Some of our ideas may not be practical nor effective in the end, but at least we are not stuck. If we keep at it, we might make a major breakthrough.

The Seven Directed-Creativity Tools for Quality Improvement: Analogies

Synopsis: Adapt concepts, approaches, and ideas from another setting into the context of our problem.

Primary creativity principles: Escape, attention, and movement.

When to use: ▪ The solution you have come up with to the original problem is unsatisfying in some way.

▪ You need some fresh directions for analysis.

Overview of method: Either (1) identify a directly analogous situation; (2) select a parallel world at random; (3) go somewhere, physically or mentally, and search for things that might relate to your problem; or (4) look at the problem through some else's eyes. Mentally free associate until something in the analogy triggers a useful thought.

Place in directed-creativity cycle: The identification of analogies and research into the world of the analogy are preparation phase activities. The generation of creative ideas is an imagination phase activity. Expect to spend some time in the development phase shaping and adapting the ideas.

Pitfalls to watch for: Giving up too easily. Dismissing far out or silly analogies. Thinking that the proposed analogy is a puzzle that, therefore, must have a correct answer.

Analogies can be powerful in problem solving, but they are also very hard mental work for some people. After introducing an analogy in a problem-solving group, consider declaring a five-minute silent time for people to think. Also do not reject analogies that seem too far out or silly. Remember that these hold the greatest potential for a truly novel idea.

Because analogies are so difficult for some people, it is wise to always use them along with several other directed-creativity tools. This will help avoid frustration and will allow everyone on the team to contribute to the creative effort, even if they never quite get the hang of analogies.

Cinematics. Since problems have visible symptoms and are the result of some concrete action by someone in an existing process, visualization techniques can be very helpful in problem solving. Wonder and Donovan (1984), Ray and Myers (1986), Higgins (1994), Michalko (1991), and VanGundy (1992) all describe tools that are variations on the theme of using the sense of sight to examine a problem scene in detail.

I mentioned this family of techniques briefly in chapter 6 in discussing the tools of imagination, but I have not said much about them since. While I am featuring them here in this chapter on problem solving, I feel that these techniques are somewhat less valuable in the other applications covered in the previous chapters. My reasoning for this goes back to our understanding of mental mechanics. Asking people to visualize scenes in design and customer-oriented innovation-needs research often ends up only reinforcing the mental valley of the current status quo. Since the future is not yet concrete to our senses, we have to work hard to conjure up a picture of it that is not clouded by the patterns of the past and present. We can certainly do it, but it requires some conscious effort that can be quite difficult for some people. In a problem-solving effort, however, we want to look closely at the past and present; that is the world of the problem.

What I am calling cinematics here is not a single tool, but a variety of techniques suggested by the various authors just cited. Cinematic techniques involve careful study of mental images, movies, photographs, or physical reenactments of situations. For example, a quality improvement team looking to reduce machine setup time and defects might videotape the manufacturing operation and play it back in slow motion to analyze each activity. The creative-thinking aspect of this lies in the fact that a slow-motion playback of the situation allows your mind more time than it usually gets to notice things and make novel connections with other stored concepts. The mind is never idle, it is always clicking away. Playing the video of the scene in slow motion has the effect of increasing the number of mental clicks per scene-second.

You can get a similar effect by simply visualizing the scene in slow motion in your mind. The caution here is that there may be things in the actual scene that you have never noticed well enough to make them part of your mental valley. If this is the case, no matter how slowly you play back the mental image, you cannot see what is not there. You can avoid this potential pitfall by simply putting in the effort to produce a video of the actual scene.

Another cinematic variation would be to act out the problem scene. The added dimension here (over that of the video) is that the participants in the role play can experience things from the points of view of the various people involved in the scene. Many people in these role plays report genuine feelings about what is going on. To the extent that these feelings are part of the problem system, this added dimension is helpful. It is particularly so when doing problem solving in service processes or any other processes that involve a high degree of human-to-human interaction. I would recommend using both a videotape and a role play in such problem-solving efforts. Each may add unique insights.

A final approach I will mention is an obvious one. Visit the problem scene and just watch. The advantage here is that you are not restricted by the field of view of the camera lens or the insight of the role players. Everything about the problem scene is there before you. In addition, you might also chat with some of the people involved to get their firsthand perspective. Finally, if people are willing to experiment, you might also manipulate the scene and observe what happens.

As a final tip on the use of cinematics in problem solving, I have always found it helpful to have people involved who know very little about the situation. (As an outside consultant to quality improvement teams, this is often the role I play.) These outsiders' often ask very interesting questions and have useful insights because they are not constrained by the mental valleys of the current paradigm. While outsiders' perspectives are generally helpful when using any improvement tool, the concreteness of watching a video of a problem scene facilitates the active participation by these outsiders. A verbal

---

The Seven Directed-Creativity Tools for Quality Improvement:
Cinematics

Synopsis: Examine the problem scene closely, in slow motion and stop action if possible.

Primary creativity principles: Attention and movement.

When to use: The process associated with the problem has a strong physical activity component, or human-to-human interaction component.

Overview of method: Shoot a video, take photographs, act out a role play, mentally imagine, or actually visit the problem scene. Notice everything. Practice active mental movement. Discuss what is going on with others. You are looking for things you have not noticed before about the problem, and for novel mental connections. Consider inviting outsiders to participate.

Place in directed-creativity cycle: The production of the video or other media is a preparation phase activity. The attention to details and mental movement are an imagination phase activity.

Pitfalls to watch for: Limited fields of views brought about by camera lens and mental blind spots.

---

explanation of the problem simply does not have the clarity and realism of a videotape, photograph, role play, or actual visit to the scene.

Random words. The random word tool is the most straightforward of the seven directed-creativity tools. We simply select a word at random and then mentally free-associate to link the mental valley of the word with that of our problem. Recall that we can use nouns, manipulative verbs, prepositions, or conjunctions. (Review chapter 6 if you need a refresher.)

For example, the automobile finish defects improvement team described earlier might supplement their use of the relatively difficult tool of analogy with the much simpler random noun tool. Using a page from any book or the random word list in the appendix, the team selects the random noun *telescope*. (Sometimes it is almost too easy!)

- Use cameras with telescopic lens to inspect finishes throughout the assembly line.

- Install magnifying sheet glass at various points along the assembly line so that workers can spot finish defects at a glance while they work.

- Use the camera or magnifying glass ideas above to inspect surfaces for small defects before finish is applied.

Remember to go for quantity of ideas when using random words. Select multiple random words and generate multiple ideas from each. This is especially important when the word you select happens to be easy to relate initially to your problem (as we just saw). The fact that the randomly selected word seems easy to relate to your problem means that your initial thoughts are not very novel. You will need to go beyond these initial thoughts to get truly creative ideas.

The Seven Directed-Creativity Tools for Quality Improvement: Random Words

Synopsis: Free associate a randomly selected noun, verb, preposition, or conjunction onto a problem situation.

Primary creativity principles: Escape and movement.

When to use: Whenever you feel stuck in your thinking.

Overview of method: Select a word at random (from a list like those provided in the appendix or from any printed material). Through mental movement, link any thoughts generated by the word back to your problem.

Place in directed-creativity cycle: On-the-spot technique for the imagination phase.

Pitfalls to watch for: Inadequate quantity of ideas.

Enhancement checklist. I introduced the idea enhancement checklist in Figure 7.4. While enhancement of ideas is always important, there is a special challenge in problem-solving and incremental improvement efforts because we are only making a focused change, leaving the basic process, product, or service intact. Therefore, it is critically important that we pay attention to how our creative idea will fit with its surroundings. We have the potential for causing more harm than good if we are not careful.

The strengthening, reinforcing, looking toward implementation, and potential faults or defects questions on the checklist demand our attention if we hope to succeed. These questions are important in quality improvement efforts regardless of the source of the change idea—whether analytical thinking or creative thinking. For this reason, practitioners of quality management might want to adopt this seventh tool of directed creativity even if they dismiss the other six.

The shaping question in the enhancement checklist reminds us that we must deal with the resistance to change that always accompanies quality improvement efforts. Whereas we might have had data to support the change if we had used analytical methods, with a creative approach we have only the intuitive appeal of the idea to rest upon. It is important, therefore, to address the comparison to current, consequences, testability and prototyping, and preevaluation questions on the checklist prior to communicating our new idea widely.

It is often useful to test the change on a small scale and temporary basis to allow people to experience it. If you are getting strong resistance, set your sights on just trying to get others to agree to a small test. This may be both the best you can hope for and all that you need.

The major pitfall in using the enhancement checklist is simply failing to use it. Creative ideas are exciting. It is easy to get caught up in the excitement and overlook critical details. The checklist provides some needed reminders.

The Seven Directed-Creativity Tools for Quality Improvement: Enhancement Checklist

Synopsis: Things to consider in developing creative ideas into implemented innovations.

Primary creativity principles: Attention (to detail) and movement (to action).

When to use: You are satisfied with the basic creative idea and are ready to move on to implementation.

Overview of method: Use the various questions on the checklist to guide thinking in developing ideas. The questions can be taken in any order. Make a final pass through them before moving on.

Place in directed-creativity cycle: Development phase.

Pitfalls to watch for: Failing to use the checklist; assuming that an idea is so good that everyone will embrace it immediately and all the details will work out on their own.

Integrating the seven tools, the directed-creativity cycle, and various quality improvement and problem-solving models. The seven tools of directed creativity for quality improvement provide a starter kit of methods for combating stuck thinking. In the preceding sections, I have concentrated on simply explaining the tools themselves and showing some examples of their use. In sharp contrast to the preceding chapters on applications, I have made only passing reference to the directed-creativity cycle. There are two reasons for this.

First, I want to clearly position these tools as supporting traditional quality improvement efforts, not replacing them. The predominant model to guide a quality improvement project should be the organization's quality improvement model, not the directed-creativity cycle. Most organizations have invested a great deal of energy into disseminating their problem-solving or quality improvement model. Asking people to now learn a new model (for directed creativity) is potentially confusing, with little incremental benefit.

The second reason for downplaying the directed-creativity cycle in the application of problem solving is related to the first. When used to complement problem solving and quality improvement, directed creativity is primarily about one phase only, imagination. Preparation happens either through nondirected noticing or as a by-product of the problem-solving effort that is now stuck. Where there is directed preparation, it happens quickly. For example, we might spend 10 minutes at a quality improvement team meeting listing rules and assumptions and then immediately use the escape tool to generate ideas. There is an immediacy to problem solving that makes the distinction between the preparation and imagination phases of academic interest only. Similarly, the development and action phases of the cycle are simply what would happen next in any problem-solving or quality improvement effort.

Of course, if you are in an organization that does not have a standardized model for problem solving and incremental improvement, and you like the directed-creativity cycle, feel free to adopt it. The model and its activities work just as well for problem solving as they have for design applications.

In the boxed summaries describing the seven tools, I have noted how each tool maps onto the phases of the directed-creativity cycle. Of perhaps greater interest, of course, is how these seven tools of directed creativity map onto your problem-solving or quality improvement model. Obviously, with the many models that exist, I cannot possibly answer that question here. I can, however, give some general guidance to enable you to do it yourself.

All successful quality improvement and problem-solving models are based on the same fundamental principles (Plsek 1993a). Without getting into too much detail, these principles are the principles of quality management (for example, focus on customer, all work is a process) and the principles of problem-solving projects (for example, universal sequence of breakthrough, convergent/divergent thinking). One such principle is that all these models involve four generic categories of activities.

1. Identification and selection of improvement opportunities

2. Determination of the causes of the problem or barriers to improvement

3. Development and implementation of improvements

4. Establishment of ongoing control

It should be relatively easy to map the steps of your organization's quality improvement model into these four categories. Figure 11.4 cross-references the seven directed-creativity tools with these four categories of activities. I'll leave it to you to make the final translation of the tools onto your specific model.

Summary of Directed Creativity in Problem Solving and Incremental Improvement

The key points about the application of directed creativity in problem-solving and incremental improvement efforts are summarized in the quick reference section at the end of this chapter.

For many readers, I suspect that this may be a natural first application of the methods of directed creativity. It is a good application in which to learn. I have made it easy for you by identifying only seven tools from among the hundreds of possibilities. While I still earnestly hope that you will invent your own adaptations of this methods, my narrowing of the field of choice may help you get started. Another factor that makes this a good application in which to learn is that it is low risk. If the team was stuck and getting nowhere, it will be no worse off even if your fail in your application of these tools. It can't hurt, so give it a shot.

	1. Identification and selection of improvement opportunities	2. Determination of the causes of the problem or barriers to improvement	3. Development and implementation of improvements	4. Establishment of ongoing control
Purpose hierarchy	X		X	
Escapes		X	X	
Alternatives from fixed points			X	X
Analogies		X	X	X
Cinematics		X		X
Random words			X	
Enhancement checklist			X	X

Figure 11.4. Cross-reference of the seven directed-creativity tools and the generic activities in quality improvement models that they support.

Quick Reference:
The Application of Directed-Creativity in Problem Solving and Incremental Quality Improvement

Key Principles to Keep in Mind

- It is useful to have skills in both analytical and creative methods.

- It is okay to retain a preferred problem-solving style; just be prepared to switch over to another style when you are stuck in your thinking.

- Figure 11.2 lists the classic symptoms of stuck thinking; all these are variations on themes of emotional reactions, belief preservation, and satisficing.

- The seven tools for directed creativity can be used to enhance your organization's quality improvement and problem-solving process.

Seven Tools for Directed Creativity

- *Purpose hierarchy.* Multiple redefinitions of the problem or underlying purpose of the effort.

- *Escapes.* Escape rules, assumptions, paradigms, and so forth that are blocking solution.

- *Alternatives from fixed points.* Everything we currently do is but a means to some end. If we are experiencing a problem, maybe we should try an alternative means to accomplish the same ends.

- *Analogies.* Adapt concepts, approaches, and ideas from another setting into the context of our problem.

- *Cinematics.* Examine the problem scene closely, in slow motion and stop action, if possible.

- *Random words.* Free-associate a randomly selected noun, verb, preposition, or conjunction onto a problem situation.

- *Enhancement checklist.* Things to consider in developing creative ideas into implemented innovations.

CHAPTER 12

Summary and Future Directions in the Application of Creative Thinking in Quality Management

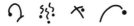

The real act of discovery consists not of finding new lands, but in seeing with new eyes.

Marcel Proust

The future ain't what it used to be.

Yogi Berra

I hope that you have enjoyed reading this book as much as I have enjoyed writing it. I also hope that you have already begun to apply some of the techniques in your work. I am excited about the endless possibilities that stem from the practice of directed creativity, specifically from its application to the field of quality management. In this final chapter, I will review the key points that I would like for you to have gotten from your study of this topic and briefly offer my views on the future role of directed creativity in quality management.

A Grand Review

In the preface I stated four objectives for this book. Let me now use those objectives as a framework to take you through a review of the major points of *Creativity, Innovation, and Quality.*

Objective 1. Enable the reader to understand recent advances from the field of cognitive science and describe how these advances unlock the creative potential in everyone. A review of the vast literature on creativity leads us to understand creativity as the connecting and rearranging of knowledge—in the minds of people who will allow themselves to think flexibly—to generate new, often surprising ideas that others judge to be useful.

Creative ideas are a product of mental processes. Quality managers know that improving the product begins with understanding the process. Understanding the mechanics of mind is, therefore, essential to the successful use of directed creativity. The key, relevant points from the research into the mechanics of mind are

- The mind is a self-organizing, patterning mechanism.

- This patterning mechanism is very efficient for day-to-day living (and that is good), but it works against creative thought.

- Our perception processes filter out most of what goes on around us and focus our attention toward signals in the environment that fit our existing patterns of how things should be.

- Our automatic memory processes rely on spreading electrical and chemical activity in the brain that reinforces the usual connections among the concepts that we have stored away.

- Our automatic judgment processes are also channeled toward reinforcing existing patterns from the past. They work automatically to ensure emotional comfort, preserve our beliefs, justify our choices, and avoid risk-taking. Judgment is never entirely rational or logical; it is always flavored with personal preferences and emotions.

- Mental processes are driven largely by heuristic rules of thumb that lead to productive thought. Heuristics are flexible, open-ended, purposefully somewhat vague pointers for thought.

While the mechanics of mind are optimized for playing back patterns in day-to-day living, everyone has the ability to temporarily break out of these patterns to make the novel mental connection essential to creative thinking. The key conclusion that we can draw from the research on mental processes and creative thought is this: If you can think, you can think creatively.

Objective 2: Enable the reader to recognize the underlying theory behind various tools of creative thinking. From our understanding of the mechanics of mind, we know that creative thinking depends on the use of heuristics that help us perceive the world freshly, make novel mental connections, and avoid the pull of judgment toward maintaining the old patterns. Specifically, a basic set of heuristics for getting started in directed creativity would include the following:

1. Make it a habit to purposefully pause and notice things.

2. Focus your creative energies on just a few topic areas that you genuinely care about and work on these purposefully for several weeks or months.

3. Avoid being too narrow in the way you define your problem or topic area; purposefully try broader definitions and see what insights you gain.

4. Try to come up with original and useful ideas by making novel associations among what you already know.

5. When you need creative ideas, remember: attention, escape, and movement.

6. Pause and carefully examine ideas that make you laugh the first time you hear them.

7. Recognize that your streams of thought and patterns of judgment are not inherently right or wrong; they are just what you think now based primarily on patterns from your past.

8. Make a deliberate effort to harvest, develop, and implement at least a few of the ideas you generate.

The models, methods, and tools of directed creativity support our efforts to exercise these mental heuristics.

The theory of creativity developed in the literature over the past 50 years further suggests that creative thought is a balance of imagination and analysis. Practitioners of quality management need not throw out their traditional, largely analytical tools in order to be creative. We simply need to supplement our tool kit.

In order to be creative, we must prepare through focus, observation, and analysis of the world around us. This preparation should lead us to a phase of purposeful imagination. It is in this imagination phase of the directed-creativity cycle that we generate new ideas. The development and action phases of the creative cycle bring our ideas to life and set us up for the next cycle of observation and imagination. Again, the various tools of directed creativity support our efforts in these four phases of the cycle.

While there are many creative-thinking tools in the literature, we need only three words to summarize the basic principles behind them all: *attention, escape,* and *movement.*

Objective 3: Enable the reader to develop his or her own techniques for generating creative ideas on demand. The attention, escape, and movement principles of directed creativity both explains the large number of methods available and enables us to invent even more. I have provided several resources to aid this invention process. Figure 4.1 summarizes the three principles of attention, escape, and movement. The preparation tools mind map in Figure 5.2 and the information in the various boxes in chapter 5, will stimulate your thinking about tools and methods for the preparation phase of the directed-creativity cycle. A mind map of the tools that support the imagination phase is given in Figure 6.2. Again, use this mind map and the boxes scattered throughout chapter 6 as you plan for specific idea generation sessions. Finally, I have also provided several checklists and matrix formats from the creativity and innovation literature for use in the development and action phases.

Whether you use a tool described here or one of your own invention, in order to be able to use a creativity tool effectively you should understand its workings relative to the mechanics of mind. If you do not understand how a particular tool works to stimulate your mind to attention, escape, or movement, select another tool. There are a nearly infinite number to choose from.

Objective 4: Enable the reader to use creative thinking techniques to stimulate innovation in the context of the challenges commonly encountered in the practice of quality management. Chapters 8 through 11 provide specific advice on the use of directed-creativity models and methods in process design, reengineering, product design, service design, customer-needs analysis, and problem-solving efforts. Review the quick reference sections at the ends of these chapters as you apply directed creativity in these various contexts. Your understanding of the basic theory, heuristics, model, and methods of directed creativity, along with these reference sections, should get you started in a useful direction.

This final objective contains the phrase "use creative thinking to stimulate innovation." Recall that it is possible to be creative (have novel ideas) without being innovative (reaping the rewards from those ideas). The difference lies in the willingness and skills to do something. I sincerely hope that after all you have learned, you are planning now to *do.*

Some Final Thoughts on Future Directions in the Application of Directed Creative Thinking in Quality Management

As I sit to write these final thoughts it is just two weeks after the 50th Annual Quality Congress (AQC) of ASQC. Futurist Alvin Toffler was the keynote speaker.

Alvin and Heidi Toffler's work has influenced many thinkers in government and industry. The Tofflers speak of the latter half of the twentieth century as the early days of the third wave of society. The first two waves saw humankind progress to an agricultural society and then to an industrial society. The third wave, the one that we in the developed world are in the midst of now, is the information society. Toffler told the AQC audience that whereas land was the key in the first wave (agricultural) and capital and equipment were the keys in the second wave (industrial), *ideas* would be the new keys to success in the third wave. Creativity, constant innovation, and the ability to produce ideas are the key skills of the information society. This is the world that the futurists envision. It is happening today.

To be sure, we have at least a little bit of time before the future fully arrives. The change that all of this will bring to our profession will be like, I think, the change that has occurred over the past 50 years. At the first annual gathering of quality control professionals in 1946, the attendees were almost exclusively focused on (to borrow from Shewhart) the control of manufactured quality. How many of them would have believed that just 40 to 50 short years later, the quality professional would be involved in strategic planning, design quality, service quality, and the like.

When we look back to the practice of quality management in the late 1990s from some future vantage point in the next century, we too will probably be amazed at how revolutionary the changes have been. I further suspect that we will not have to go very far out into the future to reach that vantage point. Scholars of the history of technology point out that the growth of technology follows an exponential, not linear, curve (the power of technology doubles every 18 months). This means that, in our technological society, the future arrives earlier and earlier each year. We may not have to wait 40 to 50 years to be able to look back and marvel at how much the practice of quality management has changed. The future will probably arrive sooner than we think.

Combining these observations about the exponential pace of change, how much quality management has and will change, and the Toffler's notion of the coming and upon us third wave, leads me to make a bold assertion. *Practitioners of quality management need to begin learning now how to produce high-quality, innovative ideas, or they risk becoming largely irrelevant over the next 10 to 15 years.*

Obviously, this comes across as an incredibly self-serving assertion. I have the integrity to admit that. Since I have learned to escape the tyranny of the I-am-right-you-are-wrong way of thinking, I do not have the need to prove or debate the matter. At the same time, the mental valleys of my judgment subprocesses make me emotionally comfortable with the notion that I am preparing myself for the future and doing my part to help prepare others. I am also comfortable leaving it to you to decide what you think the future holds. Whatever you believe the future to be, I hope that you are actively preparing yourself for it now. It will be here sooner than you think.

In my picture of the future, I see practitioners of quality management playing a key role in facilitating the production of high-quality concepts and ideas. We will train others to be innovative in their daily work. We will facilitate groups searching for innovative ideas. Innovation, like quality, will be everyone's responsibility. Our role will be to help design the processes and system structures that enable innovative ideas to emerge. Importantly, we will also find a role in ensuring that the voice of the customer is brought into the process of the production of ideas. Finally, though we will struggle mightily to do it, we will find ways to measure the process of innovation itself, the quality of ideas, and the cost of poor ideas.

That is what I see for the future. I could be wrong, but right now I do not think so. The theory, heuristics, models, methods, and tools in this book are intended as an elementary text for preparing for this future scenario.

Forget about the future, though. As I pointed out in chapter 1, I believe that we have an obligation to our organizations to learn how to be more innovative today. Customers want innovative products and services. How can we say that we are customer advocates and not know something about the process of bringing about innovation? History shows that success in the competitive marketplace depends, at least in part, on an organization's ability to innovate. After insisting for so long that the quality message must be heard because it is essential to success in the competitive marketplace, how can we now dismiss the need to focus on such a critical marketplace success factor?

I believe that the topic of directed creativity is not only timely for the future, it is timely for today. I leave it to you to make up your own mind. What ever you decide, act on your belief.

There is much more that could be said, and much more that will be learned, about the application of directed creativity in quality management. I invite you to document your efforts and publish your work for others to see. I would be happy to help in any way I can; contact me as described in the preface.

In addition to knowing something new, I hope that you are now motivated to do something new. I believe that there is a compelling, customer-oriented, competition-driven case for more innovation in our organizations today and in the future. I also believe that it will not happen on its own.

In the end, remember the wisdom that the alien sage Yoda offered to the young Jedi knight, Luke Skywalker, in *The Empire Strikes Back*. After learning the techniques of the Jedi, Luke told his teacher Yoda that he would try to put them into practice. "Try?" Yoda retorted sternly, "There is no try. There is only do and not do."

Happy creating!

APPENDIX

Resources for Continued Practice and Learning

List of Manipulative Verbs

(Sources: Osborn 1953; Koberg and Bagnall 1981; Higgins 1994; von Oech 1986)

magnify	minify	rearrange	alter	adapt
modify	substitute	reverse	combine	harden
multiply	divide	subdue	squeeze	separate
transpose	compare	rotate	invert	soften
by-pass	widen	thicken	protect	integrate
dissect	eliminate	repel	flatten	symbolize

List of Relational Words
(Prepositions and Conjunctions)

(Sources: Crovitz 1970; VanGundy 1992)

about	above	after	against	along
among	and	around	as	at
because	before	behind	beside	between
beyond	but	by	down	during
except	for	from	if	in
into	near	not	now	of
off	on	opposite	or	out
over	past	round	since	so
still	then	though	through	till
to	toward	under	up	when
where	while	with	within	without

List of Random Nouns

(Sources: de Bono 1967, 1969, 1992; von Oech 1983, 1986; Michalko 1991)

tongue	plastic	wrench	star	gourmet
money	flashlight	dice	windsurfer	ribbon
camera	can	pencil	pin	watermelon
soda	tape	necklace	mold	gutter
jewel	house	gully	fuel	music
wastebasket	x-ray	cup	paint	lamb
stomach	rain	telescope	knee	pole
champagne	top	beans	angel	student
lips	salmon	lungs	gasoline	tub
fox	chimney	bikini	prison	tax
igloo	fireplace	ax	smoke	referee
cork	stream	strip	jellyfish	vines
bomb	umbrella	cone	flood	frog
rib	table	flower	towel	window
locker	toy	podium	saucer	rainbow
amoebae	disk	snail	rice	grass
fence	horse	shed	leaves	bird
tractor	Olympics	straw	mirror	chapter
vacuum	bread	cyclone	gravy	emerald
gang	pliers	binoculars	studio	parakeet
fingernail	meadow	bat	curb	zipper
gutter	outlet	elbow	weeds	paper
wig	road	sauna	cord	duck
floor	book	announcer	diaper	cake
terrorist	sandwich	lightning	candle	crown
jelly	fossil	pet	ruler	circus
plug	coach	wallpaper	ham	envelope
actor	riot	clay	train	television
garage	stadium	mold	detective	magazine
medal	refrigerator	sonar	planet	hostage

List of Parallel Worlds for Random Analogies

(Excerpted from *Thinkertoys,* copyright 1991, by Michael Michalko, with permission from Ten Speed Press, P.O. Box 7123, Berkeley, CA 94707.)

Accounting	Acupuncture	Animal kingdom	Architecture
Art	Astrology	Astronomy	Ballet
Baseball	Basketball	Biography	Biology
Birds	Cancer	Bowling	Calculus
Cartoons	Cardiology	Caribbean	Chiropractors
Chemistry	China	Composers	Civil rights
Civil war	Comics	Computers	Dance
Deserts	Dentistry	Economics	England
Entertainment	Evolution	Fast food	Farming
Fishing	Fine cooking	Funeral homes	Finance
Football	Flying	Geology	Geography
Government	Golf	Grocery stores	Garbage collection
Germany	Great Depression	Great books	Hunting
Hawaii	History	Hypnosis	I.R.S.
India	Inventions	Interior decorating	Insects
Japan	Jungles	Journalism	Korea
Law	Literature	Law enforcement	Mafia
Math	Medicine	Manufacturing	Military
Mining	Meteorology	Monuments	Moon
Monasteries	Music	Mythology	Movies
Nutrition	Nuclear physics	Oceans	Olympics
Old West	Pharmacology	Photography	Physical fitness
Philosophy	Physics	Planets	Physical therapy
Political science	Politics	Plumbing	Printing
Psychiatry	Pornography	Publishing	Psychology
Religion	Restaurants	Revolutionary war	Resorts
Sculpture	Seminars	Sailing	Skiing
Soap operas	Shakespeare plays	South America	Space
Sociology	Stars	Special education	Steel industry
TV news	Taverns	Talk radio	Television
Tennis	Transportation	Terrorism	Theater
Travel industry	Sun	Unions	Vatican
Vietnam war	Wall Street	World War I	World War II
Wine	Warehousing	Yukon	Zoo

Internet Web Sites on Creativity and Innovation

The World Wide Web on the Internet is a constantly changing network of both great information and useless junk. Compiling a list of Internet web sites for a book that will be used over a several-year period is a hopeless task. By the time you read this, some of the sites may have either disappeared or become transformed from information into junk. Conversely, some of the sites that I visited, but discarded, in preparing this list may have now turned from junk into information. Of course, there are new sites being created each day. (For reference, I visited and verified all of the sites below on July 20–25, 1996. I visited several hundred sites during that period and selected the 25 that are cited.)

So consider my list as only a starting point for your exploration. Use an Internet search engine like Yahoo! or AltaVista and search on the words *creativity* or *innovation* to see what you come up with. I purposefully chose to designate the first three sites listed below as starting points because they appear to be regularly updated and contain links to many other web pages. I personally maintain the first site and will post new information there as I uncover it.

Starting Points

http://www.DirectedCreativity.com/

> This is my web site. Includes descriptions of the models and tools covered in this book; along with other resources such as random word lists, application examples, and downloadable articles. Contact me through the site to get advice on the use of directed creativity in the specific situations you face. I encourage you to contribute to the site to make it the interactive communications center for practitioners of directed creativity.

http://www.ozemail.com.au/~caveman/Creative/

The Creativity Web Page is a creation of Charles Cave in Sydney, Australia. Great page with lots of good information that is updated regularly. Extensive list of books on creativity. Fabulous resource describing the various software products that are available to support creative thinking. Regularly updated instructions on how to subscribe to the various Internet list servers on creativity-related topics; for example, there is a de Bono list server. Extensive list of links to other great web sites.

http://www.mcmaster.ca/busdocs/irc.html

Home page of the Innovation Research Center at the Michael G. DeGroote School of Business at McMaster University, Hamilton, Ontario, Canada. Contains a list of links to over two dozen web pages on the topic of innovation.

Sites with Content That Can Be Used to Provoke Creative Thinking

http://www.thetech.org/

Home page of the Tech Museum of Innovation in San Jose, California. Contains interactive, on-line exhibits on subjects related to technology and innovation. Gives a good, basic level of understanding that can be useful in generating analogies in the preparation phase of the directed-creativity cycle.

http://users.aol.com/granius/essays.htm

A collection of creative essays taking unique points of view on topics ranging from classical Greek philosophy to reducing health care costs. You will not agree with most of what is said, but remember directed creativity heuristic 7: no inherent right or wrong. Consider using the ideas expressed as stepping-stone provocations in the imagination phase of the directed-creativity cycle.

http://mixteca.com/

Home page for Creative Living. Well-designed page. The mind matters section contains puzzles, mind teasers, and information on creativity enhancement. Potentially useful in imagination phase.

http://www.helicon.com/simplex/simplex.htm

Information on Min Basadur's SIMPLEX creative problem-solving model. While the words are different, you'll have no trouble relating it to the cycle in this book. The page contains advice that spans the creative process.

http://www.quantumbooks.com/Creativity.html

Very nice site containing hypertext guidelines for creativity thinking and lots of interesting historical examples. The guidelines can be helpful in all phases of the directed-creativity cycle. The historical examples can be used as provocation and analogies to explore in the preparation and imagination phases.

http://galileo.metatech.com/ideaweb.htm

Home page of The Idea Web—Creativity Explorer containing an on-line creativity course and lots of examples. Again, potentially useful as analogies and provocations.

http://world.brain.com/index.cgi/UN/Index.html

Very nice site produced by BrainTainment Resources, Inc. Creativity games, resources, and a quick survey instrument. Potentially useful for analogies and provocations.

Associations and Educational Institutions

http://indyunix.iupui.edu/~ncci/ncci.html

Home page of the National Center for Creativity and Innovation in Indianapolis. This organization was established to "help facilitate the growing interest in the field of creativity and innovation." They are a strong advocate for the teachings of Edward de Bono. Information on membership, conferences, and so on.

http://www.thinksmart.com/itn/
Home page of the Innovative Thinking Network in Santa Barbara, California. Information on membership, conferences, the organization's journal, and so forth.

http://www.cre8con.org/
Web site for the annual Portland Creativity Conference.

http://web.mit.edu/icrmot/www/
Home page for MIT's International Center for Research on the Management of Technology. Describes the center and its course offerings. Links to working papers and books published by students and faculty at the center.

http://www.wisdom-inc.com/~wisdom1/btt.shtml
Home page for the Center for Breakthrough Thinking. Readings, events, services, and so on.

http://www.ideas.wis.net/
Home page for the Ideas Digest Online Center for Innovation. Features examples of innovative products, a bookstore, and announcements of innovation/creative conferences. Oriented toward small business and entrepreneurs. Good information, nice web site.

http://www.pol.com/GoCreate/
Web site of The Right Brain Works (located in Hawaii, I think). The page boldly declares that it was "established in 1990 as the creative center of the universe." Lots of good resources and links to other sites. Good list of creativity-enhancing software. The big plus is the cool picture of the baby.

http://www.webscope.com/project_mind/project_mind.html
Home page of a self-declared "creativity think tank" dedicated to improving the human condition and answering deep philosophical questions. Interesting stuff.

http://www.euronet.nl/users/xplore/creativity/EACI.HTML
Home page of the European Association for Creativity and Innovation. Information on membership, conferences, and so forth.

http://dawww.epfl.ch/info/enseignement/3e_cycles_ESST/c2.html
   Information on a masters program entitled "The Strategic Management
   of Innovation" offered by the European Inter-University Association on
   Society, Science, and Technology.

http://wire.co.uk/innovation/
   The Innovation Site is a British-based web page offering information
   about innovation seminars in the United Kingdom and international studies of innovation competitiveness.

http://ourworld.compuserve.com/homepages/cci_ltd/
   Home page for CCI Teletraining International in Holland. The group
   offers a creativity teletraining course that you can complete via e-mail.

Competitions and Idea Databases

http://newciv.org/worldtrans/BOV/BOVTOP.HTML
   The Global Idea Bank is a project of the Institute for Social Inventions in
   London. The page invites you to submit creative ideas in a variety of categories and offers a £1000 prize (about $1500 U.S.). Great place to get
   some recognition for your ideas.

http://www.x-com.de/missing-things/
   This web page is dedicated to an international competition to design creative products and services to improve public transportation. Send e-mail to
   Peter Ruthenberg in Berlin at sutter@x-com.de for information about the
   winner of the competition and notices about future creative competitions.

http://www.seussville.com/contestinfo.html
   Use your creativity to design a new Dr. Seuss character. But be careful
   that he or she is not too much like your boss, ex-spouse, or in-laws! ;-)

Organizations That Support Creative Thinking

National Center for Creativity and Innovation
17 West Market, Suite 980
Indianapolis, IN 46203

Creative Education Foundation
1050 Union Road
Buffalo, NY 14224

Center for Studies in Creativity
Buffalo State College
1300 Elmwood Avenue
Buffalo, NY 14224

The Graduate Program in Creativity, School of Education
University of Massachusetts at Amherst
Amherst, MA 01003

Alden B. Dow Creativity Center
Northwood University
3225 Cook Road
Midland, MI 48640

Creative Thinking Association of America
P.O. Box 308013
Cleveland, OH 44130

American Creativity Association
P.O. Box 26068
St. Paul, MN 55126

Center for Creative Leadership
1 Leadership Place
4152 Independence Court, #C-7
Sarasota, FL 34234

Center for Creative Studies
201 East Kirby
Detroit, MI 48202

Center for Research in Applied Creativity
184 Lovers Lane
Ancaster, Ontario, Canada L9G 1G8

Creativity Consortium
116 Galley Avenue
Toronto, Ontario, Canada M6R 1H1

The Institute for Social Invention
20 Heber Road
London, England NW2 6AA

European Association for Creativity and Innovation (EACI)
c/o Patrick Colemont
P.O. Box 112 6400 AC
Heerlen, The Netherlands

European Foundation for Creativity and Innovation
Oude Kuringerbaan 13 B B-3500
Hasselt, Belgium

Essential Recommended Reading on the Topic of Creativity

The following five books will give you a deeper understanding of the theory and tools of creativity. Anyone who is serious about being a more creative thinker should have these books in his or her personal library.

1. D. N. Perkins, *The Mind's Best Work.* Cambridge, Mass.: Harvard Univ. Press, 1981.

This classic text takes you through the essential theory behind the modern view that creativity is not the result of some magical genius that only a few possess. While Perkins is a great scholar and there are extensive endnotes for those who are interested in the primary references, the book itself is written in an easy-to-read populist style.

2. Edward de Bono, *Serious Creativity.* New York: HarperCollins, 1992.

Edward de Bono is prolific writer on the topic of thinking in general and creative thinking in particular. Part 1 of this text will introduce you to such classic de Bono-ims as "lateral thinking" and the "self-organizing mechanism of mind." Though de Bono never refers directly to the research from the cognitive sciences, you will find his work consistent with it. Part 2 covers tools and techniques for creative thinking, while part 3 discusses issues of organizationwide creative thinking. de Bono's style is crisp, sometimes too crisp, but the book is fun to read.

3. Robert J. Sternberg, ed. *The Nature of Creativity.* Cambridge: Cambridge University Press, 1988.

This is the most up-to-date, comprehensive scholarly reference on the topic. Sternberg is an incredible synthesizer of others' work, as well as a major contributor to the field himself. The 17 chapters are well-written and relatively free from the repetition one sometimes finds in a collected work such as this. The contributor's list reads like a who's who of psychologists, educators, philosophers, and computer scientists who are currently working in the field of thinking about creativity.

4. James Higgins, *101 Creative Problem Solving Techniques.* Winter Park, Fla.: New Management Publishing Company, 1994.

This is my favorite catalogue of creative thinking tools. Each of the 101 tools is explained in detail; the book should provide you with plenty of food for thought. The presentation is organized around the Creative Problem Solving (CPS) model, but the translation to the model we have used in this book is easy.

5. Arthur VanGundy, *Idea Power.* New York: American Management Association, 1992.

Like the Higgins book, this is another great catalogue of tools. In addition, VanGundy has more to say about group and organizational creativity. The appendix alone justifies the cost of the book. It contains an exhaustive list of videotapes, training programs, and software for creative thinking.

Bibliography

Ackoff, R. L. 1978. *The art of problem solving.* New York: Wiley.

———. 1995. Keynote address to the ASQC 49th Annual Quality Congress, 13 May, Cincinnati, Ohio.

Ackoff, R. L., E. Finnel, and J. Gharajedaghi. 1984. *A guide to controlling your corporation's future.* New York: John Wiley & Sons.

Adams, J. L. 1974. *Conceptual blockbusting.* Reading, Mass.: Addison-Wesley.

———. 1986. *The care and feeding of ideas.* Reading, Mass.: Addison-Wesley.

Agor, W. H. 1989. *Intuition in organizations: Leading and managing productively.* Newbury Park, Calif.: Sage Publications.

Amabile, T. M. 1983. *The social psychology of creativity.* New York: Springer-Verlag.

———. 1989. *Growing up creative: Nurturing a life of creativity.* New York: Crown.

Amabile, T. M., W. DeJong, and M. R. Lepper. 1976. Effects of externally imposed deadlines on subsequent intrinsic motivation. *Journal of Personality and Social Psychology* 34: 92–98.

Anderson, J. R. 1983. *The architecture of cognition.* Cambridge, Mass.: Harvard University Press.

Argyris, C. 1990. *Overcoming organizational defenses.* Boston, Mass.: Allyn and Bacon.

Arieti, S. 1976. *Creativity: The magical synthesis.* New York: Basic Books.

Atkinson, P. E. 1990. *Creating culture change: The key to successful total quality management.* London: IFS Ltd.

Barker, J. A. 1992. *Future edge.* New York: Morrow.

Basadur, M. 1995. *The power of innovation: How to make innovation a way of life and put creative solutions to work.* London: Pitmann Publishing.

Beckhard, R., and R. T. Harris. 1987. *Organizational transitions: Managing complex change.* 2d ed. Reading, Mass.: Addison-Wesley.

Bower, J. L., and C. M. Christensen. 1995. Disruptive technologies: catching the wave. *Harvard Business Review* 73, no. 1: 43–53.

Brassard, M. 1989. *The memory jogger plus.* Methuen, Mass.: GOAL/QPC.

Brightman, H. 1988. *Group problem solving: An improved managerial approach.* Atlanta, Ga.: Georgia State University Press.

Buzan, T. 1989. *Use both sides of your brain.* 3d ed. New York: Penguin Books.

Camp, R. C. 1989. *Benchmarking: The search for industry best practices that lead to superior performance.* Milwaukee, Wisc.: ASQC Quality Press.

Carr, C. 1994. *The competitive power of constant creativity.* New York: AMACOM.

Cerf, C., and V. Navasky. 1984. *The experts speak.* New York: Pantheon Books.

Cherniak, C. 1986. *Minimal rationality.* Cambridge, Mass.: MIT Press.

Chi, M. T. H., R. Glaser, and E. Rees. 1982. Expertise in problem solving. In *Advances in the psychology of human intelligence,* Vol. 1, edited by R. J. Sternberg. Hillsdale, N.J.: Erlbaum.

Churchland, P. M. 1990. Cognitive activity in artificial neural networks. In *An invitation to cognitive science: Thinking,* Vol. 3, edited by D. N. Osherson and E. E. Smith. Cambridge, Mass.: MIT Press.

Clark, C. H. 1958. *Brainstorming: How to create ideas.* North Hollywood, Calif.: Wilshire Book Company.

Crawford, R. P. 1954. *The techniques of creative thinking.* Burlington, Vt.: Fraser Publishing.

———. 1964. *Direct creativity with attribute listing.* Burlington, Vt.: Fraser Publishing.

Crosby, P. 1979. *Quality is free: The art of making quality certain.* New York: McGraw-Hill.

Crovitz, H. F. 1970. *Galton's walk.* New York: Harper & Row.

Csikszentmihalyi, M. 1988. Society, culture, and person: A systems view of creativity. In *The nature of creativity,* edited by R. J. Sternberg. Cambridge: Cambridge University Press.

Currid, C. 1994. *The reengineering Toolkit: 15 tools and technologies for reengineering your organization.* Rocklin, Calif.: Prima Publishing.

Dalziel, M. M. and S. C. Schoonover. 1988. *Changing ways: A practical tool for implementing change within organizations.* New York: AMACOM.

Davenport, T. H. 1993. *Process innovation: Reengineering work through information technology.* Boston: Harvard University Press.

de Bono, E. 1967. *Use of lateral thinking.* London: Penguin Books.

———. 1969. *Mechanism of mind.* London: Penguin Books.

———. 1972. *Po: Beyond yes and no.* London: Penguin Books.

———. 1985. *Six thinking hats.* London: Penguin Books.

———. 1990. *I am right you are wrong.* London: Penguin Books.

———. 1992. *Serious creativity.* New York: HarperCollins Publishing.

———. 1994. Creativity and quality. *Quality Management in Health Care* 2, no. 3: 1–4.

de Geus, A. 1988. Planning as learning. *Harvard Business Review* 66, no. 2: 70–74.

De Groot, A. D. 1965. *Thought and choice in chess.* The Hague: Mouton.

Deming, W. E. 1986. *Out of the crisis.* Cambridge, Mass.: MIT Center for Advanced Engineering Study.

———. 1993. *The new economics.* Cambridge, Mass.: MIT Center for Advanced Engineering Study.

Drucker, P. 1995. The information executives truly need. *Harvard Business Review* 73, no. 1: 54–62.

Eureka, W. E., and N. E. Ryan. 1988. *The customer-driven company: Managerial perspectives on QFD.* Dearborn, Mich.: ASI Press.

Fiero, J. 1992. The Crawford slip method. *Quality Progress* 25, no. 5: 40–43.

Fisher, A. B. 1995. Creating stockholder wealth. *Fortune,* December 11, 105–116.

Foster, R. 1986. *Innovation: The attacker's advantage.* New York: Summit Books.

Fritz, R. 1991. *Creating.* New York: Fawcett.

Gardner, H. 1985. *The mind's new science.* New York: Basic Books.

———. 1993. *Creating minds.* New York: Basic Books.

Garvin, D. A. 1988. *Managing quality: The strategic and competitive edge.* New York: Free Press.

Getzels, J. and M. Csikszentmihalyi. 1976. *The creative vision: A longitudinal study of problem finding in art.* New York: Wiley.

Ghiselin, B. ed. 1952. *The creative process.* Berkeley, Calif.: University of California Press.

Gordon, W. J. J. 1961. *Synectics: The development of creative capacity.* New York: Harper & Row.

Guilford, J. P. 1950. Creativity. *American Psychologist* 5, no. 9: 444–445.

Haefele, J. W. 1962. *Creativity and innovation.* New York: Van Nostrand Reinhold.

Hall, G., J. Rosenthal, and J. Wade. 1993. How to make reengineering really work. *Harvard Business Review* 71, no. 6: 119–131.

Hammer, M. 1990. Reengineering work: Don't automate, obliterate. *Harvard Business Review* 68, no. 4: 104–122.

Hammer, M., and J. Champy. 1993. *Reengineering the corporation.* New York: HarperCollins.

Hammer, M., with S. A. Stanton. 1995. *The reengineering revolution.* New York: HarperCollins.

Harrington, H. J. 1991. *Business process improvement.* New York: McGraw-Hill.

Hebb, D. O. 1949. *The organization of behavior.* New York: Wiley.

Higgins, J. M. 1994. *101 creative problem solving techniques.* Winter Park, Fla.: New Management Publishing Company.

Holyoak, K. J. 1990. Problem solving. In *An invitation to cognitive science: Thinking,* Vol. 3, edited by D. N. Osherson and E. E. Smith. Cambridge, Mass.: MIT Press.

Hutton, D. W. 1995. *The change agents' handbook: A survival guide for quality improvement champions.* Milwaukee, Wisc.: ASQC Quality Press.

Isaksen, S. G., and D. J. Trefflinger. 1985. *Creative problem solving: The basic course.* Buffalo, N.Y.: Bearly Publishing.

Ishikawa, K. 1985. *What is total quality control: The Japanese way.* Translated by David J. Lu. Englewood Cliffs, N.J.: Prentice-Hall.

Johnson, G. 1991. *In the palaces of memory.* New York: Vintage Books.

Johnson, P. T. 1988. Why I race against phantom competitors. *Harvard Business Review* (September–October): 106–112.

Johnson-Laird, P. N. 1983. *Mental models: Towards a cognitive science of language, inference, and consciousness.* Cambridge, Mass.: Harvard University Press.

Juran, J.M. 1964. *Managerial breakthrough.* New York: McGraw-Hill.

———. 1989. *Juran on leadership for quality.* New York: Free Press.

———. 1992. *Juran on quality by design.* New York: Free Press.

Juran, J. M., and F. M. Gryna. 1980. *Quality planning and analysis.* New York: McGraw-Hill.

Kano, N., N. Seraku, F. Takahashi, and S. Tsuji. 1984. Attractive quality and must-be quality. *Quality* 14, no. 2: 39–48.

Kanter, R. M. 1983. *The change masters: Innovation and entrepeneurship in the American corporation.* New York: Simon & Schuster.

Kanter, R. M., B. Stein, and T. Jick. 1992. *The challenge of organizational change.* New York: Simon & Schuster.

Kiechel, W. III. 1988. The politics of innovation. *Fortune,* 11 April, 131–132.

Kepner, C., and B. S. Tregoe. 1963. *The rational manager.* New York: McGraw-Hill.

———. 1981. *The new rational manager.* Princeton, N.J.: Princeton Research Press.

Kidder, T. 1981. *The soul of the new machine.* Boston: Little, Brown and Co.

King, B. 1987. *Better designs in half the time: Implementing quality function deployment in America.* Methuen, Mass.: GOAL/QPC.

Koberg, D., and J. Bagnall. 1981. *The all new universal traveler: A soft-systems guide to creativity, problem-solving, and the process of reaching goals.* Los Altos, Calif.: William Kaufmann, Inc.

Koestler, A. 1964. *The act of creation.* London: Arkana.

Kohn, A. 1990. *The brighter side of human nature: Altruism and empathy in everyday life.* New York: Basic Books.

———. 1992. *No contest: The case against competition.* New York: Houghton-Mifflin.

———. 1993. *Punished by rewards: The trouble with gold stars, incentive plans, praise, and other bribes.* New York: Houghton-Mifflin.

Kotter, J. P. 1995. Leading change: why transformation efforts fail. *Harvard Business Review* 73, no. 2: 59–67.

Krone, R. M. 1990. Improving brainpower productivity. *Journal of Quality and Participation* (December): 80–84.

Kuhn, T. S. 1962. *The structure of scientific revolution.* Chicago: University of Chicago Press.

Langley, P., and R. Jones. 1988. A computational model of scientific insight. In *The nature of creativity,* edited by R. J. Sternberg. Cambridge: Cambridge University Press.

Larkin, J. H., J. McDermott, D. P. Simon, and H. A. Simon. 1980. Expert and novice performance in solving physics problems. *Science* 208: 1335–1342.

LeBoeuf, M. 1980. *Imagineering: How to profit from your creative powers.* New York: McGraw-Hill.

Lesgold, A. 1988. Expertise in a complex skill: diagnosing X-ray pictures. In *The nature of expertise,* edited by M. T. H. Chi, R. Glaser, and M. J. Farr. Hillsdale, N.J.: Erlbaum.

Lewis, C. I. 1929. *Mind and the world order.* New York: Scribner.

Majaro, S. 1988. *The creative gap: Managing ideas for profit.* New York: McGraw-Hill.

Mattimore, B. W. 1991. Brainstormer's boot camp. *Success* (October): 24.

McClelland, J. L., and D. E. Rumelhart. 1986. *Parallel distributed processing: Explorations in the microstructure of cognition. Volume 2, psychological and biological models.* Cambridge, Mass.: MIT Press.

McGartland, G. 1994. *Thunderbolt thinking: Transform your insights and options into powerful results.* Austin, Tex.: Bernard-Davis.

Michalko, M. 1991. *Thinkertoys: A handbook of business creativity for the '90s.* Berkeley, Calif.: Ten Speed Press.

Mizuno, S., ed. 1988. *Management for quality improvement: The seven new QC tools.* Cambridge, Mass.: Productivity Press.

Morris, J. 1992. *Creative breakthroughs: Tap the power of your unconscious mind.* New York: Warner Books.

Nadler, G., and S. Hibino. 1994. *Breakthrough thinking.* 2d ed. Roklin, Calif.: Prima.

Neisser, U. 1967. *Cognitive psychology.* New York: Appleton Century Crofts.

Newell, A., and H. A. Simon. 1972. *Human problem solving.* Englewood Cliffs, N.J.: Prentice-Hall.

Nowlin, D. L. 1994. Creating a culture of innovation and quality at 3M. *Quality Management in Health Care* 2, no. 3: 36–43.

Osborn, A. 1953. *Applied imagination.* New York: Charles Scribner.

Osherson, D. N. (1990) Judgment. In *An invitation to cognitive science: Thinking,* Vol. 3, edited by D. N. Osherson and E. E. Smith. Cambridge, Mass.: MIT Press.

Osherson, D. N., and E. E. Smith. 1990. *An invitation to cognitive science: Thinking,* Vol. 3. Cambridge, Mass.: MIT Press.

O'Toole, J. 1995. *Leading change: Overcoming the ideology of comfort and the tyranny of custom.* San Fransisco: Jossey-Bass.

Parnes, S. J. 1992. *Sourcebook for creative problem solving.* Buffalo, N.Y.: Creative Education Foundation Press.

Pearson, A. F. 1979. Communication, creativity, and commitment: A look at the collective notebook approach. In *Proceedings of Creativity Week, I 1978,* edited by S. S. Gryskiewicz. Greensboro, N.C.: Center for Creative Leadership.

Perkins, D. N. 1981. *The mind's best work.* Cambridge, Mass.: Harvard University Press.

Petroski, H. 1985. *To engineer is human: The role of failure in successful design.* New York: Barnes & Noble.

Petrozzo, D. P,. and J. C. Stepper. 1994. *Successful reengineering: Now you know what it is—Here is how to do it!* New York: Van Nostrand.

Placek, D. J. 1989. Creativity survey shows who is doing what: How to get your teams on the road to creativity. *Marketing News,* 6 November, 14.

Plsek, P. E. 1987. Defining quality at the marketing-development interface. *Quality Progress* 20, no. 6: 28–36.

———. 1993a. Quality improvement models. *Quality Management in Health Care* 1, no. 2: 69–81.

———. 1993b. Management and planning tools of TQM. *Quality Management in Health Care* 1, no. 3: 59–72.

———. 1994. Directed creativity. *Quality Management in Health Care* 2, no. 3: 62–76.

———. 1995. Tapping creativity in healthcare organizations. In *The quality letter for healthcare leaders: CQI annual 1995.* Rockville, Md.: Bader & Associates.

———. 1996. Bringing creativity to the pursuit of quality. In *ASQC 50th Annual Quality Congress proceedings.* Milwaukee, Wisc.: ASQC.

Polya, G. 1957. *How to solve it: A new aspect of mathematical method.* 2d ed. Princeton, N.J.: Princeton University Press.

Porter, M. E. 1980. *Competitive strategy: Techniques for analyzing industries and competitors.* New York: Free Press.

Potter, M. C. 1990. Remembering. In *An invitation to cognitive science: Thinking, Volume 3,* edited by D. N. Osherson and E. E Smith. Cambridge, Mass.: MIT Press.

Prince, G. M. 1970. *The practice of creativity.* New York: Harper & Row.

Quillian, M. R. 1986. Semantic memory. In *Semantic information processing,* edited by M. L. Minsky. Cambridge, Mass.: MIT Press.

Ray, M. L., and R. Myers. 1986. *Creativity in business.* New York: Doubleday.

Restak, R. M. 1991. *The brain has a mind of its own: Insights from a practicing neurologist.* New York: Crown.

Rice, B. 1984. Imagination to go. *Psychology Today* (May): 48.

Roberts, H. V., and B. F. Sergesketter. 1993. *Quality is personal: A foundation for total quality management.* New York: Free Press.

Rowen, R. 1986. *The intuitive manager.* New York: Little, Brown & Co.

Ryan, K. D., and D. K. Oestreich. 1991. *Driving fear out of the workplace.* San Francisco: Jossey-Bass.

Scheffler, I. 1967. *Science and subjectivity.* Indianapolis, Ind.: Bobbs-Merrill.

Schoenfeld, A. H. 1979. Explicit heuristic training as a variable in problem solving performance. *Journal of Research in Mathematics Education* 10, no. 3: 173–187.

Scholtes, P. R. 1988. *The team handbook.* Madison, Wisc.: Joiner Associates.

Schumpeter, J. 1939. *Business cycles: A theoretical, historical, and statistical analysis of the capitalist process.* New York: McGraw-Hill.

Senge, P. M. 1990. *The fifth discipline: The art and practice of the learning organization.* New York: Doubleday.

Senge, P. M., R. Roberts, R. B. Ross, B. J. Smith, and A. Kleiner. 1994. *The fifth discipline fieldbook: Strategies and tools for building a learning organization.* New York: Doubleday.

Shekerjian, D. 1990. *Uncommon genius: How great ideas are born.* New York: Penguin Books.

Shewhart, W. A. [1939] 1986. *Statistical method from the viewpoint of quality control.* New York: Dover.

Simon, H. A. 1981. *The sciences of the artificial.* 2d ed. Cambridge, Mass.: MIT Press.

Sperling, G. 1960. The information available in brief visual presentations. *Psychological monographs* 24, no. 11.

Sternberg, R. J. 1988. *The triarchic mind.* New York: Penguin.

———, ed. 1988. *The nature of creativity.* Cambridge: Cambridge University Press.

Sternberg, R. J., and T. I. Lubart. 1995. *Defying the crowd: Cultivating creativity in a culture of conformity.* New York: Free Press.

Stich, S. P. 1990. Rationality. In *An invitation to cognitive science: Thinking,* Vol. 3, edited by D. N. Osherson and E. E. Smith. Cambridge, Mass.: MIT Press.

Tardif, T. Z., and R. J. Sternberg. 1988. What do we know about creativity? In *The nature of creativity,* edited by R. J. Sternberg. Cambridge, England: Cambridge University Press.

Tatsuno, S. M. 1990. *Created in Japan: From imitators to world-class innovators.* New York: Harper & Row.

Taylor, C. W. 1964. *Widening horizons in creativity.* New York: Wiley.

Tempe, A. D., ed. 1987. *Creativity: Volume 4 in the Facts On File series on the art and science of business management.* New York: KEND Publishing.

Torrence, E. P. 1987. *The blazing drive: The creative personality.* Buffalo, N.Y.: Bearly Limited.

Tversky, A., and D. Kahneman. 1973. Judgment under uncertainty: heuristics and biases. *Science* 185:1124–1131.

————. 1981. The framing of decisions and the psychology of choice. *Science* 211:453–458.

Usrey, M. W., and K. J. Dooley. 1996. The dimensions of software quality. *Quality Management Journal* 3, no. 3:67–86.

Utterbeck, J. M. 1994. *Mastering the Dynamics of Innovation.* Boston: Harvard Business School Press.

VanGundy, A. B. 1987. *Creative problem solving.* New York: Quorum Books.

————. 1992. *Idea power.* New York: American Management Association.

von Hipple, E. 1988. *The sources of innovation.* New York: Oxford University Press.

von Oech, R. 1983. *A whack on the side of the head.* New York: Warner Books.

————. 1986. *A kick in the seat of the pants.* New York: Harper Perriniel.

Wack, P. 1985. Scenarios: Uncharted waters ahead. *Harvard Business Review* 63, no. 5: 73–89.

Wallas, G. 1926. *The art of thought.* New York: Harcourt Brace.

Wallace, D. B., and H. E. Gruber. 1989. *Creative people at work.* New York: Oxford University Press.

Wason, P., and P. N. Johnson-Laird. 1970. A conflict between selecting and evaluating information in an inferential task. *British Journal of Psychology* 61: 509–515.

Weisberg, R. W. 1993. *Creativity: Beyond the myth of genius.* New York: W. H. Freeman.

Wonder, J., and P. Donovan. 1984. *Whole brain thinking.* New York: Ballantine.

Wycoff, J. 1991. *Mindmapping: Your personal guide to exploring creativity and problem solving.* New York: Berkley.

Zeithaml, A., A. Parasuraman, and L. L. Berry. 1990. *Delivering quality service: Balancing customer perceptions and expectations.* New York: Free Press.

Zwicky, F. 1966. *Discovery, invention, research through the morphological approach.* New York: MacMillan.

Index

Leonardo da Vinci, 135
Lepper, M. R., 58
Lewis, C. I., viii
Limits, establishing, 58–59, 104–5,
123, 162–63, 234
Logic, and judgment, 44–45
Looking closer, 105–10, 190, 191, 214
Lubart, T. I., 159

M
Majaro, S., 172, 177, 203
Malthus, T., 30
Manipulative verbs, 80–81, 132–33,
279
Market research, 209–10
Mattimore, B. W., 112, 135
McGartland, G., 55, 78, 135
McPherson, J., 28
Mechanics of mind, theory of,
32–48, 272
Medical clinic example, 189–205
Medication, delivery of, 2–3, 4
Meditative philosophy, 36
Memory, 33, 34, 35, 37–42
Mental actions, in creativity, 4–6
Mental ruts, 40, 49
Methods. *See* Tools
Michalko, M., 78, 80
on development stage, 177, 178
on imagination phase, 130, 135, 146
on preparation phase, 100, 108
on visualization, 135, 261
Mind, theory of, 32–48, 272
Mind maps, 146–47, 196
Models, ix
compared to heuristics, 69–70
of the creative process, 71–72, 125
of customer perceptions, 212–13,
220

of mechanics of mind, 32–34, 37–40
of organizational change, 164–69
of quality improvement, 267
Moral truths, 66
More-is-better quality, 212
Morphological combinations, 144–45,
196, 202
Motivation, 57
Movement
heuristic on, 61–62
principle of, 85, 88, 90, 120, 125,
216, 274
Movies, mental, 36, 84, 261–62
Multimodal thinking, 221–22
Must-be quality, 212, 220–21
Myers, R., 36, 178, 234, 261

N
Nadler, G., 15, 59, 84, 103, 250
Narrowness, avoidance of, 59
Needs. *See* Customer needs
Neisser, U., 35
Neural network, 38–39, 42, 63
New worlds, creating of, 113–16,
190, 191
Nine-dots problem, 252–53
Notebooks, of ideas, 145–46,
154–55, 196, 229–31.
See also Recording
Noticing. *See* Pausing and noticing
Novel-associations heuristic, 61, 120
Nowlin, D., 161
NR (not ready) ideas, 150, 233

O
Observation, in creative process
model, 71. *See also* Pausing
and noticing
Obvious, seeing the, 107–8, 191

READER FEEDBACK
Fax to ASQ Quality Press Acquisitions: 414-272-1734

Comments and Areas for Improvement:
Creativity, Innovation, and Quality

Please give us your comments, feedback, and suggestions for making this book more useful. We believe in the importance of continuous improvement and in meeting your needs. Your comments will help determine what improvements can be made in all ASQ Quality Press books.

Please share your opinion by circling the number below:

Ratings of the book	Needs Work		Satisfactory		Excellent	Comments
Stucture, flow, and logic	1	2	3	4	5	
Content, ideas, and information	1	2	3	4	5	
Style, clarity, ease of reading	1	2	3	4	5	
Held my interest	1	2	3	4	5	
Met my overall expectations	1	2	3	4	5	

I read the book because:

The best part of the book was:

The least satisfactory part of the book was:

Other suggestions for improvement:

General comments:

Thank you for your feedback. If you do not have access to a fax machine, please mail this form to:
ASQ Quality Press, 611 East Wisconsin Avenue, P.O. Box 3005, Milwaukee, WI 53201-3005   Phone: 414-272-8575